Dear Jeni

Thank you for your valued business
throughout 2012.
All the best and kind regards.
From all at
Freeway Tools and Fixings

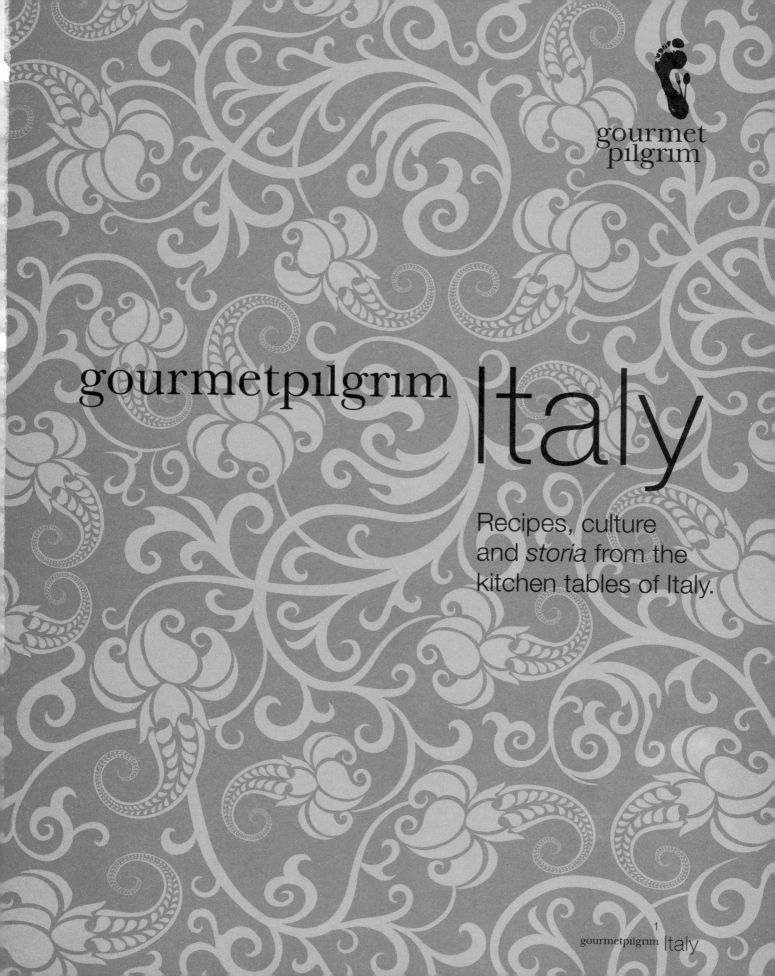

gourmet
pılgrım

gourmetpılgrım Italy

Recipes, culture
and *storia* from the
kitchen tables of Italy.

Gourmet Pilgrim would like to thank the many Italian cooks who have generously offered their family recipes for inclusion in this book and who put many hours into translating and sharing their culinary heritage.

Grazie

(Thankyou)

gourmet
pilgrim

Contenuti
(Contents)

La tavola Italiana
(The Italian table)

Think of Italian food as being a family recipe. Handed down from nonna to mamma to bambina, each one adding her own touch; a new ingredient here, a better way of cooking there, to become a richly satisfying dish to be shared by millions around the world.

So many cultures and peoples have inhabited Italy over its lengthy and varied history. So many conquerors and invaders have arrived – Phoenicians, Turks, Arabs, Normans, French, Spanish and Austrians – each imposing their own tastes and desires on whichever area they settled. They were hungry, too. Hungry for food, as well as for domination.

They came with an appetite – a meal-plan – arriving with cooks and recipes for dishes from their homeland, some with seeds and grains to grow in this newly acquired land.

This long peninsula, washed by five seas and stretching from the Alps almost to Africa, is blessed by a wide range of climates, allowing it to grow and raise almost anything. Yet it is cursed, too. Frequently rocked by catastrophic earthquakes and volcanic eruptions, its often-inhospitable terrain and soil have limited what it can grow – along with the poverty imposed by occupying nations over the centuries.

Where it all began

Many people don't realise that the Italy we know today did not even begin to form as an entity until the mid-19th century. The last few regions were incorporated only in the mid-20th century. But the landmass was here, the soil had been growing various food crops since civilisation began, and many of the ancestors of today's people were working in the fields, much as they still do in many parts today.

Snow fell in the mountains, the hot Mediterranean sun scorched the south. Game roamed the forests, mushrooms popped up in damp woodland areas, and doubtless people ground some sort of grain, possibly *faro*, to make rudimentary bread. Was this the first pizza? And did they make wine, too?

Some believe the almost-mythical Etruscans brought wine to Italy, but no one knows exactly how or when, although it may have been as early as the 12th century BC. We can be more certain about how some of the keystones of Italy's cuisine arrived.

A rich history, fertile lands, abundant seafood and a people who are passionate about food and wine have combined to ensure Italy's place at the forefront of gastronomy.

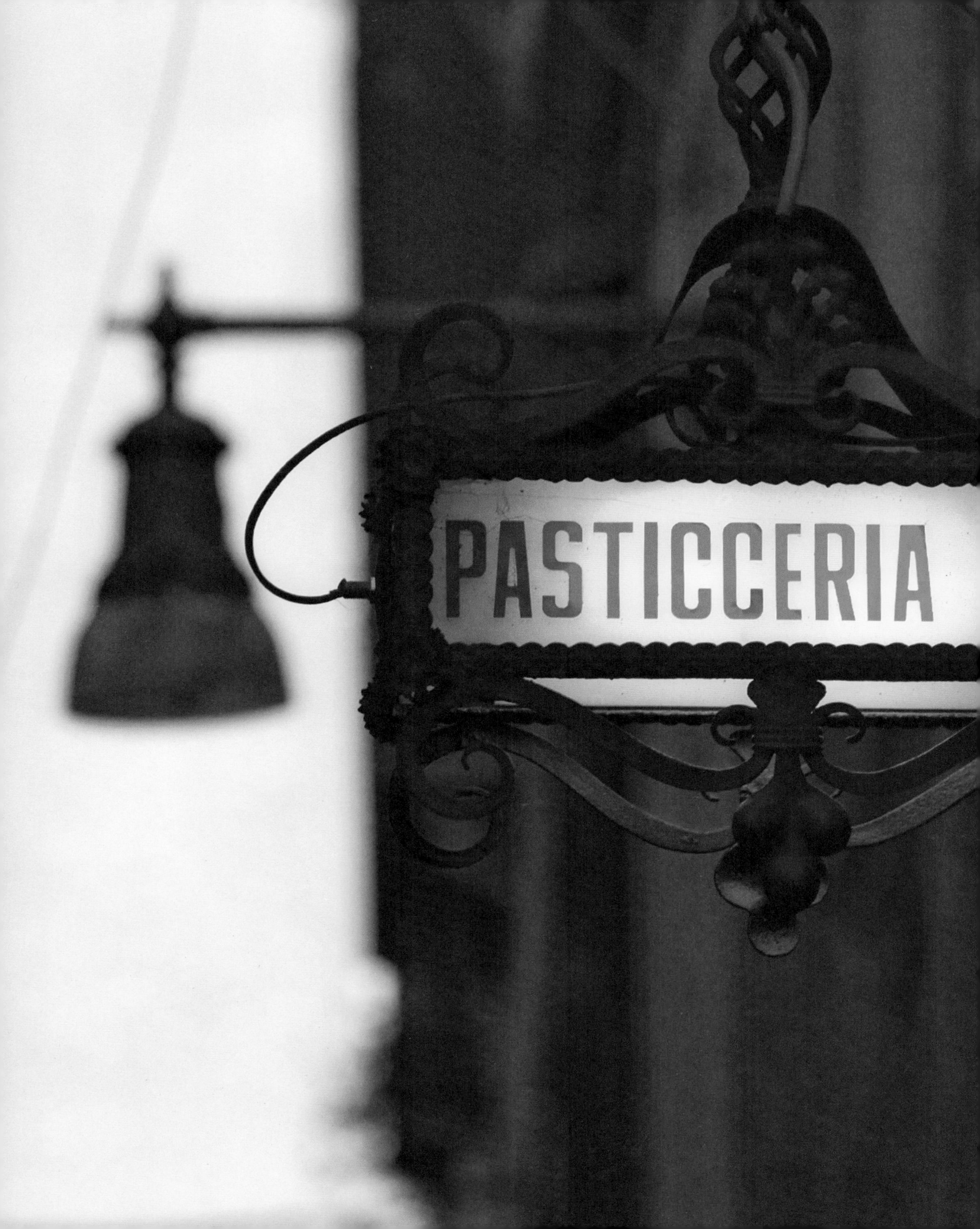
PASTICCERIA

Italy's recorded food history stretches back almost 2500 years to the fourth century BC when Archestratus, a Greek Sicilian from Syracuse, wrote a poem about food called *Life of luxury.*

Olives and the production of olive oil was one of ancient Greece's major contributions. And who can imagine an Italian menu without tomatoes, chillies, peppers and corn (and to a lesser degree, chocolate, eggplant and potatoes)? Although Christopher Columbus came from Genoa (today the capital of the province of Liguria), the four voyages on which he discovered and explored the Americas were funded by Spain. Early in the 16th century, news of his food discoveries began to be known by other European countries. Italians were nonplussed, many fearful of these strangely shaped and exotically coloured fruits and vegetables, and cooks mostly left them alone for a few centuries.

Another Italian mainstay, coffee, arrived via the Islamic world, from Turkey, entering Venice with traders who knew and understood its value, though for decades clerics and others remained suspicious of this inky black mood-altering potion. From here it spread to the rest of Italy and into Europe.

This has been the scenario for much of Italy's history. Seafaring merchants to the east brought back exotic products and techniques. Thirteenth-century Italian explorer Marco Polo may or may not have brought back from China the technique for making noodles, which morphed into pasta; many say Italy had already mastered this art.

When in Rome …

The ancient Romans loved their food, and the emperors especially enjoyed large and lengthy banquets packed with intricate dishes washed down with endless jugs of wine. They mopped up the rich game sauces with bread from Greek bakers, and became very fond of honey – thus starting a long tradition of the Italian love of ultra-sweet foods. Recipes from this time were recorded in a cookbook attributed to Apicius from the first century BC.

When the Arab Muslims invaded Sicily during the 9th century, they brought rice, almonds and spinach. They may have also brought a form of pasta. Three centuries later in a survey of the island, a Norman king mentioned seeing "long strings made from flour and water". The Normans from Europe's far north, already experts in the long-term preservation of foods by drying, smoking or salting, also brought *baccalà* and stockfish and shared their knowledge of slow-cooked casseroles.

Today, Sicily is a food-centric island and, as early as the Middle Ages, it was tapping into ancient Greek and Roman culinary traditions, beginning to evolve the most distant ancestor of an identifiable Italian cuisine. Perhaps some of this influenced the 13th-century Neapolitan writer of *Liber de coquina*, said to be the first book on Italian cuisine, which included recipes for dishes that are still made today.

During the Middle Ages, what we now call Italy was – particularly in the north – a fragmented collection of sovereign states belonging to either royalty, aristocracy or the church, or operating as republics. While coastal places had contact with sailors and seamen from other ports and other countries, people living in inland valleys, without easy communication, progressed along their own lines. Mountain chains separate entire parts of the Italian peninsula, and regional cuisines grew up, based on what the land could support or produce. This is why some people say, there is no *Italian* cuisine and that we should talk about regional food and cooking.

As time went on, generations of families perfected different recipes and methods. Some shaped their pasta in lengths, others flattened small pieces and made them ear-shaped; some filled squares of pasta with meat or mushrooms, others layered it with meat, cheese and vegetables. In other regions it was endless variations of potato dishes or rice, lamb or pork.

Trade, too, was important. Spices entered from the east, while Italian pasta spread towards central Europe. This interaction of ideas, as well as ingredients, was vital for new recipes. The maritime republics of Venice, Genoa, Pisa and Amalfi became leaders in the food fashions of the time, and it was in these places that fine glassware and tableware was first seen.

The nation we call 'Italy' is quite new - but its varied cuisine evolved in farmhouses and villages, often in isolation from other regions and influences.

A 15th-century manuscript points to a refinement in menus at this time. The author, Maestro Martino, a Vatican chef, seemed to favour herbs in preference to the spices introduced by Arab invaders some centuries previously, and macaroni had obviously been developed. There was evidence of developing regionality too, as he included dishes from Florence, Genoa and Rome. And rice had begun to be grown in the Po Valley.

At about the same time another book with a title that translates as *On Honest Pleasure and Good Health* included Martino's manuscript as well as information on local produce – fish, snails, poultry, olives, figs, oil, honey and wine – from a wide range of regions.

With the rise of royal and papal courts and the aristocracy in Italy, dining took another turn – at least for the upper classes. For those labouring in the fields it may have worsened their lot, as serfdom continued with added demands for more food for the princely tables.

Better food and more skilled cooks meant extravagant banqueting at courts in Rome, Venice and Florence. Whereas game and fish had been the main meats consumed on special occasions until the late 16th century, now domestic animals and poultry were mentioned in manuscripts, as well as recipes for their various cuts and offal.

In conjunction with this refinement of food, table settings became fashionable. In the Middle Ages, people would hack at meat or bread with their knife and use their fingers for eating. In 1533, the wealthy Florentine Catherine de Medici, married Henry II, who would later become King of France. She is credited with introducing many foods she would have grown up with in Italy, and brought to the French court something else very useful – the fork, already in use in her homeland.

A culinary evolution

About this time, in Naples, a recipe that would change the world's eating habits was being developed. Pizza – minus tomato, which had been discovered, but was still thought to be poisonous – began its life as a sweet flatbread.

We know that by the early 17th century, vegetables, herbs and fruit were popular because of a book written by a chef from Modena, Giangiacomo Castelvetro. Then, as now, cooks simmered vegetables in water, then drained and dressed them with olive oil before serving them warm or cold. The look of the table was evolving too, with plates replacing bowls, and table napkins laid out for each diner.

Previous spread - left: Ruins of Greek temple from 700 BC, Selinunte, Sicily.

Below: The port of Pozzuoli (also known as Puteoli) on the Bay of Naples. 170 miles by road from Rome, Puteoli was the offloading port of the Alexandrian fleet bringing grain to the capital of the Roman empire, and the landing place of St Paul on his journey to Rome as a prisoner.

Carbohydrate-rich, heavy food was the fare of the 18th-century peasant. They needed energy for their hard daily work, so filling and economical foods such as pasta, *gnocchi*, rice and vegetables were consumed in large quantities. Meat was a luxury, a special-occasion food for many poorer people. Potatoes became popular in the 19th century, finally shaking off the suspicion that they were poisonous and in 1871, the first pesto recipe appeared in a book. An easy, tasty dish was born.

As Italy was changing through the centuries, so too was the rest of Europe, and dining habits and recipes from occupying countries – Austria, France, and Spain – were adopted. It is important to remember that for a long time, Italy's borders ebbed and flowed as parts of various countries changed sides. Piedmont was once considered part of France; Lombardy was at different times under Austrian, Spanish and French rule – then Austrian again until 1859. Sicily had a succession of conquerors, and its cuisine shows this with Greek, Roman, Norman, Moorish and Arab influences. Islamic Saracens are responsible for Sicily's sweetmeats, such as *torrone* (nougat) and marzipan. This vast and intricate web of Italian regionalism was united in the new Kingdom of Italy in 1861, under King Victor Emmanuel II.

Food on the move

Movement of many people from the south of Italy to the north in the 20th century brought about a merging and introduction of cooking habits, dishes and foods, such as pizza and pasta. Once the north used mainly butter in cooking, while the centre favoured pork fat (*lardo*) and the south used olive oil. But this now began to change.

Another important factor was Italian migration to other countries in the 19th and 20th centuries, a reversal of the previous 2000-plus years, and caused Italian food to 'go global'. Pizza, pasta and eggplant dishes arrived in the Americas migrants opened *pizzerie* and *pasticcerie* and began to make pasta, *salami* and *salume* in their adopted homelands.

Soon the world was won over to Italian cuisine, and the Italian *attitude* to food and dining. The relaxed approach to meals – casual sharing, welcoming all generations of extended families, and their abundance and generosity – forever changed the perception of hospitality in Anglo-Celtic countries. Their wine, too, slowly infiltrated beer-drinking cultures. Vines were planted and grapes harvested under new skies, but in similar ways and to the same tempo of their forebears.

Early in the 20th century, Italian cuisine began its global emigration into kitchens and restaurants around the world.

With the increase in travel between countries during the late 20th and early 21st centuries, Italy became a highly popular destination. People learnt the taste of true *gelati,* understood *al dente* pasta and realised that real pizza is not centimetres thick.

Like the many recipes that have evolved over the years, Italy's cuisine is the sum of all the myriad influences, experiences and developments over more than two millennia. New techniques and technology have generally only improved its use of the produce on which it has based its food culture of handmade, home-made foods.

The Italian table is rich with history, crammed with individual visionaries, and full of exceptional recipes. But most of all it is composed – as any Italian will tell you – of the cooks in the kitchen working in unison to create a meal; and the family and friends, from the *nonno* and *nonna* to the smallest *bambini*, around the table, talking, laughing, eating and drinking.

That is truly the Italian table.

Antipasti
Antipasto

Every Italian meal is
a journey - the first
shared course of
antipasto shows
the way.

Antipasti (Antipasto)

The only rule you may need to follow is to pace yourself. Remember, this is only the beginning ...

Literally translating as "before the meal", antipasto dishes are meant to stimulate the tastebuds without filling the stomach. The simplest antipasto might contain cheese, cured meats, pickled or stuffed vegetables, olives and bruschetta or grissini. Wedges of frittata and seafood (cooked, pickled or raw) are also common.

Antipasto varies according to the region and the whims of the cook. In Emilia-Romagna you're likely to find a broad selection of cured meats including prosciutto di Parma, Italy's best known ham. Reflecting the region's coastal location, Ligurian antipasti often feature seafood - stuffed mussels, insalata di mare (seafood salad) – while in the poorer regions of the south, including Puglia, Basilicata and Sicily, antipasti are heavy on vegetables but include regional cheeses such as burrata, a creamy-centred stretched curd cheese.

Ingredients

500g fresh buffalo mozzarella* or baby bocconcini*
500g ripe cherry tomatoes
100g black olives
100g green Italian olives
200g sliced prosciutto crudo*
200g sliced bresaola* or salami
Fresh rucola* (arugula or rocket) leaves
Grissini or crusty bread, to serve

Method

Serves 4-6

Chop mozzarella into small pieces (if using bocconcini leave whole).

Arrange cheese, tomatoes, olives, sliced meats and rucola onto a serving platter.

Serve with grissini and or crusty bread.

Variation – Alternatively, cut tomatoes in half and drizzle with oil and balsamic vinegar and season to taste.

* Refer to Glossary – Page 470

Fiori di zucchine ripiene
Stuffed zucchini flowers

Ingredients

Vegetable oil, for deep-frying

12 zucchini* (courgette) flowers and small taped body

2 eggs

Flaked salt

Freshly cracked black pepper

75g plain (all-purpose) flour

60ml-80ml cold water

120g provolone* cheese

1 tablespoons freshly picked lemon thyme leaves

Zucchini flowers, stuffed with mozzarella cheese and anchovies then dipped in batter and deep-fried, are a specialty of Roman Jewish cooking. Found throughout Italy, these delicate blossoms are also often stuffed with ricotta and herbs, goat's cheese or sharp semi-hard cheeses, like provolone as in this recipe. In the Piedmontese dish caponet, zucchini flowers are filled with minced pork and veal then baked. They can also be steamed or sautéed and used in salads, frittatas and risottos. The male flower, which is attached to the plant by a thin stem, is said to have a slightly sweeter flavour than the female flower, which is attached to the zucchini itself.

Method

Heat the oil in a heavy-based frying pan or deep fryer. Remove stamens from the zucchini flowers and discard.

Make the batter by placing the eggs into a medium-sized bowl and lightly beating, season with salt and pepper then add the flour a bit at a time and stir well. Lastly, stir in the water to form a smooth batter. Set aside.

Cut the cheese into batons about 2cm long x 1cm wide x 1 cm deep. Fold back zucchini petals, place cheese into the cavity with a few thyme leaves then fold back petals to enclose filling. Twist the tip of the flower to assist in holding the cheese in.

Preheat oven to 150°C.

Dip the flowers into the batter one at a time and cook in the hot oil until lightly golden. The flowers will float to the top as they cook.

Remove with a slotted spoon and place cooked flowers onto a wire rack, which is sitting on an oven tray (to collect oil drips) to drain.

Keep warm in preheated oven as all the flowers continue to be cooked.

Season with salt and serve immediately.

* Refer to Glossary – Page 470

Insalata Caprese
Tomato & bocconccini salad

Ingredients

3 large ripe tomatoes

250g large bocconcini cheese*

1 large red onion, halved and thinly sliced

2-3 tablespoons extra virgin olive oil

1 tablespoon balsamic vinegar

2 tablespoons roughly chopped fresh oregano leaves

Flaked salt

Freshly cracked black pepper

Fresh sweet basil leaves, to serve (optional)

Comprising three ingredients – tomatoes, mozzarella and basil – drizzled with olive oil and vinegar, insalata caprese is proof that the simplest things in life are often the best. It hails from the island of Capri, just off the Amalfi Coast near Naples, but can be found throughout Italy. The tastiest versions come from Campania, where the sun-ripened tomatoes grow on volcanic soil and the melt-in-your mouth mozzarella di bufala (buffalo-milk mozzarella) is made daily.

Method

Slice tomatoes and cheese into ½cm slices. Arrange tomato, cheese and onion alternating onto a serving plate.

Drizzle the salad with olive oil and vinegar. Top with oregano leaves and season to taste. Serve with basil.

Tip: Serve the tomatoes at room temperature for the best flavour.

* Refer to Glossary – Page 470

Asparagi in salsa di acciughe e limone
Asparagus with anchovy lemon sauce

Ingredients

500g fresh asparagus

80ml olive oil

1 garlic clove, finely chopped

4 anchovy fillets*

1 tablespoon chopped fresh flat-leaf (Italian) parsley

1-2 tablespoons lemon juice, to taste

Flaked salt

Freshly cracked black pepper

Extra virgin olive oil, to serve

Method

Trim asparagus and steam until tender. Refresh under cold water and drain, then place onto a serving plate and keep at room temperature.

Heat oil in a medium frying pan and cook the garlic over a low-medium heat for about 3 minutes until slightly tender. Add the anchovies and breakdown with the back of a spoon. Stir into the garlic cook a further 2 minutes. Add the parsley and lemon juice to taste. Lastly, season to taste.

Pour the sauce over the asparagus and finish with a drizzle of extra virgin olive oil.

Serve immediately.

Tip – Green or white asparagus are ideal. This sauce is also perfect for steamed green beans, broad beans, potatoes and artichokes.

* Refer to Glossary – Page 470

Bruschetta
Garlic toast

Ingredients

1 Italian bread loaf (such as ciabatta), thinly sliced

2-3 garlic cloves, peeled and halved

100ml extra virgin olive oil

Flaked salt

Method

Place sliced bread onto a hot char-grill or under a griller until golden on both sides.

While warm, rub one side of the bread with the cut surface of the garlic, drizzle with olive oil and sprinkle lightly with salt.

Serve immediately.

Insalata di finocchio, arancia e rucola
Fennel, orange & rocket salad

Ingredients

2 large oranges
2 small fennel bulbs
2 bunches rucola* (arugula or rocket) leaves
100g black Liguria olives
60ml extra virgin olive oil
1 tablespoon red wine vinegar
Flaked salt
Freshly cracked black pepper
40g parmesan cheese, shaved, to serve

Method

Peel oranges and remove all the white pith, cut in half then thinly slice. Trim the tops of the fennel, cut them in half then very thinly slice.

Place the washed and dried rucola onto a large platter and top with the orange and fennel slices. Add the olives then gently toss to combine.

Combine oil and vinegar and season to taste. Pour dressing over salad and serve immediately with parmesan.

* Refer to Glossary – Page 470

Insalata mista con gorgonzola e noccioline
Mixed salad with gorgonzola & hazelnuts

Serves 4-6

Ingredients

250g sliced pancetta*

2 tablespoons water

60ml extra virgin olive oil

80ml red wine vinegar

Flaked salt

Freshly cracked black pepper

100g rucola (arugula or rocket) leaves*

100g radicchio leaves*

60g roasted hazelnuts, skins removed and roughly chopped

120g gorgonzola cheese*, crumbled

Method

Heat a large frying pan over medium-high heat and cook the pancetta in batches, if required, until crisp. Remove and drain on kitchen paper towel.

Allow the pan to cook a little before deglazing with the water. Allow the water to simmer for 2-3 minutes then remove pan from the heat.

Pour 1 tablespoon of the pan juices into a bowl and add the oil and vinegar. Season to taste.

Rinse and dry all the salad leaves and place into a large bowl or onto a large platter, tearing any large radicchio leaves into pieces. Add the hazelnuts, broken pieces of pancetta and dressing, toss gently to combine.

Finish with cheese and serve.

Tip: Prosciutto* can be used instead of pancetta.

* Refer to Glossary – Page 470

Crostini
Croutons

Ingredients

6 slices day-old white bread

Extra virgin olive oil

100g fontina*, provolone* or gruyere cheese, thinly sliced

½ roasted red pepper* (capsicum), cut into strips

½ roasted yellow pepper* (capsicum), cut into strips

50g semi-dried tomatoes*, cut into pieces

8-10 anchovy fillets

Small fresh basil leaves (optional)

Freshly cracked pepper

Method

Preheat oven to 190°C.

Cut the bread into various shapes, such as circles and triangles, trying to get a couple of shapes out of each slice. Then place onto baking trays and lightly brush with olive oil. Bake in preheated oven for 3-5 minutes or until lightly golden.

Remove bread from oven and drizzle with a little more olive oil then begin to add the toppings – cut cheese to shape and sit on the bread. Add your choice of pepper strips, tomato and/or anchovies. Mix it up for colour and variety.

Place into oven again and cook for about 10 minutes or until cheese is just melted.

Top with basil leaves, season with pepper and serve immediately.

Tip: Crostini can have many toppings – this cheesy variety is best served warm but other toppings can be served cold.

* Refer to Glossary – Page 470

Frittata di porri e pomodori secchi
Frittata with leek & sun-dried tomatoes

Serves 3-4

Ingredients

30g sun-dried tomatoes*

1 small leek

2 tablespoons olive oil

6 free-range eggs*

1 tablespoon freshly picked thyme leaves

1 tablespoon roughly chopped fresh oregano leaves

60g parmesan cheese, grated

Flaked salt

Freshly cracked black pepper

Method

Place the tomatoes into a small bowl and just cover with hot water. Allow to stand for about 15 minutes. Remove from the water and thinly slice.

Cut the white base from the leek and cut in half lengthways, wash and dry then thinly slice to achieve 1 cup of leek.

Heat the oil in a medium 26cm non-stick frying pan, add leek and cook over a low heat for 3 minutes or until lightly golden.

Meanwhile, place the eggs into a bowl and lightly beat. Add the herbs, cheese and season well with salt and pepper.

With the heat still on medium, add the eggs to the frying pan. Mix quickly to incorporate the leek then stop stirring. Cook for 5-7 minutes on the first side or until the frittata looks puffed and set a little in the middle.

Take a plate and place it upside down above the frittata in the frying pan. Turn the frying pan upside down to flip and turn the frittata over onto the plate (the golden side should now be face up).

Slide the frittata back into the hot frying pan to cook the other side for 2-3 minutes or until lightly golden.

Frittata can be served hot, at room temperature or chilled to enjoy later.

Cut into wedges or pieces to serve.

* Refer to Glossary – Page 470

Fritto misto di mare
Fried mixed seafood

Serves 2-4

Ingredients

300g whole baby octopus, cleaned

Vegetable oil, for deep-frying

300g whole squid, cleaned and cut into rings

200g fresh whole whitebait

15-20 whole medium green shrimp* (prawns), peeled and de-veined

150g plain (all-purpose) flour

110g cornflour (cornstarch)

250ml milk

Flaked salt and lemon wedges, to serve

Fritto misto is the generic name for an assortment of small fried bites, usually vegetables, which are coated in a light batter or dusted with seasoned flour, and then flash fried. Fritto misto di mare is a seafood version, found all over coastal Italy, especially along the Adriatic coast. Anchovies, calamari, prawns, octopus and chunks of firm-fleshed white fish are the star players; vegetables are sometimes included. Serve with herby mayonnaise.

Method

Cut octopus bodies into small pieces. Place into a bowl and cover with boiling water to blanch for 1 minute to help tenderise (see tip). Drain and pat dry.

Heat the oil in a heavy-based frying pan or deep fryer. Pat all the seafood dry with kitchen paper towel.

Preheat oven to 150°C.

Combine and sift the flours into a large bowl. Place the milk into a second bowl. Begin to coat the seafood in flour, shaking off excess, then into milk allowing excess to drip away, then recoat in flour.

Place onto a tray – it is best to coat all the seafood before you begin cooking.

Cook the seafood in batches in the hot oil until lightly golden. Remove with a slotted spoon and place onto a wire rack, which is sitting on an oven tray (to collect oil drips), to drain. Keep warm in a preheated oven until all the seafood is cooked.

Season with salt and serve immediately with lemon wedges.

Tip: Blanching octopus helps tenderise when cooking quickly, such as deep-frying or barbecuing.

Note – Whitebait are such small fish that they are cooked whole (not cleaned or scaled), with the head intact.

* Refer to Glossary – Page 470

Crocchetti di baccalà
Salted cod fish cakes

Ingredients

500g baccalà* (salted cod), prepared
2 garlic cloves, peeled
1 small bunch fresh flat-leaf (Italian) parsley
1 tablespoon olive oil
125g plain (all-purpose) flour
2 eggs, lightly beaten
60ml milk
1 tablespoon finely chopped parsley, extra
Freshly cracked black pepper
Vegetable oil, for deep-frying
Lemon wedges, to serve

Baccalà (salt cod) has long played an important role in Italian (and Mediterranean) cooking, even though the fish is actually caught in the icy waters of the north Atlantic, from Norway to Newfoundland. As a traded commodity, baccalà has a fascinating history; the ships that offloaded the salted and dried cod in Mediterranean ports would then transport salt (as well as dried fruits, wine and spices) back to northern Europe and the New World. Start preparing the salt cod several days before you plan to cook these moreish fritters, as you need to soak it for up to 48 hours, changing the water regularly, to eliminate the salt.

Method

Prepare the baccalà as described below. Cut into pieces.

Place the fish, whole garlic cloves, parsley stalks and leaves, and oil into a large saucepan and add enough water to just cover. Bring to a gentle boil and cook, partly covered for 30 minutes.

Remove from heat and allow the fish to cool in the water then drain well, discarding garlic and parsley. Flake fish by hand, removing skin and any bones.

Place the fish into a large bowl and add the flour, eggs and milk, then add the extra parsley. Season with pepper. Stir to combine and mix to a creamy paste.

Heat the oil in a heavy-based frying pan or deep fryer.

Preheat oven to 150°C.

Begin to add fish mixture in tablespoon amounts to the hot oil. Cook in batches until lightly golden. Remove with a slotted spoon, as it is easier to scoop the fish cakes up.

Place cooked fish onto a wire rack, which is sitting on an oven tray (to collect oil drips) to drain. Keep warm in a preheated oven as all the fish cakes continues to be cooked.

Serve immediately with lemon wedges.

Tip: To prepare the baccalà first rinse the fish under running cold water, brushing off all the salt on the surface. Put the fish into a large bowl of cold water (cut into pieces to fit) and leave for it for 48 hours, changing the water often especially during the first 3-4 hours. After 48 hours, drain and cook according to the recipe.*

* Refer to Glossary – Page 470

Insalata Rossa
Fresh fig & prosciutto salad

Serves 4-6

Ingredients

1 radicchio lettuce*

100g rucola* (arugula, or rocket)* or mixed salad leaves

6 fresh ripe figs, quartered

150g thinly sliced prosciutto crudo*

60ml extra virgin olive oil

1 tablespoon balsamic vinegar

2 teaspoons honey

Flaked salt

Freshly cracked black pepper

50g parmesan cheese, thinly shaved

Crusty bread, to serve

Method

Wash radicchio and tear leaves into pieces. Place onto a large platter or into a bowl with rucola and gently toss to combine. Add figs and prosciutto.

Place oil, vinegar and honey in a covered container and shake well to combine. Season to taste.

Pour dressing over the salad and finish with parmesan.

Serve with crusty bread.

Tip: An easy way to shave the parmesan is with a vegetable peeler.

* Refer to Glossary – Page 470

Panzanella Toscana
Tuscan panzanella salad

Serves 4-6

Ingredients

300g stale Italian-style bread, crust on

1 medium red onion, cut into thin wedges

500g baby trussed tomatoes, halved

1 handful fresh flat-leaf (Italian) parsley leaves, torn

1 handful of small fresh sweet basil leaves

60ml white wine vinegar

80ml extra-virgin olive oil

1 teaspoon flaked salt

Freshly cracked black pepper

60g whole caper berries*

A Tuscan peasant dish, panzanella dates back to medieval times. It's an excellent way to use up leftover good-quality bread, which is soaked in water to soften, then infused with juice from ripe tomatoes, olive oil and vinegar. You can add fresh herbs, capsicum, cucumber or, as in this recipe, caper berries to the basic panzanella recipe for extra flavour and texture.

Method

Break the bread into large chunks and place into a large bowl. Add just enough cold water to cover the bread. Set aside to soak for about 15 minutes.

Meanwhile combine the onion, tomatoes, parsley and basil in a large serving bowl. Drain the bread and add it to the tomatoes.

Combine the vinegar, oil and salt and whisk to combine. Adjust seasoning to taste.

Pour dressing over the salad add caper berries and toss well to combine. Serve.

Variation – Slice the bread into 2cm slices, then toast or char-grill them before breaking it up and placing into a bowl with the vinegar and olive oil. Stand while preparing the remaining vegetables. Combine all ingredients and toss to combine. Serve.

* Refer to Glossary – Page 470

Funghi marinati alla maggiorana
Marinated mushrooms with marjoram

Ingredients

500g cap, portabello or large, flat
mushrooms

80ml olive oil

2 garlic cloves, crushed

125ml red wine

2 tablespoons roughly chopped fresh
marjoram or oregano leaves

60ml balsamic vinegar

Flaked salt

Freshly cracked black pepper

Extra virgin olive oil, to drizzle

Extra marjoram or oregano, to serve

Method

Wipe mushrooms with a slightly damp cloth then cut into medium-thick slices and place into a large bowl.

Heat the oil in a small frying pan over low-medium heat. Add garlic and cook for 1-2 minutes until very lightly golden. Add wine and cook a further 1 minute.

Remove from heat and add the marjoram and vinegar.

Pour liquid over the mushrooms and season to taste. Mix well, cover and allow to marinate for at least 1 hour or overnight in the refrigerator. Stir and turn occasionally.

Serve drizzled with extra olive oil and sprinkle with extra marjoram.

Tip: Large button or Swiss brown mushrooms would also be suitable.

Insalata Russa
Russian salad

Serves 8-10

Ingredients

1 kg all-purpose potatoes

320g can tuna in olive oil

565g giardiniera*

100g whole green olives

300g fresh egg mayonnaise*

300g fresh egg mayonnaise*, extra

Hard-boiled eggs, green olives, cherry tomatoes, to garnish

Method

Peel and boil the potatoes in lightly salted water until soft. Drain and place into a large bowl and mash well.

Drain the tuna and the giardiniera and whizz together with the pitted olives in a food processor until just chopped but not totally smooth.

Add tuna mixture and mayonnaise to the potatoes and stir until well combined. Spoon into a serving dish, smooth the surface and leave to cool. Refrigerate until ready to serve – up to two days, if necessary.

Just before serving, top the potato mixture with the extra mayonnaise, then garnish to taste with hard-boiled eggs, green olives and cherry tomatoes. Serve immediately.

* Refer to Glossary – Page 470

Frittata al tartufo
Truffle omelet

Ingredients

1 medium sized black truffle*

5 free-range eggs*

100ml pure (single) cream

2 tablespoons chopped fresh flat-leaf
(Italian) parsley

Flaked salt

Freshly cracked black pepper

20g butter

1 tablespoon olive oil

Crusty bread, to serve

The heady aroma and flavour of truffle transforms this simple omelette into a truly decadent dish. In Italy, there are two types of this highly prized fungus: black truffles from the Umbrian town of Norcia (in season from late November to March) and white truffles from Piedmont (in season in October and November). Truffles occur naturally in many parts of Europe, including France and Croatia, and are now cultivated in Australia, New Zealand and the United States, among other countries. Preserved truffles are a poor imitation of the real thing.

Method

If using a fresh truffle, wipe over with a piece of slightly damp paper towel and then slice very thinly (as thin as prosciutto). If using a truffle from a jar, remove and wipe over and again cut into thin slices. Keep 6-8 slices for serving and finely dice the remaining.

Place eggs and cream into a bowl and whisk to combine. Add the diced truffle, parsley and season with salt and pepper.

Heat butter and oil in a cast-iron omelette pan or non-stick frying pan. Add the egg mixture and swirl to coat the base of the frying pan as it begins to set around the outside.

Use a spatula to pull one of the edges of the cooking omelette towards the middle; this should then allow the still uncooked egg to run towards to hot pan and begin to cook too.

Cover with a lid (this can just be the lid of a large saucepan, it doesn't need to fit the frying pan as it just needs to trap some steam under it to cook the omelette top). Cook until set or place under a preheated grill to finish the cooking.

Loosen the omelette and then fold in half.

Serve immediately with the remaining truffle and crusty bread.

* Refer to Glossary – Page 470

Carpaccio di tonno con finocchio affettato
Tuna carpaccio with shaved fennel

Serves 4-6

Ingredients

2-3 fresh tuna steaks (about 400g and about 1cm in thickness)
60ml extra virgin olive oil
1 tablespoon lemon juice
1 tablespoon white wine vinegar
2 bulbs small fennel, tops trimmed
1 bunch fresh chives, finely chopped
1 teaspoon baby capers*
Flaked salt
Freshly cracked pepper

Carpaccio is a modern invention, most commonly made with wafer-thin slices of raw beef. It was devised around 1950 by Giuseppe Cipriani, owner of the famous Harry's Bar in Venice, for an aristocratic customer who, for health reasons, had to eat raw meat. Cipriani named the dish after the Renaissance painter Vittore Carpaccio, known for his use of rich crimsons and other colours. Tuna carpaccio is a derivation of the original, and especially popular in Sicily, where most of Italy's tuna is caught. Be sure to use the freshest sashimi-quality tuna you can find.

Method

Remove any skin from the tuna steaks. Then place each steak between two pieces of plastic wrap. Use the flat side of a meat mallet or a rolling pin to gently pound and flatten the steaks out to a thickness of about 2mm. Remove the top layer of plastic and discard.

Next, roll the tuna up lengthways (as you would a Swiss roll) as tightly as possible. Then wrap each roll individually and tightly in the plastic wrap and place into the freezer for 2-3 hours or until just firm.

Meanwhile, prepare the dressing by combining the oil, lemon juice and vinegar in a small bowl.

Next, shave the fennel with a mandolin or slice very thinly with a knife and place into a bowl with the chives and capers. Season to taste.

To serve, remove the tuna from the freezer, unwrap and cut the thinnest slices possible from each roll. Flatten each piece with the flat blade side of the knife if they appear a little too thick and arrange around the outside edge of a serving platter.

Add the dressing to the fennel salad, stir well to combine then place into the middle of the platter.

Serve immediately, drizzling the tuna with a little extra olive oil.

Tip: Sashimi-quality fish is perfect for this recipe, as you can be assured it is the freshest available.

* Refer to Glossary – Page 470

Olive e olio d'oliva

(Olives & olive oil)

"Except for the vine, there is no plant which bears a fruit of as great importance as the olive".

- Pliny the Elder, Roman Empire (23-79AD)

Opposite: harvesting olives for oil in Bisceglie, Puglia.

The jury is out on when olive cultivation began in Italy. Some say that as early as 700 BC Phoenician colonists planted olive trees on the Iberian Peninsula, so it stands to reason that Italy's first groves may well have been begun about that time as well. Olives are native to the entire Mediterranean region though, so wild ones were possibly growing there already.

In 149 BC, we know that the Roman statesman Cato the Elder died, leaving papers urging the local farmers to plant grapes and olives rather than grains, because they fared better in drought. In the first century AD, historian Pliny reported that Italy had "excellent olive oil at reasonable prices", calling it "the best in the Mediterranean".

Extending the olive branch

Olives are believed to have been growing for several thousand years. According to the Bible, at the end of the Great Flood, Noah sent out a dove from the ark. When it returned bearing an olive branch, he knew that the flood was over. Since then olive branches have been seen as symbols of peace and reconciliation. Ramses II of Egypt used olive oil liberally for medicinal purposes, and ancient Greek athletes rubbed it on their bodies. In Homer's time it was considered a luxury and used only as an ointment after bathing. "Liquid gold" he called it. In fact, the recipe for luxury in Roman times was "wine within, and olive oil without".

Certainly, the Italian climate is ideal for the propagation of olives. There are places all around the Mediterranean where ancient olive trees are still alive and bearing fruit, some of which are reputed to be more than 2000 years old. The "Olive Tree of Magliano" in Tuscany is said to be 3500 years old. If this were true, that tree would have been ancient even in 1500 AD when the Medici family (the Granduca Cosimo I) granted land to all families so they could plant their own olive groves. Tuscany is still a major producer of olives today.

In the Dark Ages, olives were called oilberries, no doubt because few people had thought to eat them, preferring instead to press out the precious oil - used as much for lamp fuel as it was for food.

In most countries around the world today, olive oil is regarded as *the* oil to use, mainly because of its known health benefits. But there is a danger that we become so olive oil conscious that we may forget the fruit from which the oil is pressed.

Although machinery is used to harvest olives on the bigger groves, many believe that handpicked olives are superior to machine-harvested ones because the fruit is not bruised. Any drive through southern Italy, in particular, will pass trees with their picking nets rolled up in the lower boughs ready for the next season, late in the year, when they will be laid out at the base of the tree ready to catch the ripe fruit as eager "shakers" send the fruit tumbling from the branches. Some olive farmers still employ the manual *bruciatura* method, using a hand-harvesting tool with comb-like teeth.

Once collected, the fruit is immediately ground to a paste between millstones in an olive mill to remove all liquid. The first non-filtered oil is called "cold pressed". The filtered liquid is allowed to settle, the oil floating to the top, the remainder settling to the bottom. The remaining pulp is spread on coarse, heavy mats, which are stacked on top of each other, and then this pile is pressed to remove any residual oil.

Quality rules

Olive oil is graded according to acidity: 0.08 per cent (some say 1 per cent) or below, is called *olio d'oliva extravergine* (extra virgin olive oil). The colour of this extra-virgin oil (sometimes abbreviated to EVOO) may range from green to deep yellow. Oil pressed from green olives is said to be fruitier, but to have more "bite". When pressed from ripe black olives, a more mild, smoother-tasting oil is generally produced.

Oil ranging from 0.08 to 2 per cent acidity (or 3.3 per cent, some say) is called virgin oil. "Pure" olive oil is a blend of virgin oil and inferior oils that have been refined to remove impurities. Inedible residue oil, sometimes called sulphur oil or olive kernel oil, is often used for the manufacture of soap.

Don't be misled by extra light olive oil. It is light only in flavour, but has the same kilojoules as all fats and oils, and is a blend of refined oil and a small amount of virgin oil.

Olive oil is an exceptionally fine oil for cooking. Its fruity flavour combines well with most vegetables, grains, cheeses and meats. Perhaps one of the main advantages of olive oil is that it is very stable for cooking at all temperatures, with a high smoking point, making it ideal for all sorts of frying.

Perennially popular

Italy still grows and consumes a vast amount of olive oil. The country's annual consumption is 48 cups per capita – a staggering 12 litres – yet the Greeks consume more than double that. By comparison, US residents manage only 2.5 cups a year. Luckily Italy produces 25 per cent of world's olive oil (second only to Spain) from just 13 per cent of the world's 19.8 million acres of olive groves. It also produces 75,000 tonnes of table olives annually.

All over the country, except for the alpine regions of Piedmont and Lombardy, the Italian landscape is punctuated by silvery groves of olives. They thrive even in inhospitable steep and terraced land such as Liguria, although Puglia is the largest producer.

About half of all olive oil produced in Italy is extra virgin. The main varieties of olives grown for oil production are *taggiasca* in Liguria; *frantoio, leccino, maurino,* and *puntino* in Tuscany; *carbonella, frantoio, leccino, maurino, moraiolo, pendolino* and *rosciale* in the Marche; *corantina, frantoio, leccino* and *ogliarola barese* in Puglia; and, in Sicily *biancolilla, nocellara etnea,* and *tonda iblea.*

It's difficult to imagine how someone discovered how to make raw olives edible. The curing by fermentation is a lengthy and involved process and may vary according to the olive variety, its colour and size, and also the desired result. Different olive varieties are grown for table use, and they range from the petite Ligurian olives to huge *ascolane* in the Marche, *cerignola, maiatica* and *molellara* in Puglia and several Spanish varieties in Sicily. When bottled or packed commercially, pitted green olives may be stuffed with peppers, while black olives will be marinated in herbs and oil.

Frantoio is a type of olive grown in Italy, but it is also the Italian word for olive press, and you will find one in almost every town where olives are grown. Growers bring in their olives as they are picked in the late autumn and early winter (January in Puglia) and, in some communities, the transaction may be as simple as a direct barter of olives for an agreed amount of oil.

Liquid gold, Homer called olive oil. And he was right.

Apulia (Puglia)

If you were to choose the region of Italy that does not fit the general pattern, it would be Puglia. Think of it as a rarely mentioned second cousin who turns up unexpectedly at family gatherings.

The Apennines, which form the spine of the country, finally sweep to the west to culminate in Sicily. The whole south-eastern area, from the Molise border, where it appears the "boot" is wearing a spur, to the heel tip, is Puglia, largely made up of wide agricultural plains and undulating hills.

Diversity and prosperity

Here, the land can be windswept and almost arid, but there is prosperity too, with large olive groves producing more extra virgin olive oil than Tuscany, extensive vineyards, fields of wheat, and pastures where sheep graze. It may not be the traditional Italian postcard scene, but Puglia has been catching people's imagination, and tourism is booming.

This large region has plenty of diversity in its cuisine to lure visitors. As with all the southern parts of Italy, successive waves of invasion and migration are preserved in fragrant spices and different cooking techniques. Greek influences are strong. This area – in fact, most of the south – was once regarded as *Magna Grecia* (Great Greece), and temple ruins are a constant reminder of the former power of today's neighbours across that narrow part of the Adriatic.

Garlic, the mainstay of Italian cookery, is replaced by onion here in the south of the peninsula and dishes may be very simple combinations, but perfectly cooked. Puglia has a wealth of pastas and sauces, and chillies are used in many of them. Dishes such as *tiella*, a paella-like mix of rice, potatoes, onions, parsley and mussels, baked in layers, are the legacy of Spanish colonisation.

In addition to exceptional olives from Cerignola, inland to the north, Puglia also produces *fava* (broad beans), chickpeas near Nardo in the far south, peppers, fennel and excellent eggplant. Lamb is still popular on menus here, as well as game, when available. Cheeses can be made with sheep's milk, such as *canestrato*, a hard cheese from Foggia and Bari, and *scamorza*, like a firm mozzarella; or from cow's milk, such as *provolone, fiordilatte*, and *burrata*, butter wrapped in firm cheese, from Andria.

Puglian bread is widely accepted as excellent, probably because it makes use of the area's strong wheat flour and is usually baked in wood-fired ovens. Best bread of all is said to be the fragrant crusty *pane di Altamura*. Small crisp ring-shaped biscuits called *taralli* are also popular and widely available.

Puglian pasta

Pasta is a staple food in this region. *Cavatelli* are flat disks, *strascinati* are also flat, a little like *orecchiette* (the 'little ears' found throughout the south), and most pastas are served with a rich tomato-based sauce, sometimes including veal or horsemeat, or *cime di rape* (turnip tops), which are often served with *orecchiette*.

Desserts and snacks include *carteddate*, fried sweet pastries like *crostoli, zeppole*, resembling doughnuts, and fried *caucuini*, filled with chickpea paste, chocolate, sugar and spice.

Bari, the capital of Puglia, has one of the oldest historic city centres, and is known for its seafood restaurants. Further north, the port city of Trani has an important fish market. *Agriturismi* (farm-stays) throughout the region serve local home-style dishes.

Puglia's excellent climate makes it possible to grow more wine grapes than Tuscany. There are many DOC wines, but Puglia's production is so large that much is exported to other regions for winemaking. Notable local wines include the light white *Locorotondo*, and the fine red *Castel del Monte*.

Perhaps it's time to catch up with the family, second cousin or not … they may be hiding some culinary treasures.

Above: The beautiful town of Locorotondo, Puglia, meaning 'round place', famous for its wine and round historical town centre.

Opposite: *Taralli* - a classic Puglian bread ring.

It may not be the prettiest region of Italy, but Puglian food is extremely enticing.

Riso e pasta
Rice & pasta

Think Italian cuisine and pasta springs immediately to mind – followed by delicious, creamy *risotto*.

Riso (Rice)

Contrary to popular legend, Italians do exist on more than a diet of pasta and pizza. Carbohydrates are important to them, but the type of carbs eaten does vary regionally. Those who live in the north of the country have long been given the derogatory name of *polentone* (polenta eaters) while in turn the southerners have been labelled *terrone* (workers of the earth).

What is often overlooked, however, is that Italy is the largest rice producer in Europe. More than 40 per cent of the rice production takes place on about 400,000 hectares of the wide, fertile valley of the Po River, which flows 650 kilometres from its source high in the Alps, almost at the French border, across the breath of Northern Italy before emptying into the northern Adriatic, just south of Venice.

The growing of grains

Several varieties of rice are grown in Italy, and each suits the soil and climate of the region in which it is grown and performs differently in the dishes in which it is used.

People from Veneto, for instance, prefer a 'wet' risotto, calling it *risotto all'onda* (wavy risotto), and the locally grown *carnaroli* rice, a strain developed in the 1950s, works best for this. Another local dish, *risi e bisi*, is just rice and peas in a soupy risotto – delicious comfort food.

Further west in Emilia-Romagna, *arborio* rice is grown, allowing cooks to make a firmer risotto. Far up-river, in Lombardy, the Lomellina region is said to produce the best rice of all. *Carnaroli* and *arborio* are grown in Piedmont, and each April, **Crocera di Barge**, close to the source of the River Po celebrates with a rice festival (*Fiera del Riso*).

Tradition has it that merchants returning from the Far East to Venice or Genoa in the Middle Ages brought along the first small grains of rice. Knowledge gained in their travels would have brought the realisation that their own climate and the wide, flat Po Valley, which could be irrigated successfully using canals, might be ideal for testing out this fledgling industry. Evidence suggests it began around 1475.

From there it was just a short step until someone's *nonna* began to work in the kitchen with this strange new food, and sooner or later the first risotto (or at least its ancestor) was created.

Historically growing rice was a hands-on labour intensive task, especially for the *mondine*, women employed to plant and tend the rice fields. Since the mid 20th century, modern techniques have prevailed and rice farmings is now predominately a mechanised activity.

A matter of strains

The strains of rice grown in Italy are particularly important. Short-grain rice is better suited for the absorption-method dishes used in Italy, and *superfino* is preferred over the other grades of rice – *comune, semifino* and *fino* – as it allows just enough starch to be released from the outside of the grain to slightly thicken the dish, but retains a small 'crunch' in the centre, as Italian cooks always prefer *al dente*. Generally, the rule is that the higher the grade, the longer it will take to cook.

Arborio, carnaroli, baldo are in the *superfino* category. *Vialone nano* from Verona is *semifino* and has a PGI (Protected Geographical Indication) designation, and also highly regarded for risotto making.

Pasta

Marco Polo may have been a Venetian, but most Italians just don't believe that he discovered pasta in the Far East. *'No!'* they say, 'we already had it.' And there is good evidence to suggest that it was already being enjoyed in Liguria and Naples when he set off to explore Asia.

Italy has a staggering variety of pastas – reportedly there are about 3500 different shapes. These can vary between villages, even between families – Italian *nonnas* are revered as cooks, and their recipes cherished as family heirlooms. Traditionally in family homes, pasta was made fresh daily. The cook would heap a large amount of fine white *tipo 00* (strong) flour on the kitchen table, make an indentation in the middle and crack in an egg, perhaps some salt (depending on the region), maybe some olive oil, and a little water, then start to draw the dry ingredients into the centre, mixing the mass by hand, adding a few drops more water if necessary, until a smooth pliable dough was created.

Pieces were then rolled thinly and cut, often by hand with a sharp knife. Some homes used a small machine clamped to the tabletop, into which sheets of pasta dough were fed, folded and fed again, over and over until the desired thinness was reached. Then, and only then, was the cutting-side used to make thin strands. Or the sheets were left whole and used as layers in huge dishes of *lasagne* or rolled around a filling to become *cannelloni*, although there is also a large tube-shaped pasta of the same name that can be used for this. Sometimes rounds would be stamped out to use as *ravioli* or some other filled pasta.

While recipe books now include almost anything as an ingredient in pasta dough, traditional recipes were relatively unadventurous. Squid ink in some places, chilli in another, vegetables occasionally to colour the dough, but generally the flavours came from fillings, or the multitude of sauces or *ragùs*, which again often relied on generations-old recipes used by individual families. Some villages might stage contests between the locals, but it would be a brave person who put their hand up to judge such an affair, because, of course, everyone thinks their *mamma* (or *nonna*) is the best cook!

In the Italian home, pasta may be made in the morning, hung over a rail, or a broomstick between chairs, or some other simple device, and allowed to dry a little, then cooked very briefly when it is time to eat. That way the fresh pasta will be ready in just a couple of minutes after adding it to boiling salted (or unsalted – ah, that is another point of argument), perhaps with a splash of oil – another conflict of views. Those who have eaten freshly made pasta appreciate its silky tenderness and flavour. It won't necessarily be *al dente*, though (literally 'to the tooth', with a firm slightly resisting bite to it), as dried pasta is meant to be.

Its origins may be disputed, but there is no disagreement on how popular pasta has become since Italy introduced it to the rest of Europe.

Shaping up

The size of pasta ranges from large flat sheets used for *lasagne*, to couscous, which technically is a teeny-tiny pasta, the size of sugar crystals. Couscous originally hails from North Africa, it has drifted north to Sicily, where it has become part of the local cuisine.

Pasta shapes are made in a variety of ways. The most common sort is hand-rolled and cut, using a rolling pin and knife, which is an ideal way to quickly produce long, flat strands – everything from the finest *capellini d'angelo* (angel hair) and *vermicelli*, to *tagliatelle*, *fettuccine* and, ultimately, the wide *pappardelle*. In Calabria and Umbria, the process may involve a box-like tool with fine wires stretched taut across the top, called a *chitarra* (guitar). Sheets of pasta are pushed through the wires to make strands of spaghetti with square edges.

Small manual pasta machines abound in Italy and these are the best way for a home cook to achieve an even pasta sheet, which is hard to make any other way. There are also electric pasta machines that extrude the dough, in much the same way that a mincer or cookie press works, which are useful for making hollow pasta or other shapes. Commercial machines may have specially burred rollers and cutters to give a certain roughness to the surface of the pasta, allowing it to better capture the sauce in which it will be served. After all, the pasta itself is just one crucial part of a dish of pasta – what would it be without a sauce or filling – or both?

Fresh or dry?

Today's Italian housewife, and most of the rest of the pasta-loving world, often opts to use dried pasta. Sure, it takes longer to cook – maybe four or five times that of fresh pasta – but it stores well, and doesn't have to be made every day.

With the arrival of 'fresh' packaged pastas in delis and gourmet stores, there is now another choice, as this, like the homemade version, will keep unopened and uncooked, for a few days in the refrigerator.

The village favourite

For centuries, in villages throughout Italy, there have been a huge range of shapes, lovingly made by hand, from ear-shaped *orecchiette* to *fileja* – discs of pasta wrapped around wires or dowels to make a homespun *maccheroni* (macaroni). Often, different regions may make the same or very similar pasta shape, but the local dialect will give it a different name.

Then there are the filled pastas – little round button-shaped *tortellini* (a cousin to the dumplings Marco Polo no doubt ate in China), and larger *tortelloni*, round or square *ravioli* and semi-circular *agnolotti*.

On Italian menus, the 'Pasta' section often includes other types of food that share carbohydrates rather than technique. Expect to find *risotto*, *gnocchi* and, in northern regions, *spätzle*, a Teutonic dish of soft noodle dough, which is pushed through a colander or similar tool directly into boiling water or broth. Others, like *canederli* from Trentino-Alto Adige are really large dumplings made using stale bread.

The names of pasta shapes usually simply descriptive, such as *fusilli* (little spirals), *conchiglie* (shaped like a large seashell and often stuffed before baking in a sauce), *rotelle* (like a wagon wheel), and *radiatore* – a tube-shaped pasta with rippled edges, that look like little radiators. Others, like *strozzapreti* (priest stranglers) or *stringozzi* (tax collector stranglers) are a little less literal!

Perfect pasta partners

Pasta dishes will be as simple or as complex as the cook wishes. At one end of the scale, *spaghetti* may be served with just melted butter or olive oil and chilli tossed through it. A gourmet twist might substitute chopped truffles and parsley with the oil instead. Add a sprinkle of grated parmesan, and that would be all. At the other of the scale, the pasta might be served with a complex, slow-braised rabbit or hare *ragù*, or it could turn up in a multi-layered lasagne bursting with layers of meat *ragù*, vegetables, béchamel sauce and cheese.

Perhaps that is the eternal attraction of pasta. Forget where it all came from. Today it has become one of the most popular of Italy's many contributions to the world's table. Whether as a light one-dish meal, or part of a multi-course banquet, pasta is possibly the simplest, most versatile, most basic – and even the most loved – food on the planet.

Shape matters

While the shapes of pasta are attractive, that is not the sole reason for their creation. Their size and shape often affect the dish for which they are mainly used, and may help to 'grab' the sauce that accompanies them. There are some rules here that Italian cooks follow. With *bucatini* (a thick hollow spaghetti), the ideal accompaniment is the rich pork cheek, tomato and pecorino *amatriciana* sauce; *carbonara* or other light sauces go best with *spaghetti*; spicy tomato *arrabbiata* partners *penne*, its ribbed exterior and tube-like shape making it ideal to absorb and be filled by rich and sometimes chunky sauces, and *cime di rapa* (turnip tops) are traditional with *orecchiette*. *Fettuccine* and *pappardelle* are said to be best with creamy sauces, although the latter is often served in Tuscany with a rich duck *ragù*.

Opposite: Two women prepare home made tortelli, Piacenza, Emilia-Romagna.

Arancini alla Siciliana
Sicilian rice oranges

Ingredients

1 tablespoon, olive oil

1 small brown onion, finely chopped

1 stick celery, finely diced

200g lean minced beef

100g fresh or frozen peas

1/3 cup tomato puree (passata)*

Flaked salt

Freshly cracked black pepper

1 litre salt-reduced chicken stock

300g carnaroli rice (or vialone nano or arborio)

30g butter

50g parmesan cheese, grated

1 egg, lightly beaten

Vegetable oil, for deep-frying

1/3 cup plain flour, for dusting

2 eggs extra, lightly beaten

150g dried fine breadcrumbs

As far as fast food goes, you can't beat Sicilian arancini, deep-fried golden orbs of rice with a rich centre of minced beef, named after the oranges they resemble. Palermo is famous for them; in the city's historic centre, crowds park their motorini daily outside Bar Touring, in Via Abramo Lincoln, opposite the Botanic Gardens, to eat them straight out of the fryer.

Method

Heat oil in a medium frying pan over medium-high heat. Add onion and celery and cook for 5 minutes or until soft. Increase heat to high and add the mince cook for 8 minutes or until lightly browned. Add peas and passata. Season to taste.

Reduce heat to low and cook uncovered for 15 minutes. Allow to cool slightly, then mash mixture with a potato masher to combine and break up.

Meanwhile, bring only half the stock to a gentle boil and pour in the rice. Cook for 15 minutes, stirring occasionally and add more stock as required until the rice is al dente* and not too wet. Stir in the butter, cheese and egg. Spread the cooked rice out onto large platter or tray to cool.

To make an arancine, take a large spoonful of rice, roll in your hand to form a ball then make a hollow in the centre. Place a small teaspoonful of the mince mixture in the centre of the rice and bring edges in to completely cover mince filling. Continue to make all the balls this way.

Heat oil in a heavy based saucepan or deep fryer. Then lightly dust rice balls in flour, shaking off any excess. Dip into extra beaten egg and roll in breadcrumbs (again shaking off excess crumb). Coat all balls in breadcrumbs before beginning to cook. When cooked the balls should resemble "little oranges" and be golden brown. Serve hot or cold.

* Refer to Glossary – Page 470

Risotto ai funghi
Mushroom risotto

Serves 4

Ingredients

40g butter

2 tablespoons olive oil

1 medium brown onion, finely chopped

120g bacon, chopped

350ml dry white wine

2 garlic cloves, finely chopped

1 tablespoon finely chopped fresh sage or rosemary leaves

400g fresh porcini*, portabello or Swiss brown mushrooms*, diced

15g dried porcini mushrooms* (soaked for 15 minutes in tepid water, drained and roughly chopped)

1.25 litre salt-reduced chicken or vegetable stock

350 carnaroli rice (or vialone nano, or arborio)

100g fontina cheese*, cut into 1cm cubes

Flaked salt

Freshly cracked black pepper

50g parmesan cheese, shaved or grated

Fresh flat-leaf (Italian) parsley, to serve

Method

Heat only half the butter and only half the olive oil in a medium saucepan over medium heat, add onion and bacon; cook for 10 minutes.

Add only 250ml of the wine and simmer, uncovered, over a low heat until almost all the liquid has reduced.

Heat remaining butter and oil in a larger saucepan, add garlic, herbs and mushrooms; cook over high heat 2-3 minutes, reduce heat to medium and cook a further 5 minutes.

Add remaining wine to the mushroom mixture and cook a further 5 minutes.

Add the onion mixture to mushroom saucepan. Pour the stock into the medium saucepan, cover and bring to a gentle boil over medium heat. Reduce heat to low and keep the lid on the stock.

Stir rice into mushroom bacon mixture. Begin to add the heated stock 500ml at a time, stirring frequently and cooking until the liquid is absorbed. About halfway through cooking time, add the fontina cheese. Continue adding the warm stock 250ml at a time and stir frequently until all the stock has been absorbed and the rice is cooked but al dente* (this will take about 15-20 minutes).

Season to taste and serve immediately with shaved parmesan and parsley.

Variation – Don't add the bacon and add a few extra mushrooms (Swiss brown or button).

Tip: If the rice still has a "bite" and needs more liquid just add ¼ to ½ cup of boiling water.

* Refer to Glossary – Page 470

Risotto alla Milanese
Milanese risotto

Ingredients

1.25 litres chicken stock
2 teaspoons saffron threads*
100g butter
1 medium brown onion, finely chopped
350g carnaroli rice (vialone nano or arborio)
100g parmesan cheese, grated
Flaked salt
Freshly ground black pepper

Northern Italy is the home of risotto, specifically Piedmont, Lombardy and the Veneto where much of the country's rice is grown. Although most risotto dishes are served as a primo (first course), this Milanese version, for which saffron provides a deep yellow colour and distinctive aroma, is often served as an accompaniment to meaty stews, such as osso buco (page 136).

Method

Place stock into a medium saucepan, cover and bring to a gentle boil over medium heat. Reduce heat to low and keep the saucepan covered throughout the cooking of the risotto. Remove a small amount of stock to a side bowl and add the saffron threads to infuse.

Heat only half the butter in a larger saucepan or frying pan over medium-high heat. Add onion and cook for 5 minutes or until soft. Add the rice and cook a further 5 minutes, stirring often.

Reduce heat to low add the infused saffron, then begin to add the stock 500ml at a time, stirring frequently and cooking until the liquid is absorbed.

Continue adding the warm stock 250ml at a time and stir frequently until all the stock has been absorbed and the rice is cooked but al dente* (this will take about 15-20 minutes).

Stir in the remaining butter, parmesan and season to taste.

Serve immediately.

* Refer to Glossary – Page 470

Risotto ai frutti di mare
Seafood risotto

Ingredients

350g fish fillet, skinned (such as cod or monkfish)

720g medium whole green shrimp* (prawns), peeled, de-veined and shells reserved

1.125 litres fish stock

400g mussels, cleaned and beards removed

50g butter

1 tablespoon olive oil

1 leek, white part only, chopped

350g carnaroli rice (vialone nano or arborio)

250ml dry white wine

¼ cup chopped fresh flat-leaf (Italian) parsley

2 tablespoons chopped fresh chives

Flaked salt

Freshly cracked black pepper

Lemon wedges, to serve

Method

Cut fish into large cubes and set aside. Place reserved shrimp shells into a large saucepan with the stock, cover and bring to a gentle boil over medium-high heat. Remove shells with a slotted spoon and discard.

Poach the fish, shrimp and mussels in the hot stock, remove, set aside and keep warm. Keep the stock covered and over a low heat while cooking the risotto.

Meanwhile, heat only half the butter and the oil in a second large saucepan or frying pan over medium-high heat. Add leek and cook for 5 minutes or until soft. Add the rice and cook a further 5 minutes, stirring often. Add the wine and cook until it is absorbed.

Begin to add the stock 500ml at a time, stirring frequently and cooking until the liquid is absorbed. Continue adding the warm stock 250ml at a time and stir frequently until all the stock has been absorbed and the rice is cooked and al dente* (this will take about 15-20 minutes). Stir the remaining butter, herbs, poached fish and seafood through the cooked risotto and season to taste.

Serve immediately with lemon wedges.

Note – Risotto gets its creamy texture from the starch in the rice and from the knocking together of the grains while stirring during cooking. This is why risotto rice is not washed before using.

Note – Traditionally, cheese is not usually served with fish or shellfish risotto.

* Refer to Glossary – Page 470

Pasta all'uovo
Fresh egg pasta

Ingredients

300g plain or strong white flour
¼ teaspoon salt
3 free-range eggs*, at room temperature

Method

Place flour directly onto a clean work surface and add the salt.

Make a well in the middle and add the eggs. Use a fork to whisk the eggs and begin to draw and combine the flour into the eggs.

Lightly flour hands and continue to mix the flour and egg together to form a soft dough. Once the dough has come together, knead until smooth, elastic and silky to look at.

Wrap in plastic wrap and refrigerate for 30 minutes to chill.

If using a pasta machine, remove dough from refrigerator and leave it to return to room temperature. Divide into small balls about the size of a tennis ball.

Start with your pasta machine on the rollers farthest (widest) setting. Run one ball of dough though the rollers, about 10 times on this setting folding the pasta top to bottom or side to side to achieve a long sheet slightly narrower than the machine rollers. Continue to guide the pasta sheet through the rollers with every diminishing setting until you achieve the thickness you wish – usually this is the smallest or second-smallest setting.

Run the finished sheets through the cutting rollers of the pasta machine. Pile loosely on kitchen baking paper until you are ready to cook.

If rolling by hand, remove dough from refrigerator and leave it to return to room temperature. Divide into small balls about the size of a tennis ball.

Place a small amount of flour onto your work surface and roll the dough ball out into as thin a circle as you can manage, roll up the circle from one edge to the other as if you were rolling a rug, and slice to desired width.

Variation

• *To make spinach pasta: at the time of adding the eggs, add about ¼ cup of cooked and well-drained spinach that has been very finely chopped. Ensure as much moisture as possible has been removed.*

• *To make squid ink pasta: add 1 teaspoon or 1x 4g sachet squid ink with the egg.*

* Refer to Glossary – Page 470

Spaghetti alla Bolognese
Spaghetti Bolognese

Ingredients

450g dried or 650g fresh, spaghetti

50g parmesan cheese, grated, to serve

Sauce

80ml olive oil

1 large brown onion, finely chopped

2 garlic cloves, crushed

100g bacon, diced

1 celery stalk, finely diced

1 medium carrot, finely diced

250g beef mince

250g pork mince

150ml dry red wine

400g can chopped tomatoes

2 teaspoons finely chopped fresh oregano leaves

1 teaspoon flaked salt

Freshly ground black pepper

Method

To make the Sauce, heat oil in a large frying pan over medium-high heat and add onion, garlic, bacon, celery and carrot. Cook for 10 minutes.

Increase heat to high and add meat, cook until lightly brown, stirring occasionally and breaking up any large pieces of meat with the back of the spoon.

Add red wine and bring to the boil. Reduce heat to medium-low and continue to cook uncovered until wine has almost evaporated. Add tomato, oregano and season to taste. Reduce heat to low and cook covered for 1½-2 hours, or until sauce has thickened, stirring occasionally. Taste and season again, if required.

Cook the spaghetti in a large saucepan of boiling salted water until al dente*. Drain pasta and return to the saucepan. Add the Bolognese sauce and toss to combine.

Serve immediately with parmesan.

Tip: The longer the cooking time, the richer and more flavoursome the sauce.

Pesto
Pesto

Ingredients

200g pine nuts
200g (about 3 bunches) fresh basil leaves
4 garlic cloves, roughly chopped
370ml extra virgin olive oil
250g parmesan cheese, finely grated
Flaked salt
Freshly ground black pepper

Although the word pesto actually refers to any sort of paste, it's become synonymous with the basil-based pesto of Liguria, which combines pine nuts, garlic, olive oil, salt and parmesan (sometimes Pecorino Romano is included), which is tossed through pasta, used in soups and on meats. The Genoese invented it and insist that authentic pesto has to be made, with the locally grown small-leaf basil, in a marble mortar. But you can make an excellent pesto in a food processor using large-leafed basil, as in this recipe.

Method

Place the pine nuts into the bowl of a food processor bowl with the chopping blade and process in short bursts until roughly chopped.

Add the basil leaves (no stems) and garlic and process until just combined. With the machine in operation begin to add the oil in a steady stream through the liquid shoot in the processor lid. Lastly, add the cheese.

Season to taste.

Serve with your favourite vegetables or stir through hot pasta.

Note – Pesto will keep for about 3 days covered in the refrigerator the top of the pesto may discolour slightly so stir the pesto before reusing.

Tip: Homemade pesto can be frozen successfully to use when basil is not easily available or in season.

Salsa d'estate
Summer tomato & olive sauce

Serves 4

Ingredients

800g ripe tomatoes, finely chopped

1 medium brown onion, finely chopped

6 green olives, pitted and chopped

1 tablespoon capers*, drained and chopped

¼ teaspoon dried oregano leaves

¼ cup small whole fresh basil leaves or torn large leaves

2 garlic cloves, crushed

120ml extra virgin olive oil

Flaked salt

Freshly cracked black pepper

400g dried or 650g fresh pasta of choice

Method

Combine the tomatoes, onion, olives, capers, oregano, basil, garlic and olive oil in a medium bowl. Season to taste. Cover and refrigerate overnight.

Remove from the fridge about an hour before serving to allow sauce to return to room temperature.

Bring a large pot of salted water to the boil, add the pasta and cook according to packet directions or until al dente*.

Drain pasta and toss with sauce and serve.

Tip: Often when basil is chopped too vigorously on a chopping board essential oils are lost into the board – this is why many recipes suggest that basil leaves be directly torn into a dish.

* Refer to Glossary – Page 470

Lasagna
Beef lasagna

Ingredients

8-10 sheets of fresh or dried sheets
lasagna*
2½ quantities béchamel sauce*
250g mozzarella cheese*, finely grated
100g parmesan cheese, finely grated
250ml water

Filling
2 tablespoons olive oil
1 large brown onion, finely chopped
1 garlic clove, finely chopped
500g minced beef
1 tablespoon tomato paste
400g can chopped tomatoes
2 teaspoons dried mixed herb leaves
150ml dry red wine
Flaked salt
Freshly cracked black pepper

The Emilians claim ownership of lasagna but there would be few households in Italy that don't have their own special recipe. Traditionally, rich meat ragu and cheesey béchamel are layered with sheets of fresh spinach pasta and baked in the oven. Plain, dried lasagna sheets generally work well (just don't tell the purists). Be careful not to overlap the pasta sheets too much or the lasagna can become stodgy.

Method

To make the Filling, heat oil in a large frying pan over medium heat and cook onion for 3-4 minutes. Increase heat to high and add garlic and beef, cooking until meat is lightly brown. Stir occasionally and break up any large pieces of meat with the back of the spoon.

Reduce heat to medium and add the tomato paste and cook uncovered for 10 minutes. Add tomatoes, herbs and wine, stir well to combine. Reduce heat to low and cook uncovered for 30 minutes (mixture should be fairly moist, add about ½ cup water, if necessary). Season to taste.

Preheat oven to 200°C.

To assemble the lasagna, use an ovenproof dish approximately 25cm x 40cm – the aim is to have 4 sheets of pasta on each layer.

Begin by placing only half the meat mixture over the base of the dish. Then lay 4-5 pasta sheets side by side (ideally, don't overlap) onto the meat. Top with only half the béchamel sauce and sprinkle with a little mozzarella and parmesan.

Repeat layering with remaining meat mixture and pasta, then pour the water evenly over the last pasta layer. Finish with the remaining béchamel sauce and cheeses.

Bake in preheated oven for 20-30 minutes or until pasta is tender and the top golden. Serve hot with a salad or green beans.

Tip: Use lasagna pasta sheets that don't need pre cooking to save time. Or make or look for fresh lasagna sheets.

Tip: It's OK to break the sheet to fit on the edges, if necessary.

Variation – Reduce the beef to 300g and use the sausage meat from 200g of Italian sausages (cut sausage skin and remove meat then discard skins). You could also add a layer of cooked and well-drained spinach in the middle.

* Refer to Glossary – Page 470

Spaghetti d'estate
Summer spaghetti

Ingredients

125ml extra virgin olive oil
1 teaspoon finely grated lemon rind
2 tablespoons lemon juice
2 garlic cloves, finely chopped
8 fresh basil leaves, torn
½ teaspoon chilli flakes, or to taste
400g dried or 650g fresh spaghetti
Flaked salt
Freshly cracked black pepper
Grated fresh parmesan, for serving

Method

Heat the oil in a large frying pan over medium heat add the lemon rind, lemon juice, garlic, basil and chilli, cook for 1 minute or until aromatic. Remove from heat.

Bring a large pot of salted water to the boil, add the pasta and cook according to packet directions or until al dente*. Drain.

Add pasta to sauce in frying pan and stir to coat in sauce. Season to taste.

Serve with parmesan.

Tip: Add small fresh basil leaves when serving

* Refer to Glossary – Page 470

Cannelloni di carne e spinaci
Cannelloni with meat & spinach

Serves 4-6

Ingredients

15 cannelloni tubes (dried)*
1 quantity béchamel sauce*
125g mozzarella cheese*, grated
2 tablespoons grated parmesan cheese

Filling

2 tablespoons olive oil
1 medium brown onion, finely chopped
1 garlic clove, crushed
250g minced beef
250g minced pork
½ teaspoon dried basil leaves
½ teaspoon dried oregano leaves
2 teaspoons tomato paste
250g frozen spinach, thawed
1 egg, lightly beaten
60ml pure (single) cream
Flaked salt
Freshly cracked black pepper

Tomato sauce

2 tablespoons olive oil
1 small brown onion, finely chopped
1 garlic clove, peeled and crushed
400g can chopped tomatoes
250ml water
2 tablespoons tomato paste
1 teaspoon, sugar
Flaked salt
Freshly cracked pepper

Method

Preheat oven to 190°C.

To make the Filling, heat oil in a large frying pan over medium heat and cook onion for 3-4 minutes. Increase heat to high and add garlic, beef and pork, cooking until meat is lightly browned. Stir occasionally and break up any large pieces of meat with the back of the spoon. Add dried herbs and tomato paste then cook, uncovered, for 10-15 minutes. Remove from heat and add spinach, egg and cream; mix well to combine. Season to taste and allow to cool slightly.

To make the Sauce, heat oil in a medium saucepan over medium-high heat, add onion and garlic and cook for 5 minutes. Add remaining ingredients, bring to the boil then reduce heat to low. Cover and simmer for 10 minutes, stirring occasionally. Season to taste.

To assemble the cannelloni, spread about ¼ cup of tomato sauce over the base of an ovenproof dish large enough to fit all the cannelloni tubes in a single layer.

Spoon meat filling into cannelloni tubes and arrange side by side into the dish and around the edges of the dish in a single layer. Cover filled cannelloni tubes with remaining tomato sauce. Spread the béchamel sauce over the top of the dish and finish with the grated cheeses.

Bake, in preheated oven for 30 minutes or until the pasta is cooked and the top golden brown. Serve with salad.

Tip: To test if pasta is cooked, a small sharp knife should easily insert into a cooked cannelloni shell.

* Refer to Glossary – Page 470

Ravioli alla stufato
Beef & spinach ravioli

Serves 4-5

Ingredients

1 quantity of pasta dough

Filling

1 tablespoon olive oil

1 small brown onion, finely diced

80g minced beef

30ml red wine

60ml beef stock

1 bay leaf

1 cinnamon stick

50g fresh spinach leaves

1 teaspoon finely chopped fresh marjoram leaves

1 eggwhite, lightly beaten

2 teaspoons finely grated parmesan

Flaked salt

Freshly cracked black pepper

Method

To make the Filling, heat oil in a small frying pan, add onion and cook for 5 minutes over medium-high heat or until soft. Increase heat to high and add meat, cooking until meat is lightly brown, stirring occasionally and breaking up any large pieces of meat with the back of the spoon. Add wine, beef stock, bay leaf and cinnamon stick. Cover and cook over a low heat for 1-1½ hours or until meat is tender and juices thick. Stir occasionally.

Meanwhile, boil spinach for 3-4 minutes in lightly salted water; drain and, using your hands, squeeze out excess liquid and finely chop. Allow the meat to cool then remove and discard bay leaf and cinnamon stick. Add spinach, marjoram, eggwhite and parmesan to the meat. Mix well, season to taste and set aside to cool. If time permits refrigerate until cold.

To make the Ravioli, cut dough into two portions, keeping the second ball covered (to prevent drying out) while rolling out the first. Roll out dough on a lightly floured surface (or use a pasta machine) to a 1-2mm thickness, cut into 20cm wide strips and place over ravioli mould*.

Add half a teaspoon of filling to each mould – no more, or they will burst during cooking. Top with another strip of dough and roll across the top of the mould firmly with a rolling pin. Turn out of mould onto a lightly floured surface and cut into individual ravioli with a fluted wheel.

Alternatively, place dough strips on a floured board and place half teaspoonfuls of filling at 5cm intervals. With a damp finger, trace lines onto the dough between the fillings. Place a second dough strip on top. Press down lightly between mounds of filling and cut into ravioli shapes with a fluted wheel. At this point you can freeze the ravioli on baking trays (then bag when frozen), or cook in plenty of boiling salted water for 6-8 minutes, until tender.

Tip: Serve with your favourite sauce (for example pesto or tomato) or simply extra virgin olive oil, fresh herbs, grated parmesan and season to taste.

Tip: Make the filling the day before so it is cold and easier to use and the flavour will be more developed too. New tip frozen ravioli should be cooked from frozen; just allow a little extra cooking time.

* Refer to Glossary – Page 470

Spaghetti ai frutti di mare
Seafood spaghetti

Serves 4

Ingredients

450g dried or 650g fresh spaghetti

60ml olive oil

2 garlic cloves, crushed

500g mixed prepared shellfish (shrimp, mussels, clams)

1 tablespoon baby capers*

½ teaspoon chilli flakes

2 teaspoons tomato paste

¼ cup chopped fresh flat-leaf (Italian) parsley

1 tablespoon lemon juice

Flaked salt

Freshly cracked black pepper

Method

Cook the spaghetti in a large saucepan of boiling salted water according to packet instructions or until al dente*.

Meanwhile, heat oil in a large frying pan over low-medium heat, add garlic and cook until for 2-3 minutes or until lightly golden. Increase heat to medium-high and add the shellfish, capers, chilli flakes and tomato paste. Stir to combine and cook for 5-10 minutes, stirring occasionally.

Add the parsley and lemon juice. Season to taste.

Drain spaghetti and place onto a serving platter or divide spaghetti between four plates, top with shellfish sauce and serve immediately.

Tip: As a timesaver, marinara mix – a mixture of prepared shellfish and calamari – can be used. It's available at fish shops.

* Refer to Glossary – Page 470

Spaghetti alla carbonara
Spaghetti carbonara

Serves 4-6

Ingredients

450g dried or 650g fresh, spaghetti
2 tablespoons olive oil
200g bacon, roughly chopped
1 garlic clove, crushed
2 free-range eggs*, at room temperature
2 free-range egg yolks*, at room temperature
80g parmesan cheese, grated
80g pecorino cheese*, grated
Flaked salt
Freshly cracked black pepper

Carbonara is a Roman dish thought to have originated in the mid-20th century. It's usually served with spaghetti, although fettuccine, rigatoni and bucatini are also used. The egg cooks and the cheese melts as they come into contact with the piping hot pasta, creating a delicious sauce. If you can get your hands on guanciale, cured pork cheek, use it instead of the bacon in this recipe.

Method

Cook the pasta in a large saucepan of boiling salted water according to packet instructions or until al dente*.

Drain, reserving 1-2 tablespoons cooking water in the saucepan. Return pasta to saucepan.

Meanwhile, heat oil in a large frying pan over medium-high heat, add bacon and cook for 3-4 minutes or until slightly crisp. Add garlic and remove from heat. In a bowl combine eggs and yolks with the grated cheeses. Ideally, prepare egg mixture as close to the time of the spaghetti being cooked as possible.

Add the bacon and the egg and cheese mixture to the hot spaghetti and toss with tongs to combine. The egg will cook as it comes into contact with the hot pasta. Season to taste and be generous with the pepper.

Serve immediately.

Note – Pancetta is the cured meat traditionally used in this dish.*

* Refer to Glossary – Page 470

Tagliatelle con salmone
Tagliatelle with smoked salmon

Serves 4

Ingredients

200g sliced smoked salmon

450g dried or 650g fresh tagliatelle*

60ml extra virgin olive oil

2 tablespoons baby capers*

1 teaspoon finely grated lemon rind

2 teaspoons lemon juice

2 tablespoons snipped fresh chives

¼ cup chopped fresh flat-leaf (Italian) parsley

Flaked salt

Freshly cracked black pepper

Method

Cut salmon slices into strips and set aside.

Cook the pasta in a large saucepan of boiling salted water according to packet instructions or until al dente*.

Drain, reserving 1-2 tablespoons cooking water in the saucepan. Return pasta to saucepan.

Add to the pasta the oil, capers, lemon rind and juice, chives and parsley. Toss with tongs to combine. Season to taste. Add the salmon and gently toss again.

Serve immediately with salad and crusty bread.

Variation – Serve pasta topped with breadcrumbs that have been lightly fried until golden and crisp. You can also serve with freshly chopped red chilli.

* Refer to Glossary – Page 470

Ragù alla Napoletana
Neopolitan beef & tomato sauce

Serves 4-6

Ingredients

1.5kg piece of beef blade, cut into large pieces

100g piece prosciutto crudo*

50g bacon, trim rind, retaining fat

2 tablespoons olive oil

1 medium brown onion, finely chopped

2 garlic cloves, crushed

200ml dry red wine

500g tomato puree (passata)*

2 tablespoons tomato paste

Flaked salt

Freshly cracked black pepper

450g dried or 650g fresh pasta

Small fresh basil leaves, to serve

Parmesan cheese, to serve

In a true Neapolitan ragu, a large piece of beef or pork is simmered slowly, with wine and stock added from time to time. It's two dishes in one: the thick, dark cooking juices are used as a sugo for ridged short pasta and the meat is eaten as a second course. The portinai (doormen) of Naples were known for having ragu bubbling away on their stovetops all day long, while they watched the comings and goings in their apartment buildings.

Method

Cut beef blade into large pieces and set aside. Cut prosciutto and bacon into strips.

Heat the oil in a heavy based saucepan over medium heat and add the prosciutto, bacon, onion and garlic, cook for 5 minutes or until soft. Increase heat to medium-high and add the beef; cook until browned on all sides.

Add the wine to the meat a little at a time, allowing it to evaporate before you add more. When all the wine is evaporated, stir in the passata and paste, cover and cook over a very low heat for 2 hours or until the meat falls apart easily. Add a little boiling water, if necessary, to prevent the meat from sticking to the bottom of the saucepan and stir occasionally.

At the end of this time the sauce should be dark, thick and glossy. Break up the meat using two forks and season to taste. Thin the sauce with a little extra boiling water if it is too thick.

Cook the pasta of your choice, preferably penne or maccheroni, in a large saucepan of boiling salted water, following the instructions on the packet or until al dente*.

Drain, and return to the saucepan. Pour over the ragu' sauce, cook stirring over low heat for 2-3 minutes. Serve garnished with fresh basil leaves and a handful of grated parmesan cheese.

Variation – The meat may be left in larger pieces and enjoyed with vegetables or, if finely torn apart, could be used for filling Ravioli

* Refer to Glossary – Page 470

Farfalle con salsiccia e radicchio rosso
Pasta bows with sausage & radicchio

Serves 4

Ingredients

450g dried farfalle* pasta

600g Italian sausage, meat removed from casing

30g butter

80ml olive oil

1 medium brown onion, finely chopped

½ teaspoon chilli flakes, or to taste

150g radicchio rosso leaves*, shredded

200ml dry white wine

200ml thickened cream*

Flaked salt

Freshly cracked black pepper

Method

Cook the pasta in a large saucepan of boiling salted water according to packet instructions or until al dente*.

Drain, reserving 1-2 tablespoons cooking water in the saucepan. Return pasta to saucepan.

Meanwhile, cut the sausage meat into bite-sized pieces. Heat butter and oil in a large frying pan over medium-high heat, cook onion and chilli for 3-4 minutes or until it just changes colour. Add the sausage, and cook until lightly browned. Add the radicchio to the pan and cook stirring, until just wilted.

Add the white wine and simmer uncovered for 2-3 minutes or until slightly reduced, then add the cream. Stir well to combine,

Add cooked mixture to the pasta. Stir, over low heat for 3-4 minutes or until heated through. Season to taste.

Serve immediately.

* Refer to Glossary – Page 470

Penne con pesce spada e finocchio
Pasta with swordfish & fennel

Serves 4

Ingredients

450g dried or 650g fresh pasta (such as penne)

600g swordfish steaks

1 leek

1 medium fennel bulb

60ml olive oil

40g butter

Finely grated rind from ½ lemon

Juice from ½ lemon

½ teaspoon chilli flakes or to taste

2 tablespoons chopped fresh flat-leaf (Italian) parsley

Flaked salt

Freshly cracked black pepper

Extra virgin olive oil, to serve

Method

Cook the pasta in a large saucepan of boiling salted water according to packet instructions or until al dente*.

Drain, reserving 1-2 tablespoons cooking water in the saucepan. Return pasta to saucepan.

Meanwhile, cut the swordfish into large cubes about 2cm and set aside. Trim and wash leek then thinly slice the white section and a little of the pale green section, discard remaining leek. Trim tips from fennel and cut in half lengthways then very thinly slice.

Heat the oil and butter in a large frying pan over medium-high heat. Cook the swordfish for 1-2 minutes each side or until lightly browned then remove to a side plate.

To the same pan add the leek and fennel cook over medium heat for 8-10 minutes or until soft. Return fish to the frying pan add the lemon rind and juice, chilli and parsley. Season to taste.

Add cooked mixture to the pasta. Stir over low heat for 3-4 minutes or until heated through.

Serve immediately drizzled with a little extra olive oil.

* Refer to Glossary – Page 470

Fettuccine nere con calamari
Pan-fried squid with squid ink fettuccine

Serves 4

Ingredients

800g whole fresh calamari (squid)

Flaked salt

Freshly cracked black pepper

1 quantity squid ink fettuccini

80ml extra virgin olive oil

1 garlic clove, crushed

1 small red chilli, halved, seeded and sliced

60ml lemon juice

1 cup fresh flat-leaf (Italian) parsley leaves, coarsely chopped

1 tablespoon capers*, coarsely chopped

Extra virgin olive oil, to serve

Lemon wedges, to serve

Method

Once the calamari is cleaned (see note), cut the calamari hoods open and lay flat on a board, inside up. Score with a sharp knife to make a crisscross pattern just into the surface of the calamari (also known as "honeycombing"), then cut the flesh into smaller pieces. Cut the tentacles into sets of two or three. Season with salt and pepper and set aside.

Add the fettuccini to a large saucepan of boiling salted water. Cook for 3 minutes or until al dente*. Drain well.

While pasta is cooking, heat only half the olive oil in a large frying pan over medium -high heat. Add only half the calamari and cook for 1-2 minutes or until curled up and lightly browned. Remove from heat and repeat with remaining olive oil and calamari.

Return all the calamari to the pan with the garlic and chilli and cook for 1 minute or until aromatic. Deglaze the pan by adding the lemon juice and while bubbling, scrape the bottom of the pan to lift any bits stuck to the base.

Add the cooked pasta, parsley and capers, and toss over heat until pasta has heated through and is well coated. Season to taste.

Serve drizzled with a little more extra virgin olive oil and serve with lemon wedges.

Tip: To prepare the calamari, gently pull the body of the squid away from the tentacles, then remove the cartilage from the body – it should pull out quite easily. Skin the body, starting from the open edge and pulling it inside out along the length of the body. Rinse the squid body under cold running water. Cut the squid head just below the eyes to remove the tentacles, discard the intestines and the ink sac (if not using for risotto or pasta). Remove the "shell-like beak" from the centre of the tentacles, pressing gently on the body to make it pop out. Cut tentacles into pieces for cooking.

* Refer to Glossary – Page 470

Polenta
Creamy polenta

Ingredients

1.5 litres salt reduced chicken stock or water

2 teaspoons flaked salt (only if using water)

350g polenta*

30g butter

2 tablespoons extra virgin olive oil

Flaked salt, extra

Freshly cracked black pepper

Method

Pour stock into a large heavy-based saucepan over medium-high heat, cover with a lid and bring to the boil.

Gradually pour the polenta into the stock, stirring continuously with a wooden spoon. Reduce heat to low and continue stirring – this process may take from 30-50 minutes. The polenta is ready when it leaves the side of the pan.

Stir in the butter, oil and season to taste. Mix well.

Serve immediately.

Variation – Add 100g finely grated parmesan cheese when adding the butter and beat well to combine.

Tip: Using a slightly wet spoon when serving will make it easier to remove the polenta from the spoon.

* Refer to Glossary – Page 470

Gnocchi alla Valdostana
Valdostana gnocchi

One of the core ingredients of this polenta-based gnocchi is fontina, an unpasteurised cow's milk cheese from the Valle d'Aosta near the French border in the north-west of Italy, after which this dish is named. They can be served with a meaty sauce or eaten as a snack on their own.

Ingredients

1 litre milk
200g polenta*
100g cornflour (cornstarch)
1 teaspoon flaked salt
150g fontina cheese*, cubed
20g butter
Pinch ground nutmeg
2 egg yolks, at room temperature
40g parmesan cheese, finely grated
Freshy ground white pepper

Method

Preheat oven to 180°C. Line 2 large baking trays with kitchen baking paper.

Place milk into a medium saucepan and bring to a gentle boil over medium heat, then slowly add polenta, cornflour and salt; whisking or stirring constantly – make sure to move vigorously as polenta thickens to ensure an even consistency. Gently squash any lumps that form by pressing them against the side of the saucepan. Cook for 20 minutes. While cooking the bottom of the saucepan will become encrusted and the polenta will begin to lift away from the encrusted base of pan – indicating that it is ready.

Remove from heat and add cheese, butter and nutmeg; mix well. Cool slightly and mix in yolks.

With a spatula spread mixture onto a flat, clean work surface to a thickness of 1cm. Cool and cut into 4 or 5cm rounds, using a round or fluted cutter.

Place rounds onto prepared trays, sprinkle with parmesan and season with pepper.

Bake for 15 minutes or until golden. Serve hot or cold.

Tip: Have a small bowl of flour at your side to dip the cutter into if it sticks to the mixture while cutting out the rounds. Just dip the cutting edge into the flour and shake off excess. After the first round of cutting the polenta dough it can be re-kneaded and more circles can be cut. Alternatively, cut polenta into squares.

* Refer to Glossary – Page 470

Venezia e Veneto
(Venice & the Veneto)

As its name suggests, this region surrounds the fabled and fabulous city of Venice. Full of romance and art, Veneto enjoys an influx of visitors, and indeed survives visits by millions of tourists annually, who heavily outnumber the locals.

The region also pokes a finger north beyond the canals, finishing at the tiny border with Austria in the Dolomites, and extending westward to Lake Garda, to include the venerable cities of Verona and Padua.

Historically grand, Venice was referred to as *La Serenissima*, meaning "the most serene" for more than 1000 years; a cultured aristocratic city filled with doges, or dukes, presiding at colossal and exquisite banquets in their *palazzi* (palaces).

Alongside all this wealth and grandeur, a constant stream of visiting sailors created a demand for simple and hearty home-cooked fare as part of its thriving merchant economy.

Today's Venice is bustling with tourists and is far from serene, but both the city itself and the Veneto region, extending from Lake Garda to the Venetian lagoon in one direction, and from the Po River to the Dolomites in the other, still manage to provide something for everyone.

Land of plenty

Vaneto's wide spread of climate and terrain means that, in terms of produce, almost anything is available. In the warmer, sunnier areas there are vineyards and olives. Cherries are best near Marostica and the Verona hills, while apples and pears flourish in the hills around Castelbaldo and **Casale di Scodosia**. Excellent chestnuts are harvested around Treviso, inland from Venice, and strawberries, melons, nectarines and even kiwi fruit are grown on the Verona plain and towards the Garda hills. Those peaches from Verona (and only white peaches, of course), are often used for Peach Bellinis, the famed cocktail devised at Harry's Bar on **Piazza San Marco** in Venice. Harry's even employs a staff member whose sole duty is to peel and pulp these remarkable peaches.

Vegetables also love the climate and soil of Veneto – red chicory (*radicchio*) hails from Treviso variegated chicory from Castelfranco, with many others from Verona, and Chioggia, at the southern end of the Venetian lagoon. **Bassano del Grappa** is noted for its fine asparagus, which is mainly grown on the plains, while potatoes are grown mainly in *terreni rossi*, the rich red soil around **Roveredo di Guà** in the heart of the region. Honey, for sweetening dishes, comes from hives situated towards the Dolomites.

Venice may be this region's star performer, but the quality produce from the surrounding region also deserves its time in the spotlight.

Opposite: Vegetables sold from a gondola in the picturesque S. Elena Quarter, Venice, Veneto.

The province of Veneto produces about 20 per cent of Italy's DOC wines.

Below: the town of Bassano del Grappa and the *Ponte degli Alpini* - a covered wooden bridge over the Brenta river, designed by the famed Venetian architect Palladio in 1568.

Opposite: Vineyards of the Soave wine region, Veneto.

Cheeses are made throughout the Veneto, notably *asiago* from Vicentino, and from the Belluno Valley in the Dolomites, *piave* and *schiz*, a fresh cheese served baked with butter or cream. The lush pastures of the region are ideal for raising pigs and dairy cattle, while the coast provides fish from the sea and cultivated eels, bass and mussels from the Venetian lagoon. Inland streams yield freshwater fish, and game is hunted and trapped in the mountains.

As is common all over Italy, cured meats are prepared in many parts of the Veneto. Stars of this region are *prosciutto Veneto*, produced between the Euganei and Berici hills, and *sopressa vicentina*, from the Pasubio valleys but also produced in many other places throughout the region.

Rice rules, polenta prevails

While *bigoli*, a thick spaghetti often served with an anchovy sauce, appears on menus, pasta is still rarer here than the ubiquitous polenta or rice. These cereal crops are generally grown in the lowlands, with barley planted in the cooler north. The local strain of rice, *vialone nano veronese*, grown near Verona is preferred as diners in Veneto prefer looser, wetter risotto, calling it *risotto all'onda*, or wavy risotto.

Polenta is king in Veneto, and used throughout the region, often flavoured with Eastern spices and raisins, similarly to couscous. *Baccalà* (salt cod), introduced by northern seafarers centuries ago, is a popular staple here, too.

Perhaps the most basic dish on the menu is *risi e bisi* (true peasant food – just rice and peas, and as simple as it gets), now becoming trendy in other countries because of its simple combination of flavours. To celebrate its patron saint, *San Marco*, Venice hosts *Risi e Bisi*, a delightful festival, each April.

The *secondi* (main courses) on menus in Veneto will be *vitello* (veal) and *pollo* (chicken), and other popular meats including guinea fowl and horse, may also be on offer. For dolci (dessert) *Tiramisù*, a dish often regarded quintessentially Italian, *pan biscotto* – a firm, long-lasting bread found all over the region, and *fougasse* – a rich pastry-like cake.

Cicchetti, however, are a typically Venetian specialty. Ideal to accompany drinks in one of the city's many bars, these small tapas-style snacks – mini meals of fish or meat dishes, sandwiches, olives, cured meats – are common, and you can make an entire meal from them if you wish, generally accompanied by a glass or two of local white wine, such as Moscato or Soave.

Dining al fresco

Venice has a relaxed style of dining. Cafes, especially those in **Piazza San Marco** and the other main tourist areas, usually provide outdoor seating and umbrellas. In the smaller streets there are bars, cafes and pizzerias, mostly geared to the tourist trade, admittedly, but still allowing space for diners to linger canalside and soak up the ambience of this unique city. There are also a number of osterias serving local specialties dotted throughout the city, which are worth searching out.

Whilst the Veneto is not generally regarded as one of the country's major wine regions, it produces about 20 per cent of Italy's DOC wines. These are mainly grown towards Lake Garda, especially in the vicinity of Verona. Prosecco, so essential to Bellinis – indeed, to most social occasions in Italy, including breakfast – comes from Treviso. Amarone, a fine red, is made near Valpolicella and Veneto also produces a fine and fragrant Bardolino.

Visitors in February will find themselves caught up in Venice's weeks-long *Carnevale*, essentially a street party before the privations of Lent. On the last day of *Carnevale* there is a massive dumpling feast in Verona. The markets of Padua, Chioggia and Venice, the latter right on the Grand Canal, are also must-sees for any visitor to the area. The fish is of the best and freshest possible quality, as is the other produce, brought directly from the fields that day, and in Venice it arrives and is taken away by boat, which alone is worth seeing.

Emilia-Romagna

The mighty Po River touches many regions throughout Italy, and here it is again, bordering Emilia-Romagna to the north. This large wedge-shaped region stretches almost right across the peninsula from the mountains near Piedmont in the west to the Adriatic coast in the east.

The sweep from mountains to sea and its abundance of fresh produce has created a region of generosity. Some call this area Italy's "gastronomic heart", and it is certainly responsible for producing some of the country's best ham and cheese, as well as much more.

The preference for dishes varies across the region. The residents of Emilia, from Piacenza to Bologna, prefer richer, more buttery dishes while their coastal neighbours in Romagna, from Ravenna to Rimini, go for meatier, stronger, more "central Italian" food.

The best of the best

Absolute star of the region's cheese is *Parmigiano-Reggiano*, called the "king of cheeses" and produced in Parma, Reggio nell'Emilia, Modena and Bologna. *Grana Padano* comes from Piacenza in the far north-western corner on the Po, as does *provolone Valpadana*. A particularly unusual local cheese is *formaggio di fossa* (meaning "pit cheese", where it is aged), which is made by entire communities in **Sogliano al Rubicone** near Rimini.

The most famous gastronomic celebrity from Emilia-Romagna is the Parma prosciutto – air-dried, salt-cured and spectacular. But in this nirvana of cured meats there are many other varieties of *charcuterie*: *coppa*, pork and fat-rich *mortadella, pancetta, salame, coppa* and *cotechini* – large nutmeg-enhanced pork sausages. The *Festival del Prosciutto di Parma* held every September to celebrate this remarkable produce.

However, there many other delicious options arising from the valleys of the river beyond *prosciutto* and *parmigiana*. There are corn and cold-climate fruits from farms and orchards in the upper Po Valley, and pears, peaches, nectarines, cherries and plums in Romagna. The **Castel del Rio** woodlands yield chestnuts, and mushrooms are collected from the woods of the **Val di Taro** and **Pontremoli**. Brisighella, near Piacenza, is famous for its olive oil.

While the deep waters of the Adriatic provide fresh fish, the fishing lagoons of Comacchio on the northern coast are also important, as are the Bologna flatlands, where rice fields have been converted for breeding fish.

Cheese and ham might sound like staple foods, but with Emilia-Romagna's magic touch they're taken to a whole new level.

Opposite: the picturesque villiage of Sestola, Emilia-Romagna, known as 'the pearl of Modena' and a paradise for winter and mountain sports.

Life in Emilia-Romagna is like a year long celebration of food, with festivals for all things culinary, from balsamic vinegar and *proscuitto* to the humble bulb of garlic.

Connoisseurs of vinegar

Modena, almost in the centre of Emilia-Romagna, is responsible for the region's third most famous product: *aceto balsamico* – balsamic vinegar, which has been made there since the eighth century. It's a true craft and some of the aged balsamics are treated as carefully as aged wines (and are as valuable). Gusto Balsamico features *balsamico* during the first week of October in Modena in collaboration with Slow Food Italia – the perfect time to explore the possibilities and tastes of the town.

Risottos become thicker again here, using arborio rice. G*nocco fritto*, fried gnocchi, may be on the menu, and this is the heartland of egg pasta, often handmade. Menus include *lasagne* and *tortellini* (plus *tortelli* and *tortelloni*, all originally from Bologna).

Above: an old fishing casone in the marshlands of the Po delta, Emilia-Romagna.

Opposite: a cheese master assesses the aging of his Parmigiano Reggiano.

A plate of *artisanal tagliatelle*, also from Bologna, may be topped with *ragù alla bolognese*, a worldwide favourite of meaty mince pork and veal sauce made with vegetables, lemon zest and nutmeg. Elsewhere it might be *maltagliati* (literally, "badly cut"), roughly chopped pasta sheets (sometimes called rag pasta) and beans, or navel-shaped stuffed pasta in a soupy broth, called *tortellini in brodo*.

Savoury snacks may be *piadina*, a fried unleavened flatbread filled with cheese and vegetables from Emilia, or *biscione reggiano* (biscuits), spongata, a short pastry with nuts, honey and candied fruits from Bussetto or Reggio nell'Emilia, and *torta di riso reggiana*, a rice cake from **Reggio nell'Emilia**.

This foodie region has so much to offer, including some of Italy's best and most artistically served gelati in *Reggio nell'Emilia*, and many *pizzicherie* stores selling *charcuterie* in Bologna.

And the only thing to toast friends, family and a little *ragù alla* is some Lambrusco, that fun and sparkling red, and the best-known wine of the region, hailing from the upper Po – although there are many other vineyards in the hills, some with a QC (Quality Controlled tag) and many with DOC labels. *Salute!*

gourmet
pilgrim

Carne

Meat

Slow cooked,
cured, minced
or turned into
sausages,
Italians love
their meat.

Carne e selvaggine
(Meat & game)

Italians love their meat. As a nation of farmers, people in most parts of the country have always raised animals that were destined to be killed for the table. It's a pragmatic approach that suits the country's way of life – Italians are not known for their squeamishness. Pigs, sheep, goats, cattle and poultry, even horse, are staple parts of the Italian diet. In some areas donkey meat is available too. In rural and remote areas game – birds, rabbit and hare, boar, venison and wild birds – are a welcome addition to the table.

The prolific pig

Pigs are raised throughout the country, and much of their meat is used for cured meat products and sausages. Pork (*maiale*) is eaten with beans or cabbage in Piedmont, in stews and casseroles and as chops and other cuts accross the nation. *Porchetta* is very popular, especially in Umbria and Lazio, where a whole adult pig will be spit-roasted, then carved to order. A popular Sardinian dish, *porceddu*, is pit-roasted suckling pig, and roasted pork loin is enjoyed everywhere.

A cut above the rest

Cuts of meat (their names often expressed in the local dialect) vary between regions. However, most Italian *macellerie* (butcher shops) will have on hand plenty of the palest *vitello* from young calves, as milk-fed tender young veal is highly prized. Veal is used for *osso buco Milanese (see page 136)*, a rich dish of veal shank, and *vitello tonnato*, an unusual dish of veal slices with a piquant tuna sauce (see page 132). It is seen on menus with sliced ham as *saltimbocca* (see page 154), or crumbed and fried as *cotoletta alla Milanese*.

Perhaps the next most-used meat is from sheep, ranging from *abbacchio* (milk-fed lamb) - a traditional Easter dish in Rome, to *agnello* (lamb) (see page 128) and *montone* (mutton). Because it is so widely raised, there are many regional dishes, including stuffed breast of lamb, lamb cutlets and many stews.

Goats are also common, particularly in harsher country where other animals find it difficult to thrive, and their meat (*capra*) is used in slow braises, *ragùs* and stews (see page 154), or else a young kid (*capretto*) is spit-roasted whole.

Some of Italy's best beef cattle, the white Chianina, are raised in the central Apennines, and their meat, and those of other similar breeds of cattle, provides much of Italy's best beef. Grilled steaks (*bistecca alla Fiorentina* see page 140) are popular in Tuscany, and a rich and unctuous braise of oxtail dates from Roman times.

It seems Italians are yet to find a piece of meat that they can't turn into a delicious dish.

Horse is the other common red meat and, for this, people must look for a shop sign saying *Carne Equina* often accompanied by a picture or sculpture of a horse's head. These butchers sell all the various cuts of *cavallo* (horsemeat) to their many aficionados, who feel it is richer and healthier than other meats. Occasionally it appears on restaurant menus in the north, and is popular in Puglia.

Chicken (*pollo*) has always been a favourite in Italy, especially in the days when people kept a few hens for eggs and then eventually killed one or two for the cooking pot. Chicken broth is a good base for many dishes and the meat appears in stews and other dishes, although it is not as widely used in Italy as in some other countries.

Duck (*anatra*) does not have quite the following that it does in neighbouring France, and geese are mainly bred in Piedmont, where in Lomellina they are raised for *fegato grasso*, or foie gras. Turkeys are usually commercially farmed, and in Lombardy are boned and stuffed, then roasted whole.

Waste not, want not

Italians are not squeamish about eating almost any part of an animal. Many believe that offal and the various off-cuts not generally favoured in some other countries are important in the diet. Hence liver, sweetbreads, blood, spleen, bone marrow, heart, brains, tongue, caul fat, kidneys, tripe, pluck (the liver, lungs and heart), tendons and gristle, and even the entire head are made use of in many, often quite delicious, dishes.

Bollito Misto

Literally 'boiled mixed meats', *bollito misto* combines several meats together (at least four, the recipe decrees) in a massive broth, rich with vegetables and 'extras' such as pig trotters, tongue or whatever else is at hand. This signature dish of all the northern regions is celebrated in Carrù, Piedmont, each December where the best *bollito misto* is chosen.

Above: A butcher in his Bologna deli.

Pig's ears, trotters, cheeks (when cured and air-dried they become *guanciale*) are delicacies, and there is even an offal dish called *pagliata*, quite similar to tripe. *Involtini* in Puglia and the south is often made mainly with offal. *Coratella*, a herbed soup-like stew from Umbria and Lazio uses lamb pluck, and *soffritto di maiale* is a Campanian dish of pork pluck.

Got game

Animals from the forest and wilder areas have long been favoured, especially in the northern regions, the Apennines, and Calabria, Sardinia and Sicily. In Sardinia much of the larger game is cooked on a spit, although *cinghiale* (wild boar) is cooked in a pit in the ground. Wild boar sausages, hams and salami are also popular in Tuscany.

Small birds are not exempt from the hunters' guns either. Sparrows, thrush, pigeons, wild quail and skylarks are hunted, as are– snipe and woodcock and larger birds such as partridge, guinea fowl, grouse and pheasant. In Tuscany small birds are spit-roasted, several together, on skewers.

Wild deer, such as roebuck, and wild goat are mostly found in the higher regions, such as the Valle d'Aosta and the Dolomites, as well as Abruzzo. A rich and spicy *ragù di capriolo* (deer) is a popular accompaniment to polenta or pasta.

Rabbit (*coniglio*) is mostly a farmed meat now in Italy, and is widely used to make a braise or a savoury *ragù* to serve with polenta. Hare (*lepre*) is also greatly esteemed by hunters. The carcasses are usually 'hung' for a couple of days before being used to make a rich *ragù* to accompany *pappardelle*, a wide flat pasta.

Sometimes sold from street stalls in Naples, *lumache di terra* (snails) can hardly be classified as 'game', although while they are raised commercially now in Italy, they are still a food that people can collect from the wild. The small snails from southern Italy are preferred, but all snails must be purged before use. A popular way to serve them is in a *sugo*, rich tomato sauce.

Lastly, and surprisingly, Italians also eat frog's legs – often lightly breaded or dusted with flour and deep-fried, or casseroled – and regard them as delicacies. Frogs are prevalent in the watery rice lands of the Po River Valley, but few people attempt to snare their own. The legs are mostly sold ready to be cooked.

For centuries game meats were often the only way of including meat in the weekly diet.

Salumi e salame
(Cured meats & sausages)

From the humble pig comes a seemingly countless selection of delicious deli meats.

Some Italians say that you can't really be considered a true Italian until you have helped your papa make his own salami (and to his own secret recipe). Consider it a coming-of-age in the food sense.

Italy's range of salted and cured meats, mainly from pork, is truly inspiring. Each Italian eats more than 20 kilograms of pork each year, and much of it will have been cured in some way. In farming communities, most families would keep a few pigs, slaughtering one or two each year, usually around December.

This way the family would have fresh meat for Christmas – plus the pig was at its best after feasting on acorns and other goodies all through the autumn, and the smallgoods had all winter to cure and dry.

The various parts of each pig would be cured or turned into sausages or salami for use throughout the coming months. As most of a pig's flesh (and internal organs) can be used for some purpose, it was a very useful animal to keep.

For generations, nearly every family in rural Italy understood the how to butcher, cure, and make sausages. With the onset of industrialisation it was a natural extension for factories to begin making many of these products commercially.

Of course, old habits die hard, and no doubt every day in Italy somebody's *nonna* shakes her head in disbelief, because she is convinced that *her* salami (or her father's) was better than today's bought one. Occasional salami festivals and regional markets will display rustic or homespun family recipes. In Italy you can usually see a region's complete range by locating the town *salumeria*, a special shop where all these preserved meat products (*salumi*) are kept and sold.

Because the two words sound so similar it is easy to confuse *salumi* (cold cuts) and *salame* (cured sausage). In fact, *salumi* is an overall name for cured meat products, which include *salame*. Almost without exception *salumi* are traditional salt-preserved pork products, many so respected that they have been awarded PDO (Protected Designation of Origin) or PGI (Protected Geographical Indication) designation.

Most *salumi* are made from pork cured in salt or brine then dry-aged, a process that can take many months. Perhaps the most famous of all *salumi* is *prosciutto di Parma* (Parma ham) from Emilia-Romagna or Lombardy. Because of its excellent reputation, very strict controls are in place to ensure it is cured and dried only according to traditional methods.

Perfect prosciutto

In Italy, *prosciutto* is available *cotto* (cooked) or *crudo* (raw). Cooked prosciutto has been pickled, pressed and cooked, while raw prosciutto, as the name suggests, has simply been salted and air-cured for up to two years. As an antipasto, *prosciutto crudo* can be served thinly sliced with fresh figs, draped over wedges of rockmelon or wrapped around *grissini*.

Pancetta, from the pig's belly, is simply unsmoked streaky bacon that has been lightly cured in the traditional way with salt, pepper and spices, including cloves, then rested in a cool, dark place. Calabrian *pancetta* and *pancetta piacentina* each have a PDO. *Pancetta* is often sold very thinly sliced, and can be used to add flavour in savoury sauces or to wrap chicken pieces, quail or other meats before baking.

Coppa (sometimes called *capocollo*) is the neck of pork that has been cured in salt brine, then wrapped and air-dried for six months. It too is served sliced thinly on an antipasto platter.

There are many variations of cured hams in Italy, sometimes varying marginally between regions – perhaps even between villages. *Culatello* ham originates from Parma, and the technique for curing and ageing is quite involved, but the resulting ham is considered a great delicacy, perhaps the best in the land.

Guanciale (salted and air-dried pork cheek) is a rich addition to many sauces such as *amatriciana* and *carbonara*. Italian speck resembles smoked bacon, but is made from the leg of the pig rather than the belly. It is seasoned then rested before smoking, and *lardo*, used in many dishes to add fat, is simply lard.

Finally, two of the very few *salumi* that are not made from pork: *violino di Chiavenna* is cured lamb or goat leg that has been seasoned and washed in red wine before air-drying for several months, while dark red *bresaola* from Valtellina is air-dried loin of beef. It is sold thinly sliced and is served as an antipasto, fanned on a plate and drizzled with olive oil and lemon juice.

Hams invariably feature amongst the *affettato* (sliced meats) on antipasto platters. These meats should be sliced thinly and consumed soon after being sliced.

All *salame* contain finely ground meat (usually pork, but there is sometimes beef, occasionally even horse), about 40 per cent fat (usually lard) and a mixture of spices according to the preference of the maker. Salt, pepper and garlic are invariably used, along with spices such as mace, fennel, cinnamon or chilli, and wine or Marsala. The mixture may have preservatives of some kind added as well as colouring. After packing into casings, the *salame* are aged in cellars for between two and four months.

In markets, *macellerie* (butcher shops) and grocery shops throughout Italy there will always be bunches of long dry-cured *salame* hanging overhead. These are ready to slice and eat, but should be consumed soon after slicing.

The size of *salame* varies enormously - *Cacciatore* is a small sausage of only one hundred grams, while *mortadella di Bologna* is the largest, weighing in at between 5 and 50 kilograms. When sliced it is studded with pieces of white fat. It may contain veal or beef and sometimes horse or donkey.

Salame selection

It would be impossible to list all the various *salame*, so better to try a short degustation. *Finocchiona* is a rich fennel-flavoured dry-aged *salame*, made with equal quantities of pork and fat, and served cut in thick slices. *Napoletano salami* is small and red and spicy, and *salsiccia Calabrese* is also spicy. *Soppressata* is another Calabrian specialty, aged for a shorter time, which allows it to remain softer. It is flattened into squares before drying. At the other end of the country in Piedmont, *salam d'la duja* is salami preserved in a terracotta pot under lard.

The basic rules for slicing *salame* for serving are that soft or cooked *salame* should be sliced thinly; hard or dry-aged salami should be cut thick. It can be served alone with hard cheese or fruit. In cooking, it can be sliced or diced and added to tomato-based pasta sauces, sprinkled on pizzas, or used in stuffings.

Alongside *salumi* and *salame, salsiccie* (fresh sausages) are another specialty among Italian meats. Of course these are perishable, and must be cooked and eaten shortly after they are made.

Cappello del prete (meaning priest's hat) is a cooked, uncured *salame* made from meat left over when *culatello* is made. *Cappello del prete* gets its name because the mixture is stuffed into skin from the top of the pig's leg and sewn up before boiling. The triangular parcel resembles, some say, a cleric's cap.

Cotechino from Modena is cooked inside pig rind, and often served with lentils, although a much spicier Puglian version is served cold.

Luganiga are metre long fresh pork sausages that are best grilled or sliced into a tomato sauce.

If the list seems endless, don't consider it overwhelming, think of it as a goal to be reached … a list of delicacies still to be experienced. If you are not able to make your own salume, the next best thing is to visit your local Italian delicatessen, thinly slice a few favourites, and serve them on a plate. All you need is a glass of pinot grigio and companion prepared to argue about politics and you will have truly arrived in Italy.

Almost every region has its own salame, made traditionally and with pride, and many have been awarded a PDO designation.

Porchetta
Roast pork

Serves 6-8

Ingredients

2kg boned pork loin

3 teaspoons fennel seeds

1 teaspoon dried chilli flakes

1 teaspoon flaked salt

1 tablespoon extra virgin olive oil

4 fresh bay leaves

6 large fresh sage leaves

1 lemon juiced

Table salt

Kitchen string

Driving through the countryside outside Rome, especially in the area south of the city known as the Castelli Romani, you'll often see big white vans parked on the side of the road. Cars pull up, disgorging passengers who buy crusty rolls filled with thick slices of succulent roast porchetta, from huge whole pigs that have been boned and rolled with a glorious aromatic, salty, herb stuffing. This stuffed loin is a little more manageable for the domestic oven than the whole hog.

Method

Preheat oven to 220°C.

Score the rind of your pork loin with a sharp knife – or ask your butcher to do it for you. Place the pork, rind side down onto a board, and open out flat.

Place the fennel, chilli and salt into a mortar bowl and gently pound with the pestle to grind.

Drizzle the pork flesh with the oil and sprinkle the spice mix evenly over the pork flesh. Lay the bay and sage leaves along the middle. Roll, secure and tie the pork loin up with kitchen string.

Place the pork on a roasting rack sitting within a baking dish. Pour the lemon juice over the scored rind and rub well into the rind. Next, add a liberal amount of salt and again rub well into the scored rind.

Cook pork in the preheated oven for 20 minutes, then reduce to 180°C. Cook for a further 1½-2 hours or until cooked to your liking.

Tip: The pan juices can be used to make a delicious gravy. Serve with roast pumpkin, potato and zucchini (courgettes*).

Note – Some butchers will prepare porchetta made from a suckling pig, small enough to fit in a large household oven. Porchetta is delicious when sliced thinly and placed in a warm ciabatta roll with plenty of cooked onions.

* Refer to Glossary – Page 470

Salsiccia con finocchio
Italian pork & fennel sausage

Makes about 20 sausages

Ingredients

125ml dry red wine
470g cold pork lard
1.9kg pork scotch fillet
300g cold pork mince
4 ice cubes
1 egg, lightly beaten
33g flaked sea salt
1 tablespoon fennel seeds
1 tablespoon chopped fresh rosemary leaves
1 teaspoon dried chilli flakes
2 teaspoons freshly cracked black pepper
160g very finely grated Romano cheese, approximately
Olive oil for cooking

Note – A butcher can help prepare the meat. Request they cut the sinew and unwanted fat from the piece of pork scotch fillet. This may require some planning ahead and you may need to pay a little extra for their time. The butcher will also be able to supply the pork lard.

This is a homemade style of Italian sausage without a casing. It will take time to prepare, so be patient and seek out a butcher who can prepare the meat and remove any sinew and unwanted fat. Many butchers and produce markets now have a great variety of sausages available, including Italian-style. It is important that the pork meat, lard and mince be kept cold and used while cold from the refrigerator so that the sausages bind well and are free from any bacteria.

Method

Place the wine into a small saucepan and simmer to reduce by half. Chill until cold.

The pork lard needs to be cut into very tiny pieces (0.5cm x 0.5cm). If necessary, cut the pieces of lard in half horizontally to make a thinner piece before you start.

Italian sausages usually have this fat showing and it is a characteristic part of the sausage, which is also usually a little more chunky. Once all the pork lard is cut, place it back into a bowl and back into the refrigerator to chill for 30 minutes.

Cut the cold, trimmed pork scotch fillet meat into 3-4cm cubes and refrigerate in a separate bowl for 30 minutes. Pass the meat through the coarse plate of a mincer if you have one or ask your butcher to do it for you. A food processor can be used with the pulsing button (however it is not the ideal appliance as it tears and mashes the meat).

Mince or process the meat in 4 batches, adding an ice cube to each batch. Process using the pulse button until it is just chopped and avoid over processing as this method can also cause the meat to become a little stringy.

Place the pork, pork mince, cooled lard, wine, egg, salt, fennel, rosemary, chilli and pepper together into a large bowl.

Next, with gloved hands begin to knead the mixture. This will need to be done for 20 minutes – turn the mixture over in the bowl as you go and knead as you would a bread dough to combine the sausage mixture. Remove any stringy or sinew pieces and discard.

Chill the mixture for 18-24 hours. As the mixture has egg in it rather than starch or flour they will not keep as long, so these sausages need to be shaped and cooked within 48 hours of being kneaded.

To make the sausages, shape 100g of the mixture firmly into a sausage shape (longer rather than too wide so they will cook more evenly) and then lightly coat in the very finely grated Romano cheese.

Heat some olive oil in a large non-stick frying pan over medium-high heat and cook the sausages in batches, turning occasionally for about 10 minutes. Serve.

Arrosto di maiale al latte
Pork cooked in milk

Serves 4-6

Ingredients

60ml olive oil

20g butter

1.5kg pork loin (boneless and pork rind removed)

1 small brown onion, finely chopped

1 stick celery, finely chopped

2 fresh bay leaves

2 teaspoons whole black peppercorns

500ml milk

Flaked salt

Method

Preheat oven to 150°C. Use a large ovenproof dish that has a lid, and that will tightly fit the pork loin snuggly.

Heat oil and butter in a large frying pan over medium-high heat, add the pork and sear well on all sides until lightly golden. Transfer to the ovenproof dish. Add the onion, celery, bay leaves and peppercorns. Pour over the milk and season well with salt.

Cook covered in preheated oven for 1½ hours or until tender. While cooking time baste every 30 minutes and turn the pork so that each side spends some time on the bottom of the dish during cooking.

Remove pork and cover with foil for 10-15 minutes to rest before carving.

Optional – To make the cooking liquid into a sauce, skim the excess fat away then strain the remaining cooking liquid through a sieve. Discard the vegetables, bay leaves and peppercorns. Pour cooking liquid to a small saucepan and reduce to a sauce consistency by simmering uncovered over a low heat. Serve with sliced pork.

Polpette
Beef & pork meatballs

Serves 4-6

Ingredients

200g lean minced beef
200g pork mince
120g fresh breadcrumbs*
50g finely grated parmesan cheese
2 garlic cloves, crushed
2 eggs, lightly beaten
2 tablespoons finely chopped fresh flat-leaf
(Italian) parsley
1 tablespoon olive oil
1 teaspoon flaked salt
Freshly cracked black pepper
Extra olive oil for pan-frying

Just about every household in Italy will have their own version of polpette. They are most often eaten as a second or main course, although spaghetti and meatballs has become an American classic. It's a good idea to test for seasoning once you've prepared the meat mixture but before you've formed all the balls. Quickly fry one polpette and taste, adjusting salt and pepper accordingly.

Method

Combine the beef, pork, breadcrumbs, cheese, garlic, eggs, parsley and oil in a large bowl. Season with salt and pepper.

Mix ingredients together well with clean hands to form a stiff mixture. Add a little more of the breadcrumbs if the mixture seems a little too wet.

Form the meat mixture into balls about the size of a walnut and set aside on a tray. Place into the refrigerator for 30 minutes to firm up.

Heat oil in a large frying pan over medium-high heat. Cook the meatballs in batches for 10-12 minutes, turning frequently to brown evenly.

Serve with a rich tomato sauce, peperonata or with cooked pasta.

* Refer to Glossary – Page 470

Agnello arrosto con aglio e erbe fresche
Roast lamb with garlic & fresh herbs

Serves 4-6

Ingredients

1.5kg leg of lamb

40ml olive oil

6 garlic cloves, halved lengthways

2 long sprigs fresh rosemary, trimmed into 6 small sprigs

2 teaspoons freshly picked thyme leaves

Flaked salt

Freshly cracked black pepper

200ml vegetable stock

Method

Preheat oven to 220°C.

Cut about 12 small (2cm) incisions into the flesh of the lamb. Rub the lamb flesh with the oil.

Place a piece of garlic into each incision and then alternate with a small sprig of rosemary and some thyme leaves pressed in with the garlic. Season generously with salt and pepper.

If possible, allow seasoned lamb to stand covered for 30 minutes before cooking.

Place lamb into a roasting rack sitting within the baking dish. Cook in preheated oven for 30 minutes turning once.

Reduce heat to 190°C. Pour only half the stock over the lamb and continue to cook for about 30-40 minutes. Turn the roast twice during cooking and add the remaining stock. At this time, baste the roast with the pan juices.

Cover with foil and allow to rest for 20-30 minutes before carving. Serve with baked potatoes and vegetables.

Agnello con olive e limone
Lamb with olives & lemon

Serves 4

Ingredients

700g cubed shoulder lamb

2 tablespoons plain (all-purpose) flour

80ml olive oil

1 large brown onion, finely chopped

250ml salt-reduced beef stock

1 small red pepper* (capsicum), halved, deseeded and chopped

3 sprigs fresh oregano leaves

1 strip lemon rind

100g pitted black olives

1 teaspoon finely grated lemon rind

1½ tablespoons lemon juice or to taste

Flaked salt

Freshly cracked black pepper

Fresh flat-leaf (Italian) parsley, to serve

Fresh oregano, to serve

Steamed potatoes, to serve

Method

Lightly dust the lamb pieces with flour, shaking off the excess. Heat only half the oil in a heavy-based saucepan over medium-high heat and cook only half the lamb until lightly browned on all sides. Remove from pan to a side plate and repeat with remaining oil and lamb. Remove lamb from pan.

Add the onion to the same saucepan and cook for 5 minutes over medium heat. Return all the lamb to the saucepan and pour over the stock. Add the pepper, oregano and strip of lemon rind. Cover and cook over a low heat for 1 hour or until meat is almost tender.

Remove the lid and add the olives, continuing to cook uncovered for a further 30 minutes or until meat is tender and sauce has reduced. Stir occasionally to prevent sticking and add a little extra water if sauce appears too thick.

Add grated lemon rind, juice and season to taste.

Serve with parsley, oregano and steamed potatoes.

* Refer to Glossary – Page 470

Vitello tonnato
Veal with tuna mayonnaise

Serves 4-6

Ingredients

800g veal (fillet or leg)

Flaked salt

Freshly cracked black pepper

2 tablespoons olive oil

500ml dry white wine

2 bay leaves

1 large stick celery, thinly sliced

1 medium carrot, thinly sliced

3 free-range eggs*, at room temperature

1 lemon, juiced

2 anchovy fillets*, finely chopped

100ml olive oil, extra

100ml sunflower oil

200g can tuna, preferably in olive oil, drained

2 tablespoons baby capers*

Paprika, to serve

Veal (vitello) is a young milk-fed calf, and the star of many fine Italian dishes. This recipe is closest to the Piedmontese version of the dish. Poached veal loin is finely sliced and served cold, topped with good mayonnaise mixed with tuna and some of the cooking liquid. A Milanese recipe uses cream rather than mayonnaise for the sauce, and a version from Lombardy serves the veal and its tuna sauce hot.

Method

Season the veal with salt and pepper. Heat the oil in a large, heavy-based saucepan or heatproof casserole dish over medium-high heat and brown meat on all sides.

Pour the wine over the meat and add bay leaves, celery and carrot. Bring to the boil and simmer, uncovered, for 3 minutes. Reduce heat to low, cover saucepan and cook for 50 minutes or until tender, turning once halfway through cooking.

Remove the veal from cooking liquid and set aside, covered with foil. Allow to cool completely before thinly slicing and arranging onto a serving platter.

In the jug of a stick blender combine eggs, lemon juice, anchovies and a pinch of salt. Whisk with the stick blender to combine then with the blender on low-medium speed gradually begin to add the combined olive and sunflower oils in a thin, steady stream. Begin slowly with the oil to ensure it emulsifies with the egg.

Season with more salt and a little extra lemon juice, if required. Add the flaked tuna to the mayonnaise and process with the stick blender once again until just combined. Adjust seasoning to taste.

Serve the tuna mayonnaise over the sliced veal, adding the capers and a light dusting of paprika.

Tip: Add crusty bread and a salad for the perfect summer lunch.

* Refer to Glossary – Page 470

Saltimbocca
Rolled veal with sage & ham

Ingredients

8 small (60g) veal escalopes/schnitzels
8 fresh large sage leaves
8 slices prosciutto*
1 tablespoon olive oil
40g butter
100ml salt-reduced chicken stock

Saltimbocca alla Romana hails from the Lazio region, but the dish is popular throughout Italy. Directly translated, saltimbocca means "jumps into the mouth", which is appropriate for these moreish veal escalopes rolled up with sage leaves and prosciutto. This recipe uses stock to deglaze the pan and create a sauce but other recipes incorporate Marsala or dry white wine.

Method

Place the veal between two pieces of plastic wrap and gently tap with the flat side of a meat mallet or rolling pin to flatten out to 5mm or less.

Place the veal onto the work surface, top with a sage leaf then prosciutto slice. Roll the veal up and secure with a toothpick.

Heat the oil and only half the butter in a large frying pan over medium-high heat. Add the veal and cook for 5-8 minutes or until cooked, turning occasionally to brown on all sides. Remove and cover with foil to keep warm.

Add the remaining butter to the frying pan with the stock. Bring to a gentle boil and use a wooden spoon to deglaze the pan and remove cooked pieces from the frying pan. Cook for 1-2 minutes uncovered to reduce slightly.

Serve sauce with veal.

Tip: This dish goes well with a crisp green salad.

* Refer to Glossary – Page 470

Ossibuchi al vino in tegame
Osso bucco in red wine

Serves 4-6

Ingredients

6 large veal leg slices with bone
(ossibuchi), about 1.2kg

2 tablespoons plain (all-purpose) flour

80ml olive oil

1 medium brown onion, finely diced

1 large carrot, finely diced

1 large stick celery, finely diced

2 garlic cloves, finely chopped

250ml dry red wine

400g can chopped tomatoes

150g small whole Swiss brown
mushrooms or sliced Portabello
mushrooms

300ml salt-reduced beef stock

1 bay leaf

Flaked salt

Freshly cracked black pepper

The traditional version of this dish, ossibuchi alla Milanese or ossibuchi in bianco, is flavoured with cinnamon and bay leaf and comes from Italy's north. The tomatoes and red wine in this modern version add a delicious depth of flavour. A gremolata of lemon zest and parsley is a perfect finishing touch.

Method

Lightly dust the veal pieces with flour, shaking off the excess.

Heat only half the oil in a large, heavy-based saucepan over medium-high heat. Add the veal and cook for 5 minutes or until browned on both sides. Remove from pan.

To the same saucepan add the remaining oil and cook the onion, carrot and celery over medium heat for 10 minutes, stirring occasionally. Add garlic and cook for 2 minutes.

Return the veal to the saucepan and pour over the wine. Cook for a further 5 minutes or until reduced by half.

Add tomatoes, mushrooms, stock and bay leaf and cook, covered, for 1-1½ hours or until meat is tender. Season to taste.

Transfer the meat to a serving plate along with the cooked vegetables.

Tip: Serve with gremolata (see below), Milanese risotto (recipe page 66) or creamy mashed potatoes.

Gremolata: Combine ¼ cup finely chopped fresh flat-leaf (Italian) parsley, finely grated rind from 1 lemon and 1 very finely chopped small garlic clove.

* Refer to Glossary – Page 470

Fegato alla Veneziana
Venetian style liver with onions

Serves 6

Veal offal is delicate and the liver is particularly prized. This Venetian specialty, which is usually served with soft polenta, combines calves' liver with sweet caramelised onions, and has been known to convert many non-offal eaters. The thinner the liver is sliced the faster it cooks and the sweeter the flavour; be very careful not to overcook it.

Ingredients

40g butter

60ml olive oil

4 large brown onions, halved and thinly sliced

2 fresh bay leaves

300g calf's livers, thinly sliced

4 fresh sage leaves, roughly chopped

1-2 tablespoons balsamic vinegar (to taste)

Flaked salt

Freshly cracked black pepper

¼ cup roughly chopped fresh flat-leaf (Italian) parsley

Extra virgin olive oil, to drizzle

Method

Heat only half the butter and only half the oil in a large frying pan over low-medium heat. Add the onions and bay leaves and cook, stirring occasionally for 30-40 minutes or until the onions are tender and lightly golden. Remove to a side plate.

To the same frying pan add the remaining butter and oil and heat over medium-high heat until the butter foams a little. If necessary, pat the liver dry with kitchen paper towel to ensure there is no excess moisture before adding to the frying pan.

Cook for 2-3 minutes each side or until lightly golden, remove livers to a side plate. Return the onions to the pan with sage and about 1 tablespoon of the vinegar; heat through, stirring well to pick up all the delicious pan juices. Season to taste and adjust vinegar to taste.

Spoon onions onto a serving plate and top with livers. Sprinkle with parsley and drizzle with extra virgin olive oil. Serve hot or warm.

Bistecca alla Fiorentina
Florentine-style beef steak

Ingredients

1kg large T-bone steak (about 4cm thick)

60ml extra virgin olive oil

1 large garlic clove, chopped

1 tablespoon freshly picked rosemary leaves, roughly chopped

1 tablespoon roughly chopped fresh flat-leaf (Italian) parsley

Flaked salt

Freshly cracked black pepper

Tuscany's classic T-bone steak, often referred to simply as la fiorentina, is deservedly famous. The meat comes from horned, greyish-white Chianina cattle, one of the world's oldest and largest breeds, which are raised in the Val de Chiana valley in eastern Tuscany. The secret to a great fiorentina is the quality of the meat, which is sliced thick and chargrilled over hot coals, or barbecued.

Method

Remove steak from refrigerator for a minimum of 1 hour prior to cooking. Cover and allow to stand at room temperature to assist in even cooking, due to the thickness of the meat.

Preheat oven to 200°C.

Heat a char-grill plate or barbecue grill to very hot. When ready to cook, rub both sides of the steak with two teaspoons oil. Place onto grill and cook each side for 4 minutes, taking care not to pierce the meat in anyway, which would allow valuable juices to escape.

Transfer the steak to an oven tray and cook in preheated oven for 30 minutes (for medium). Cook the steak less or a little longer in the oven depending on your preference.

Meanwhile, place the remaining oil, garlic, rosemary and parsley into a tray or serving platter with a shallow rim to hold the liquid. Place the cooked steak into the oil and spoon the oil and herbs over the top. Season to taste.

Cover with foil and allow to stand for 5-10 minutes before carving into pieces from the bone and serving.

Tip: This is delicious served with salad and crusty bread.

Note – Ask your butcher to cut this steak, and to include the porterhouse section.

* Refer to Glossary – Page 470

Brasato al barolo
Beef in wine

Ingredients

1.5kg beef (bolar blade)
6 small brown onions, peeled and left whole
6 small baby carrots, peeled and left whole
2 celery stalks, cut into thick slices
¼ cup freshly picked rosemary leaves
3-4 garlic cloves, peeled and left whole
1 cinnamon stick
750ml dry red wine
Flaked salt
Freshly cracked black pepper
80ml olive oil
150g bacon, roughly chopped

A classic dish from Piedmont, this slow braise uses a large piece of beef – blade, chuck or rolled brisket all work well – which is browned then cooked for several hours in red wine. The authentic recipe incorporates full-bodied Barbera or Barolo and the success of the finished dish depends largely on the quality of the wine. In this recipe, the beef and vegetables are marinated in wine overnight, although not all brasato recipes do this. Break up any leftover beef and toss it through the pasta.

Method

Combine the beef, onions, carrots, celery, rosemary, garlic and cinnamon stick in a large non-metallic bowl. Pour the wine over the meat, cover and refrigerate for 12 hours.

Remove meat from the bowl and reserve the marinade. Pat meat dry with kitchen paper towel. Season with salt and pepper.

Heat the oil in a large saucepan or flameproof dish over medium-high heat. Brown the beef with the bacon until seared and browned on all sides. Add only half the reserved wine and all the vegetables from the marinade bowl and cook uncovered until the wine has evaporated.

Add the remaining wine, cover and cook over a low heat for 2 hours or until tender. Check the pan from time to time to see that there is enough liquid; if necessary, add some water to ensure the pan does not boil dry.

Alternatively, cook beef in a slow cooker or in a 150°C oven for 2 hours or until tender.

Serve the vegetables on the side or process with the meat juices to make a sauce.

Tip: When choosing your beef cut ask for bolar blade, which is from the shoulder and comparatively inexpensive. A rolled and tied beef brisket would also be suitable. Both these cuts contain a lot of connective tissue, which becomes tender when simmered gently for a long period of time.

* Refer to Glossary – Page 470

Pollo arrosto con finocchio e origano
Roast chicken with fennel & oregano

Serves 4-6

Ingredients

1.5kg free-range chicken
1 lemon, halved
1 small brown onion, cut into quarters
2 tablespoons olive oil
1 teaspoon dried oregano leaves
1 teaspoon fennel seeds
1 teaspoon flaked salt
Freshly cracked black pepper
125ml white wine
125ml water
2 tablespoons olive oil, extra

Method

Preheat oven to 180°C.

Pat the chicken, including the cavity, dry with kitchen paper towel. Place the lemon and onion into the chicken cavity. Then place chicken onto a roasting rack sitting in a baking dish.

Combine the oil, oregano, fennel and salt in a small bowl. Season with pepper and mix well. Rub this herb mixture evenly all over the skin of the chicken, ensuring the area down near the thigh area is well covered.

Pour wine and water into the base of the baking dish, ensuring it doesn't come in contact with the bottom of the chicken.

Cook in preheated oven for 60-70 minutes or until the juices run clear from the flesh when it is tested at the thick area near the thigh and breast. During cooking, baste the breast area with the extra oil. Add extra water to the baking dish, if required, during cooking.

Remove from the oven, cover with foil and allow to rest for 15 minutes before carving.

Tip: For variety, lay some thin slices of pancetta* or prosciutto across the breast area of the chicken prior to cooking. And place some small onions onto the rack holding the chicken and then cook at the same time.

Pollo al marsala
Chicken marsala

Ingredients

40g butter

1 tablespoon olive oil

4 single chicken breasts fillets, skinned

125g fresh mozzarella*, thinly sliced into 4 pieces

1 tablespoon baby capers*

8 anchovy fillets*

2 tablespoons Marsala*

200ml pure (single) cream

Flaked salt

Freshly cracked black pepper

2 tablespoons roughly chopped fresh-flat leaf (Italian) parsley

The fortified wine Marsala, produced in and around the Sicilian town of the same name, is often used in Italian cooking from all regions. Marsala was actually discovered in 1773 by an Englishman, John Woodhouse, who exported it to the English market, and is aged for at least a year (and up to 10 years) before being bottled. Most versions of Pollo al marsala include prosciutto and mushrooms, some also incorporate cream into the sauce. This variation tops each chicken breast with a slice of mozzarella cheese.

Method

Heat the butter and oil in a large frying pan over medium-high heat and cook chicken for 2 minutes each side or until lightly golden. Top each chicken breast with a slice of mozzarella, a few capers and anchovy fillets.

Cover the frying pan and cook over medium heat for 5 minutes. Transfer chicken to a serving dish, cover with foil and keep warm.

Increase heat to high and add the Marsala to the same frying pan, stir well, scraping the bottom of the pan to dislodge any cooked pieces pan. Reduce heat to low, add cream and simmer gently until sauce thickens slightly. Season to taste.

Spoon the sauce over the chicken, sprinkle with parsley and serve.

* Refer to Glossary – Page 470

Diavola alla Toscana
Tuscan-style spatchcock

Serves 4

Ingredients

2 tablespoons olive oil

4 spatchcock, cleaned and prepared

1 medium brown onion, finely diced

1 large carrot, finely diced

100g bacon, finely diced

150ml dry white wine

4 sprigs fresh thyme leaves

½ teaspoon dried marjoram leaves

150ml salt-reduced chicken stock

12 Sicilian green olives, pitted and finely chopped

Flaked salt

Freshly cracked black pepper

40ml brandy

1 tablespoon roughly chopped fresh flat-leaf (Italian) parsley

This recipe is a derivation of the typical Tuscan dish pollo alla diavola where a whole chicken is butterflied (flattened), marinated in olive oil, herbs and chilli then grilled over an open fire, the skin becoming crisp and caramelised. In this version the succulent baby chickens are gently braised.

Method

Heat oil in a large frying pan over medium-high heat and cook spatchcock until well browned on all sides. Remove from pan and set aside.

Reduce heat to medium and add onion, carrot and bacon and cook for 5 minutes. Add wine, thyme and marjoram and cook a further 5 minutes.

Return spatchcock to the pan and add stock and olives; cover, reduce heat to low and simmer for 20-30 minutes, turning once during cooking. The liquid should reduce by half and the spatchcock should be tender. Season with salt and pepper.

Heat brandy in a small saucepan then pour over spatchcock and ignite (for extra flavour). Transfer to a serving dish and serve with sauce. Sprinkle with parsley.

Tip: Serve with rice or Creamy Polenta (see recipe page 100)

Variation – Substitute 8 quail for the spatchcock and reduce the cooking time to 15 minutes. The spatchcock can also be butterflied open and cooked this way, browning the flesh side well.

* Refer to Glossary – Page 470

Anatra con castagne e cavolo cappuccio
Duck with chestnuts & cabbage

Serves 4

Ingredients

4 duck breasts, skin on

100g bacon, diced

150g whole canned unsweetened chestnuts, drained, or fresh, peeled

250ml salt-reduced chicken stock

¼ teaspoon fennel seeds

200g green cabbage, finely shredded

Flaked salt

Freshly cracked black pepper

1/3 cup chopped fresh flat-leaf (Italian) parsley

100g orange marmalade

60ml water

Method

Score the fat on each duck breast in a crisscross pattern – try not to go too deep and through to the flesh. The idea is to score the fat only. Set aside.

Heat a large saucepan over medium heat and add the bacon (if there is not much fat on the bacon add a little olive oil), cook for 3 minutes or until bacon begins to lightly brown.

Add the whole chestnuts, stock and fennel and cook covered over a low heat for 20 minutes.

Add the cabbage and stir to combine. Cover and cook a further 20 minutes. Season to taste and stir through parsley. Keep warm.

Heat a medium frying pan over high heat. Place duck breasts into the frying pan skin side down and cook for 5 minutes until skin is crisp. During this time fat will come out of the skin – drain or spoon some of this away during cooking, if excessive.

Remove duck to a side plate and drain most of the fat into a heatproof bowl.

Return duck to frying pan, flesh side down and cook a further 8-10 minutes. Remove to a side plate, cover with foil and set aside to rest for 5 minutes before cutting into slices.

Once again remove any excess fat from the frying pan by spooning it out, not wiping with paper towel. Add the marmalade and water to the frying pan return to low heat and de-glaze pan juices while warming the citrus glaze.

To serve, place some chestnut and cabbage onto each plate, top with sliced duck and drizzle with marmalade glaze.

Coniglio al limone
Braised rabbit with lemon & fresh herbs

Serves 4

Ingredients

1 rabbit, cut into pieces

2 tablespoons plain (all-purpose) flour

40g butter

2 tablespoons olive oil

500g small new potatoes, washed and halved

2 eschallots*, chopped

200ml dry white wine

375ml salt-reduced chicken stock

1 tablespoon chopped fresh flat-leaf (Italian) parsley

1 tablespoon shredded fresh sage leaves

1 tablespoon chopped fresh rosemary leaves

1 lemon, rind finely grated and juiced

1 teaspoon flaked salt

Freshly cracked black pepper

Extra chopped flat-leaf (Italian) parsley, to serve

Method

Lightly dust the rabbit pieces with flour, shaking off the excess. Set aside.

Heat only half the butter and only half the oil in a large heatproof casserole or heavy-based saucepan over medium-high heat. Add the potatoes and cook for 10 minutes or until lightly browned all over; remove to a side plate.

Add the remaining butter and oil and cook the rabbit over medium-high heat for about 6 minutes or until lightly browned on both sides. Add the eshallots and wine, and cook uncovered until the wine has reduced by half.

Pour in the stock, herbs, lemon rind and juice. Season with salt and pepper. Cover and cook over a low heat for 40 minutes turning once during cooking.

Remove the lid, increase the heat to high and simmer for 10 minutes to reduce and thicken the sauce. Return the potatoes to the pan and cook a further 10 minutes.

Adjust seasoning to taste. Serve with extra chopped parsley.

* Refer to Glossary – Page 470

Capretto di gambellara
Kid (goat) stew with pea risotto

Serves 8-10

Ingredients

2kg boned piece of kid
1 cup chopped mixed fresh herbs
(parsley, mint, chives)
4 strips lemon rind
2 medium brown onions, finely chopped
Flaked salt
Freshly cracked black pepper
1 litre dry white wine
100g butter
60ml olive oil

Pea Risotto
800ml vegetable stock
60ml olive oil
2 spring onions*, finely chopped
320g arborio or short-grain rice
200ml dry white wine
240g fresh or frozen peas, cooked and
mashed
50g butter
200g grated parmesan cheese
Lemon rind threads to serve

Method

Cut the meat into bite-size pieces; place in a non-metallic bowl with the chopped mixed herbs, lemon rind, onions, salt, pepper and the wine. Cover and refrigerate for 2 hours to marinate.

Drain the marinade from the meat and reserve. Melt only half the butter and only half the oil in a large heatproof casserole dish or large heavy-based saucepan and brown half the meat. Remove meat from the dish and repeat with remaining butter, oil and meat.

Return all the meat to the dish and pour in the reserved marinade. Bring to the boil, cover and cook over low heat for 1½-2 hours or until meat is tender.

Remove meat with a slotted spoon to a side plate cover and keep warm. Return the dish to a medium heat and simmer the pan juices uncovered until reduced and slightly thickened.

To make the Risotto, heat the stock in a small, covered saucepan over low heat. Heat the olive oil in a large saucepan over medium heat. Add the spring onions and cook until just starting to colour.

Add the rice and stir continuously to coat rice in the hot oil. Pour in the wine, salt and pepper, and cook stirring until the wine has almost completely evaporated. Add the stock a little at a time and continue stirring between each addition until the stock is absorbed. Continue adding stock until the rice is tender or al dente*.

Remove risotto from the heat, and add the mashed peas, butter and parmesan cheese. Mix well then shape spoonfuls of the risotto between two large spoons to make 'quenelles' or elongated balls (see photo).

Place the quenelles on a serving plate with the stewed kid, drizzled with the reduced pan juices.

Garnish with julienne strips of lemon rind and serve with steamed beans.

Note – This is a very typical Easter dish. The meat is generally very lean, but has a more pronounced flavour than lamb.

* Refer to Glossary – Page 470

Latium e Roma
(Lazio & Rome)

How do you define a city that is just so old? Rome – often called 'the Eternal City' – has seen so much, watched so many cultures come and go, and in turn sent its legions off to conquer so many others. This ebb and flow inevitably brought back to Rome different foods in the pockets of soldiers' tunics, and new ideas from things they had seen and eaten in faraway lands.

Today's Rome is even more cosmopolitan. Millions of people visit this ancient city each year, tramping its streets and working up an appetite. Yet even though this is the national capital, it is not easy to find glossy, glitzy restaurants here. This place is 'trattoria-central', and no other city does fuss-free, honest food better than Rome.

Dishes from Rome and the region of Lazio are noted for having fewer ingredients than those of some other regions. That is the essence of Roman cuisine – the dishes are simple, and the servings are not excessive, it's the good food of the common people. It makes more sense when you learn that the original eating places here were *osterie*, unpretentious family-run inns.

The region of Lazio, surrounding Rome, is intensely farmed, mostly raising sheep, and growing wine grapes on the rich, fertile volcanic soil. Bordered by the Tyrrhenian Sea to the west and the mountains of the Apennines, to the east, Lazio has everything – lakes, hills, plains and a small island, Ponza, about a hundred kilometres off the coast.

Residents of Rome often take day trips away from the capital, heading north along the coast towards Civitavécchia on the Tuscan border, and Anzio to the south, as well as the rich agricultural countryside of the Campagna Romana on the banks of the Tiber. In summer they seek refuge in the cooler temperatures and lush surroundings of the lakes and hill towns to the north and east.

The food of Lazio can tend to be a little salty – a by-product of ancient times when the *Via Salaria* – still so-named today – was the beginning of the salt-trading route of the Roman Empire.

Trust the trattorias

In the city, the best place to go for good pasta and meat dishes is a *trattoria*, particularly one tucked away off the main tourist routes. Beware of tourist traps – the phrase 'when in Rome – do as Rome does...' is possibly never so true as when choosing where to dine here. Eat where the Romans eat, in small places packed with locals and full of the aromas of the dishes being served, and you can't go wrong.

"When in Rome…
…do as Rome does" - it's time to eat, drink and be merry.

Opposite: The Roman Forum, Rome. For centuries the Forum was the center of the Roman Empire: the site of triumphal processions and elections, venue for public speeches and nucleus of commercial affairs.

For a glass of wine and some bar snacks, an *enoteca* (a wine bar) is ideal; and at breakfast, or for a quick hit of caffeine, a café is the answer. A popular snack for sightseers is *pizza al taglio* (by the slice) – crispy, cheesy and readily available from little hole-in-the-wall vendors. Some of the country's best *gelati* can be found in Rome – it may be clichéd, but there is still something delicious about buying a gelati, and walking down the Spanish Steps absorbing the sights and sounds of the Imperial City.

Fertile soil, fresh produce

Because of the warmer climate and fertile soils, chefs here have a wide range of flavourful produce to work with. Even kiwi fruit grow in Lazio, and the best strawberries come from lakeside Nemi, just south-east of Rome. Locals generally agree that the finest table olives are grown at San Gregorio on the far southern coast; and good olive oils hail from Viterbo in the north, Rieti near Umbria, and also groves near to Rome itself.

The cuisine of Lazio relies heavily on vegetables, doubtless because the quality grown here is exceptional. Chefs use locally grown garlic, onion, basil, rosemary and other herbs to emphasise the flavours of artichokes from Cerveteri and Sezze, and peppers, beans, peas, and lentils from Onano. Local produce even travels well, and Romana lettuce (aka cos or romaine) is found in fruit markets worldwide.

Local cheeses feature sheep's milk, so *pecorino Romano, fiordilatte* and *ricotta Romana* tend to prevail, and the buffalo mozzarella from Frosinone and Latina is well worth trying.

Because of the warmer climate and fertile soils, chefs here have a wide range of flavourful produce to work with.

Opposite: a takeaway food van in Rome.

Above: a market garden in the shadow of the ancient Felice aqueduct on the *Via Appia* (Appian Way), one of the earliest and most strategic Roman roads (built 312BC), running south from Rome itself.

Meat lovers

Romans love plenty of meat in their cuisine, and that means the *entire* beast. Visiting diners need to be prepared for offal – and lots of it. A dish of *coratella* can mean it has been prepared from heart, lungs and kidneys. Lard is widely used in dishes, and rich *guanciale* (pig's cheek) and bacon are often used as flavourings, and some dishes might feature the local, highly prized black truffle. Naturally, a wide selection of seafood will be found in villages along the coast.

Then, as in every other Italian region, there are the cured meats and sausages. *Coppiette* are very snackable strips of flesh cut with special knives, seasoned with salt and natural spices, then matured for 60 days. Once the 'salted nuts' of the Roman *osterie*, designed to foster the thirst of patrons, *coppiette* were originally made with donkey or horsemeat, but today it is more likely to be pork.

Lazio is definitely the dominion of pasta, so rice and polenta appear only briefly. Local menus are dominated by *spaghetti alla carbonara*, *fettuccine* (a Roman version of tagliatelle), *penne*, *gnocchi alla Romana* – discs of semolina dough baked with cheese – and *bucatini alla amatriciana*, served in a rich sauce of olive oil, pig cheek and fresh tomatoes.

Lazio has known many influences from other cultures in its colourful career. The Jewish diasporas brought dishes such as *mammola alla giudia*, a ghetto recipe of artichokes cooked twice in olive oil, and *coda alla vaccinara*, an almost middle eastern flavoured recipe of unctuous oxtail with spices, pine nuts and sultanas; while *stracciatella* is an egg-strand soup with a strong lashing of Greek tastes.

The locals are especially proud of the bread of Lazio, *pane casareccio di Genzano* – round loaves or long sticks baked in wood-fired ovens known as *soccie* – which retains its fresh fragrance for up to a week.

Lazio produces many DOC wines, but they are not generally regarded as particularly superior to those of other regions. This, too, is fine with the locals, as they better suit the region's dining preferences of good home style, or trattoria, meals.

Not all roads may lead to Rome nowadays, but many a good honest meal can be found hidden within its cobbled streets.

Fruili-Venezia Guilia

Friuli-Venezia Giulia is sometimes known as the 'centre of Europe', a term that might not be correct geographically, but perhaps metaphorically. This 'new' region of Italy (the capital – Trieste – only joined the Italian Federation in 1947, the rest of the region in 1963) is a melting pot that brings together the Latin, Slavic and Teutonic cultures.

Almost a mirror-image of Liguria, but with the Dolomites, not the Alps, as its high point, this region adjoins Austria and Slovenia. Trieste, more Eastern European than Italian, is a narrow band, dipping down on the other side of the Adriatic, and facing back towards the Italian peninsula.

Consequently, there are many different cultural influences here, not least in the local cuisine. And, as with every region of Italy, the cuisine is dictated by the local produce, which in turn depends on the terrain and the climate. The *Comitato per la Difesa delle Osterie Tradizionali* has been formed to protect the traditional *osteria* (local restaurant) dining, where you will find the classic dishes of the region on offer – be sure to check them out if you are fortunate enough to travel in this part of the world.

In many ways, foods here are similar to the Trentino-Alto Adige, featuring Habsburg, Slavic and Oriental influences, and *agrodolce* – sweet and sour flavours, and spices are a distinctly notable feature of local dishes.

Cold weather fare

The Carnia Mountains to the north are a bastion of good cold weather fare, such as *minestrone d'orzo e fagioli*, a stick-to-your-ribs barley and bean soup. *Montasio*, a soft and delicate cheese that has been made with the milk of the local Friulian *pezzate rosse* cows for the past four centuries is highly prized, along with *formaggio salata della Carnia*, a salted alpine cheese.

Carnia beans are well known, and there are potatoes and cabbages, wild game from the woods, and salmon trout from the cold mountain streams.

The alpine foothills form a massive natural amphitheatre that curves around the flatlands cut by rivers flowing into the Gulf of Trieste. On these irrigated flats orchard fruits, corn and vines grow well, before the land melts away to a coastline of Adriatic lagoons and the wild Carso plateau.

Perhaps the most notable regional specialty is the tasty sweet *prosciutto di San Daniele* (San Daniele Ham) from Udine, bordering Slovenia to the east.

With Eastern European and Oriental influences, Fruili-Venezia Guilia is truly a multicultural melting pot.

Above: Rocca Bernarda winery vineyards in Friuli-Venezia Giulia.

Opposite: Piazza dell'Unita d'Italia, Trieste.

The coastal areas give rise to dishes such as a fish broth (*brodetto di pesce bianco di Grado*), razor clams, John Dory and much more, and many Dalmatian-style dishes. *Cotto e cren* (cooked ham and horseradish) is as popular here as it is in Trentino, and the proximity of Austria ensures that *gulasch* (here made with larger pieces of meat and more spices) is firmly on the menu.

Trieste, like any capital, is especially multi-ethnic. Restaurants (or *buffets*, which are like *osterie*) serve *iota*, an Austrian-style bean and vegetable soup flavoured with cumin, *cevapcici* (a Slavic spicy sausage), and *rape* – turnips pickled in marc. Meals may end with *gubana*, a rich spiral bun laced with chocolate and nuts, a signature recipe of Gorizia, on the Slovenian border. Other local dishes include *mesta e fasoi* (polenta beans and butter), and *frico* (fried cheese cakes or fritters). And the coffee is very good, as this is the home of illycaffé.

Ravioli and risotto

Still not in the true pasta zone, carbohydrates come in the form of *cialzons*, a meat and herb-filled ravioli from Carnia in the alpine north, or made sweet with candied citron, chocolate and ricotta. On the flatlands it will be more likely to be *risotto*, often flavoured with locally grown asparagus in season. *Polenta* is widely eaten and there will be *gnocchi* (possibly made with bread) on many menus.

Take the time to sit, eat, drink and discuss politics with the locals here, and you may be left with little doubt that Friuli-Venezia Giulia is not only the centre of Europe, but the centre of the civilised world. Life doesn't get much better than this.

Pesce e frutti di mare

Italy's vast shoreline has made a large contribution to the country's culinary history and present-day menu.

Fish & seafood

Pesce (Fish)

Italy is blessed by waters on almost every side, stretching from high alpine climates in the north to hot Mediterranean conditions in the south. It has a coastline of around 8000 kilometres, which allows easy access to a staggering variety of fish and seafood.

Unfortunately some of the waters of the Mediterranean and Italy's four adjoining seas – the Tyrrhenian, Ionian, Adriatic and Ligurian seas – are in danger of being over-fished. Some would say they already are, as catch numbers have dropped dramatically in recent decades. There are still, however, more than 800 ports and marinas from which boats leave to fish locally or in deep waters further away and they still return laden with fresh catches. In addition to this, small freshwater fish are found in the lakes and rivers in the north of the country, and there are lagoon fish around Venice.

The freshwater fish include *goregone* (lake fish), favoured for its delicate flesh, as well as *luccio* (large pike), bony and sometimes muddy-tasting *carpa* (carp), *pesce persico* (perch), *salmone* (salmon) and *trota* (trout), the latter often served simply fried or grilled. Large *anguille* (eels) from the mouth of the Po River are particularly prized and are farmed in the area. These may be eaten grilled, fried, or baked, and are cured and grilled as a traditional Christmas dish.

Italians have valued fresh fish since Roman times, when the locals would come to the market in Rome to select live seafood from huge fish tanks. This is even more apparent in fishing ports around the peninsula and in Sardinia and Sicily, where boats sell to locals or chefs directly from their decks or nearby fish markets. Italy also has more than 1000 fish farms, mostly in the north of the country.

Preserved and salted fish

Seafood has been a part of almost every Italian's diet for centuries. However, fresh fish was not always available before modern refrigeration made transportation easy. This tradition means that many people still enjoy *stoccafisso* (stockfish), whole air-dried cod as a meal option.

Preserving in salt was also a favourite technique as far back as the middle ages, when *baccalà*, or cod that has been salted at sea, cut into pieces and dried, was introduced to the Mediterranean parts by Nordic seafarers.

From tiny anchovies to the mighty swordfish – there is always something in Italy's daily catch to satiate the seafood lover.

Right: *La Mattanza*, Trapani, Sicily.

Once seen as food for poor people, *baccalà* remains popular today and is coming back into fashion as a peasant-style food favourite. *Baccalà alla Vicentina*, a dish from Vicenza in Veneto, which is served with white polenta, uses stockfish, in spite of its name, unlike Rome's *baccalà alla Romana*, which does feature salted cod.

Sarda (sardines) and *acciuga* (anchovies) are also preserved in oil and salt, while carp, lake fish, eels and trout, and the extremely small whitebait (*neonati*), may be pickled in vinegar. In Calabria, tiny immature blue fish (an overall name for anchovies because of their colour) are marinated in salt and chilli to produce *rosamarina* (or *sardella*), a prized delicacy that some fear may ultimately deplete the numbers of this species.

The hearty fish stew

All Italian maritime regions have specific local dishes that make use of an often-varied catch, often a fish stew or soup into which go a variety of fish and seafood depending on the catch or the season. *Cacciucco* is a soupy fish stew from Livorno in Tuscany. In Liguria, it's called *burrida (see page 188)*. Other regions have local *brodetti* (fish broths) and these vary from place to place, but the best ones will be made with fish only and will include several varieties.

burrida (see page 188)

La Mattanza

La Mattanza is an ancient technique used to harvest migrating bluefin tuna in the outer islands of Sicily and Sardinia each summer.

Thought to have originated in the Phoenician or Carthaginian eras, *la mattanza* uses a complex series of nets organised into a vast trap (the *tonnara*), gradually reducing in width and depth to shepherd the passing tuna into a central pool - *la camera della morte* (chamber of death). Once the tuna are corralled, the floor of the pool is raised and the frantic fish are harpooned.

Some of the more common fish found off Italy's coasts include *orata* (bream), which is ideal for baking, *cernia* (groper), a large fish found in deeper waters, and *nasello* (hake), often served poached whole in a broth as *nasello in brodetto*.

Pesce San Pietro (John Dory, or 'St Peter's fish') has an interesting name. According to legend this is the fish in whose mouth St Peter found the stater to pay taxes, when the Lord Jesus Christ told him to 'go to the sea and cast a hook, and take the first fish that comes up, and when thou hast opened its mouth thou wilt find a stater' (Matthew 17:27).

Other Italian fish include *sgombro* (mackerel), consumed more than any other fish in the country, *cefalo* (grey mullet) and *triglia* (red mullet), best grilled or baked, *spigola* (the large and delicious sea bass) and *dentice* (sea bream), both of which may be prepared in a number of ways.

Razza (skate) is an unusual flat fish of which only the large 'wings' are used, often simply crumbed and fried. *Sogliola* (sole), another flat fish, is often fried or baked and served whole.

Sarda (sardines), which are actually young pilchards, come from the waters around Sardinia, and the South. For centuries Sardinians mostly inhabited the inland and their diet was based on wild game. It is only in relatively recent history that they have begun to make use of the rich bounty of the sea that surrounds their island.

Prize catch

Two mighty ocean dwellers are the undisputed kings of Italian seafood - swordfish and tuna. *Pesce spada* is a transliteration of swordfish. In markets in Sicily, thick steaks of the pinkish flesh are displayed beside the severed head, which is positioned with the 'sword' pointing upwards. Tuna, also from Calabria and Sicily, are corralled by a maze of nets and then harpooned in an ancient fishing ritual known as *La Mattanza* (see previous page). A decline in the numbers of the bluefin – a huge fish which can reach 800kgs and a length of 14 feet – has seen legal restrictions placed on the annual harvest, and the days of *la mattanza* may yet be numbered.

The flesh of tuna mostly goes to canneries, although it is delicious fresh, lightly grilled, or raw and thinly sliced as carpaccio. It may also be air-dried in fillets called *mosciame*.

Finally – whitebait. These may be either young herrings, a few centimetres long, which are dusted with flour, fried and eaten whole, or tiny fragile newly hatched herring (bianchetti), which are made into fritters with eggs and flour.

Anchovies (*Acciuga*, or *Alice*)

Called 'blue fish' because of the colour of their skin, anchovies are widely used, especially in the south, with the best from Naples and Sicily. The smallest, newly hatched *neonati* may be used in delicate fritters, while the mature fish (up to 20 centimetres) are delicious lightly sautéed or marinated uncooked in oil and lemon juice.

The preserving process sees anchovies layered in salt for three months, rinsed, dried, hand-packed into jars, then covered with oil before sealing. Anchovies are exported worldwide and are popular on pizzas and in many other dishes. When sautéed at the beginning of a sauce, they add a subtle but delicious flavour.

Opposite: Fish seller at the market of Casale sul Sile, Veneto. Casale sul Sile lies on the Via Claudia Augusta, built under the Roman Emperor Claudius in 46AD to create a trade route from the Adriatic sea to the Danube river, in present day Austria.

Frutti di mare (Seafood)

Richly named "fruits of the sea" - Italian seafood is even more delicious than it sounds.

Above: Scallops for sale in a market.

Opposite: Crates of fresh seafood at the harbour of Ancona, Marche.

Richly named 'fruit of the sea', the seafood found along Italy's coasts and in her waters is rich and delicious, and is used to great advantage in a plethora of wonderful dishes.

A simple seafood antipasto of octopus, prawns and scallops, creates marvellous memories when served at a coastal bar or restaurant, while *seppie* (cuttlefish) simmered in a broth of their own black 'ink' is perhaps as dramatic a dish as anyone can ever hope to eat. Cuttlefish 'ink' is so permanent that artists of medieval Europe used it in their paintings, and it appears in many dishes, staining risotto or pasta a deep black and adding contrast to other ingredients. One example is *seppie in nero con polenta*, where light polenta sets off the dark cuttlefish.

Polpo (octopus), also a cephalopod, is found in most coastal areas around the country. In southern Italy it is often cooked slowly, stewed with tomatoes and olives, or it may be lightly cooked and served in a salad. Sometimes vendors sell pieces of cooked octopus from stands in markets or on the streets.

Prized shellfish and crustaceans

Italy enjoys a number of shellfish. *Vongole* (clams) are most popular in Naples and the south, and are often added to pasta sauces. *Datteri di mare* (literally the 'dates of the sea') from Puglia are an unusual brown mollusc considered to be a delicacy. These may be eaten on their own or cooked in a *sauté misto* (mixed fry) with clams or other shellfish.

Others include *aliotide*, often added to soups or pasta sauces, *cozze* (mussels), farmed extensively in the Venetian lagoon area, and delicate *conchiglia di San Giacomo* (St James scallops), from the same area, named for the saint who is always associated with their fan-shaped shell. The oyster, *ostrica*, has been popular in Italy since Roman times, and is now farmed off the coast of Puglia.

Italian crustaceans are highly respected, and every good Italian chef has a favourite *scampi* recipe. Similar to *langoustines*, these long creatures are somewhat like small lobsters, have delicious flesh, and are best simply poached or grilled, or added to a fish stew or broth. Their nearest cousins are the lobster (*astice* or *aragosta*) and prawns (*gambero* or *gamberone*), both of which are used extensively in a variety of dishes from soups to pasta sauces, or in dishes of their own. Italy's waters also have many varieties of crab (*granchio*), and the best ones come from Venice.

Sardine alla pescatore
Fisherman-style sardines

Ingredients

16 whole fresh sardines, cleaned and butterflied*

35g plain (all-purpose) flour

180ml olive oil

1 small brown onion, finely chopped

1 garlic clove, crushed

450g ripe tomatoes, chopped

1 tablespoon chopped fresh flat-leaf (Italian) parsley

200ml dry white wine

1 teaspoon white (granulated) sugar

Flaked salt

Freshly cracked black pepper

Extra virgin olive oil, to drizzle

2 tablespoons chopped fresh basil leaves

2 teaspoons freshly picked fresh thyme leaves

Sardines are caught in southern Italian waters, so it's no surprise that most recipes for them originate in Sicily and other parts of the south. The two most famous Sicilian sardine dishes are pasta con le sarde (the sardines are braised with fennel, pine nuts, currants, herbs and spices to create a wonderful sugo) and sarde a beccafico (stuffed sardines which are rolled up to resemble small warbler birds). This simpler recipe showcases the delicate flavour of very fresh sardines.

Method

Pat fish dry with kitchen paper towel. Dust lightly in flour, shaking off the excess.

Preheat oven to 150°C.

Heat only half the oil in a large frying pan over medium-high heat. Pan-fry only half the sardines for 2-3 minutes each side or until lightly browned. Remove and drain on crumbled kitchen paper towel. Keep warm in preheated oven.

Heat the remaining oil and cook the remaining sardines. Remove.

Pour and discard most of the cooking oil from the frying pan, reserving about 2 tablespoons. Add the onion and cook over a medium heat for 5 minutes, then add the garlic and cook a further 2 minutes. Add tomatoes, parsley, wine and sugar. Cook uncovered over low heat for 8-10 minutes, or until the tomato has reduced slightly to form a sauce. Season to taste.

Serve sauce with sardines. Drizzle with olive oil and sprinkle with basil and thyme.

Tip: Alternatively, return the sardines to the frying pan and spoon over the hot sauce and serve.

* Refer to Glossary – Page 470

Trancio di pesce spada alla Mediterranea
Swordfish steaks in tomato & herb sauce

Serves 4

Ingredients

4 x 160g steaks or pieces of fish (such as swordfish, tuna or cod)

75g plain (all-purpose) flour

80ml olive oil

2 garlic cloves, finely chopped

300g very ripe tomatoes, finely chopped

200ml dry white wine

Flaked salt

Freshly cracked black pepper

¼ cup chopped fresh flat-leaf (Italian) parsley

2 teaspoons picked fresh thyme leaves

Extra virgin olive oil, to drizzle

Baked potatoes or polenta, to serve

The Mediterranean, Tyrrhenian and Ionian Seas surrounding the boot of Italy are rich fishing grounds for species such as swordfish and tuna. This recipe works equally well with either fish, and brings the flavours of the Mediterranean summer – tomato, garlic and fresh herbs – to the table. Be careful not to overcook the swordfish, which is best served slightly pink in the centre.

Method

Lightly dust the fish in flour, shaking off the excess, and place onto a side plate.

Heat only half the oil in a large saucepan over low-medium heat, add the garlic and cook for 2 minutes until tender. Add the tomatoes and wine, cover with a lid and cook over a low heat for 15-20 minutes or until a sauce has formed. Season to taste. Stir in the parsley and thyme.

Heat the remaining oil in a large frying pan and cook the fish for 2-3 minutes per side, depending on thickness, and until well browned.

Place onto a serving platter with the sauce. Drizzle with olive oil and serve.

Serve with baked potatoes or polenta.

Pesce al sale
Salt-baked fish

Ingredients

2kg large fish (such as snapper, bream or salmon), cleaned and scaled

3kg coarse rock salt

125ml water

2-4 fresh garlic cloves, peeled and halved

3 sprigs of each fresh herb (dill, thyme, flat-leaf (Italian) parsley)

½ lemon, sliced

This is a spectacular way to cook fish. The entire fish is encased in sea salt, baked in the oven and presented whole at the table. The salt crust acts like an oven within an oven, sealing in the moisture, the fish steams and when the crust is cracked open it reveals a succulent, aromatic flesh. It works well with snapper, bream, salmon or trout.

Method

Preheat oven to 200°C.

Rinse fish cavity with cold water then pat fish dry inside and out with kitchen paper towel. This fish dish is presented as a whole fish so leave the head and tail intact.

Place only half the salt in a large lidded ovenproof dish or into an oven-baking tray and dampen with only half the water. Place the fish onto the salt and pack the cavity of fish with the garlic, herbs and lemon slices.

Cover the fish with the remaining salt and dampen with remaining water, especially around the main body of the fish.

Cover with a lid or seal well with foil and bake in preheated oven for 40 minutes. Remove and allow to stand for 15 minutes.

The salt should form a solid block. When ready to serve the fish, break the salt away from the body of the fish with the back of a large spoon or heavy bladed large knife. Scrape as much salt away from the fish and to the side before removing the flesh.

Remove the flesh from the fish and serve.

Pull the backbone/spine out by pulling from the tail end of the fish towards the head. Discard. Then serve the second fillet of the fish.

Trota ai funghi
Trout with mushrooms

Serves 4

Ingredients

4 whole medium baby trout, cleaned and scaled

35g plain (all-purpose) flour

80g butter

60ml olive oil

Flaked salt

Freshly cracked black pepper

300g button mushrooms, thinly sliced

200ml dry white wine

2 garlic cloves, crushed

125ml thickened cream*

¼ cup chopped fresh flat-leaf (Italian) parsley

Method

Pat fish dry with kitchen paper towel. Dust lightly in flour, shaking off the excess.

Preheat oven to 150°C.

Heat only half the butter and the oil in a large frying pan over medium-high heat; pan fry trout for 6-8 minutes each side and until lightly browned. Season with salt and pepper. Remove fish to a serving plate and keep warm in preheated oven.

Wipe the frying pan clean with kitchen paper towel. Then heat the remaining butter over medium-high heat and lightly brown the mushrooms cook for 3-4 minutes, season to taste.

Add wine and garlic cook until the wine is almost evaporated. Stir in the cream and cook for 2-3 minutes.

Serve mushroom sauce with trout and top with parsley.

Tip: If the fish are too big to cook in the frying pan together simply cook in two batches.

* Refer to Glossary – Page 470

Pesce al forno con pomodorini ciliegia
Fish with fennel & cherry tomatoes

Serves 4

Ingredients

4 x 140g pieces monkfish or cod fillets (see note)

100ml extra virgin olive oil

¼ cup chopped fresh flat-leaf (Italian) parsley

2 whole baby fennel, thinly sliced

12 cherry tomatoes, halved

80g parmesan cheese, grated

Flaked salt

Freshly cracked black pepper

Method

Preheat oven to 200°C.

Pat fish dry with kitchen paper towel. Place only half the oil into a large ovenproof dish. Sprinkle the bottom of the dish with only half the parsley then add only half the fennel as a layer over the parsley. Add all the tomatoes and only half the parmesan.

Layer the remaining fennel and fish over the top of the tomatoes. Sprinkle with remaining parsley and parmesan.

Drizzle with remaining oil, season with salt and pepper.

Cover with lid or foil and bake in preheated oven for 30-35 minutes. Remove foil and cook a further 10-15 minutes to lightly brown.

Serve.

Note - Any firm white fish fillet could be used.

Baccalà alla Romana
Roman-style salted cod

Serves 4

Ingredients

500g baccalà* (salted cod), prepared
50g sultanas
80ml olive oil
5 garlic cloves, peeled and halved
150g whole Ligurian black olives
50g pine nuts
500g tomato puree (passata)*
400ml water
35g plain (all-purpose) flour
Extra 2 tablespoons olive oil
Freshly cracked black pepper

Method

Prepare the baccalà as described below. Cut into pieces about 8cm long, leaving skin intact.

Place the sultanas in a small bowl with a little warm water and leave for 5 minutes.

Heat the oil in a large frying pan and cook garlic over medium heat until it just changes colour. Remove the garlic and discard.

To the same oil add the olives, pine nuts and drained sultanas. Cook for 2 minutes, then add the passata and water, bring to a gentle boil then reduce to a low heat and cook uncovered for about 20 minutes.

In the meantime, dust fish lightly in flour, shaking off the excess.

Heat extra oil in a large frying pan over medium-high heat and cook fish for 1-2 minute on each side to or until lightly golden.

Add the fish to the sauce, and cook over low heat uncovered for a further 25 minutes. Taste and adjust the salt, if necessary. Season with pepper.

If the sauce gets too thick, thin it with a little water.

Serve the fish in the sauce.

Tip: This dish is delicious served with a green salad, mashed potato or a plain risotto.

Note – To prepare the baccalà first rinse the fish under running cold water, brushing off all the salt on the surface. Put the fish into a large bowl of cold water (cut into pieces to fit) and leave for it for 48 hours, changing the water often, especially during the first 3-4 hours. After 48 hours, drain and cook according to the recipe.*

* Refer to Glossary – Page 470

Sgombri alla Sarda
Sardinian-style mackerel

Serves 4

Ingredients

4-6 whole medium mackerel, cleaned and butterflied*

80ml olive oil

1 large brown onion, thinly sliced

1 teaspoon dried oregano leaf

1 teaspoon finely grated lemon rind

1 tablespoon lemon juice

3 bay leaves

Flaked salt

Freshly cracked black pepper

250ml dry white wine

Lemon wedges, to serve

Crusty bread, to serve

An oily fish plentiful in Mediterranean waters and served throughout Italy, mackerel belongs to the same family as sardines and pilchards. They are often simply grilled or lightly fried, or cooked then marinated in cider vinegar, white wine, olives, fennel and fresh herbs. This recipe comes from the island of Sardinia; the oregano, lemon rind and bay leaves add layers of flavour to the fish.

Method

Preheat oven to 200°C.

Pat fish dry with kitchen paper towel. Heat only half the oil in a large frying pan, add onion and oregano and cook over high heat for 3-4 minutes or until soft and lightly browned. Remove from heat, stir in lemon rind, juice and bay leaves.

In an ovenproof dish, layer only half the mackerel, skin side up, and top with only half the onion mixture, season with salt and pepper then repeat layers.

Drizzle with remaining oil and pour over the wine. Bake, uncovered in preheated oven for 20 minutes or until fish is cooked.

Serve with lemon wedges and crusty bread.

* Refer to Glossary – Page 470

Insalata di merluzzo e pomodori
Mediterranean cod & tomato salad

Ingredients

500g baccalà* (salted cod) prepared (see note)

300g fresh roma tomatoes, deseeded and chopped

3 anchovy fillets*, chopped

¼ cup shredded fresh basil leaves

30g pitted black olives, halved

1 tablespoon baby capers*

2 tablespoons extra virgin olive oil

2-3 teaspoons white wine vinegar, to taste

Freshly cracked black pepper

Extra small basil leaves, to serve

Method

Prepare baccalà as described below and cut into 5cm squares.

Place fish into a large saucepan of boiling water and cook over medium-high heat for 5 minutes. Remove fish to a colander, cool and drain well. Remove all the skin and bones and flake the flesh with your fingers.

Place fish, tomatoes, anchovies, basil, olives and capers into a large bowl and toss to combine. Drizzle the oil and vinegar over the fish mixture, season with pepper and toss again.

Serve with extra basil.

Note – To prepare the baccalà* first rinse the fish under running cold water, brushing off all the salt on the surface. Put the fish into a large bowl of cold water (cut into pieces to fit) and leave for it for 48 hours, changing the water often, especially during the first 3-4 hours. After 48 hours, drain and cook according to the recipe.

Teglia di alici e patate
Anchovy & potato bake

Serves 4

Ingredients

600g fresh anchovies, cleaned and butterflied*

4 all-purpose potatoes, peeled and sliced
thinly

60ml fish stock

1 teaspoon fennel seeds, dry roasted*

1 bunch fresh flat-leaf (Italian) parsley
leaves, chopped

2 garlic cloves, crushed

Flaked salt

Freshly cracked black pepper

2 tablespoons extra virgin olive oil

Green salad, to serve

Method

Preheat oven to 200°C.

Pat fish dry with kitchen paper towel. Place potatoes in a medium saucepan and just cover with cold water. Parboil* potato slices over medium heat for 5 minutes or until just tender when tested with a skewer. Allow to cool slightly.

Lightly grease an ovenproof dish. Layer potato slices over the base and pour over the stock then sprinkle with only half the fennel seeds, only half the parsley and only half the garlic. Season with salt and pepper.

Next, cover the potatoes with anchovies (closed and layered side by side). Top with remaining fennel seeds, parsley and garlic.

Drizzle the oil over the top of the fish and cook covered with foil in preheated oven for 15 minutes. Remove foil and cook a further 10 minutes or until fish is cooked.

Serve with a crisp green salad.

Tip: If anchovies are unavailable use fresh sardines.

* Refer to Glossary – Page 470

Buridda
Fish stew

Ingredients

2 small-medium Spanish mackerel or red mullet, cleaned

1-2 red mullet, cleaned and scaled

300g whole baby octopus, cleaned and halved

400g whole medium green shrimp* (prawns), peeled and de-veined

250g whole medium squid, cleaned, skinned and cut into pieces

2 tablespoons olive oil

500g brown onions, thinly sliced

400g ripe tomatoes, roughly chopped (see note)

Flaked salt

Freshly cracked black pepper

2 tablespoons fresh flat-leaf (Italian) parsley

2 tablespoons chopped fresh oregano leaves

200ml dry white wine

Extra 2 tablespoons extra virgin olive oil

Crusty bread, to serve

This hearty stew is a classic Ligurian dish which combines a variety of fish and seafood with tomatoes, onions and herbs. Use whatever fish is fresh and in season. Whole fish give better flavour than fillets but if you use the latter, don't add them to the stew until the final 10 minutes of cooking. Make sure you have finger bowls at the ready – this can be messy to eat – and plenty of crusty bread to mop up the juices.

Method

Place all the prepared seafood onto a large plate.

Heat oil in a large deep frying pan or saucepan over medium heat. Add the onions and cook over low heat for 15-20 minutes or until tender. Remove only half the onions and set aside.

Add only half the tomatoes, the fish, octopus, shrimp and squid to the pan. Season with salt and pepper and add only half the herbs. Top with the remaining onion and tomato. Season again and add the remaining herbs.

Pour the wine over the fish and onion and drizzle with the extra olive oil. Cover with a lid and reduce heat to very low. Cook for 30 minutes then a further 10 minutes uncovered.

Serve the Buridda directly from the pan with plenty of crusty bread.

Note – For the best flavour use canned tomatoes when fresh tomatoes aren't in season.

* Refer to Glossary – Page 470

Scampi all'aglio
Shrimp with lemon, garlic & parsley

Serves 4

Ingredients

1.5kg whole medium green shrimp* (king prawns)

80g butter

80ml extra virgin olive oil

2 spring onions*, finely chopped

2 large garlic cloves, crushed

1 tablespoon lemon juice

Pinch flaked salt

¼ cup chopped fresh flat-leaf (Italian) parsley

Pinch chilli flakes or to taste

1 teaspoon finely grated lemon rind

Lemon wedges, to serve

Crusty bread, to serve

Method

Peel and de-vein shrimp leaving the tails intact.

Heat butter and oil in a large frying pan over medium heat and add spring onions, garlic and lemon juice. Cook for 1-2 minutes or until aromatic. Season with salt.

Add shrimp and cook on medium-high heat for about 5 minutes or until they are pale orange in colour. Stir in parsley, chilli and lemon rind.

Serve with lemon wedges and crusty bread to dip into pan juices.

Note – Shrimp are also known as prawns in some countries.

* Refer to Glossary – Page 470

Calamari ripieni grigliati
Stuffed grilled squid

Serves 4

Ingredients

12 whole small or 6 medium calamari (squid)

2 slices fresh Italian bread (e.g. ciabatta)

2 teaspoons baby capers*

1 tablespoon chopped fresh flat-leaf (Italian) parsley

2 teaspoons freshly picked lemon thyme leaves

1 tablespoon lemon juice

2 tablespoons olive oil

Flaked salt

Freshly cracked black pepper

Extra virgin olive oil

Chopped flat-leaf (Italian) parsley, to serve

Toothpicks

Method

Prepare and clean calamari as described below. Place the bread into a food processor bowl and chop to form breadcrumbs. Place breadcrumbs into a medium bowl and add the capers, parsley, thyme and lemon juice.

Heat only half the oil in a small frying pan and over medium heat and cook the chopped squid tentacles for 2 minutes. Remove and add all the squid and cooking liquid to the breadcrumbs, season with salt and pepper.

Use a small spoon to fill and stuff the bodies of the squid. Don't pack too firmly as the squid bodies shrink a little during cooking. Secure the open end with a wooden toothpick. Season squid with salt and pepper, and drizzle with remaining oil.

Cook squid on a hot char-grill or barbecue for 10-12 minutes, turning 1-2 times. Drizzle with extra virgin olive and serve with extra parsley.

Note – To prepare the squid, gently pull the body of the squid away from the tentacles, then remove the cartilage from the body – it should pull out quite easily. Skin the body, starting from the open edge and pulling it inside out along the length of the body. Rinse the squid body under cold running water. Cut the squid head just below the eyes to remove the tentacles, discard the intestines and the ink sac (if not using for risotto or pasta). Remove the "shell-like beak" from the centre of the tentacles, pressing gently on the body to make it pop out. Cut tentacles into pieces for cooking.

* Refer to Glossary – Page 470

Cozze in umido
Mussels with wine, garlic & chilli

Serves 4

Ingredients

2kg mussels in shell

2 tablespoons olive oil

200ml dry white wine

60g butter

2 garlic cloves, crushed

1 small red chilli pepper, seeded and finely chopped (optional)

¼ cup chopped fresh flat-leaf (Italian) parsley

Crusty bread, to serve

Green salad, to serve

Method

Clean and de-beard mussels (see below) then rinse under cold water and drain.

Heat the oil in a large saucepan over medium heat and add the mussels and the wine. Cover and cook for 3-5 minutes, tossing the mussels occasionally with tongs. Check and discard any mussels that have not opened, remove opened mussels in their shells to a large side bowl. Pour the mussel cooking liquid into a second small bowl.

In the same saucepan melt the butter over medium heat and add the garlic. Cook for 1 minute, removing from heat as soon as the garlic starts to colour. Add the reserved mussel liquid, chilli and parsley. Stir to combine. Return mussels to the saucepan and toss to coat in the liquid.

Serve immediately, with plenty of crusty bread and a large green salad.

Note – to prepare your mussels, place them in a bowl of clean water. Check them individually, scraping any filaments (or fibrous beard) away with a small, strong knife. Then scrub them individually with a wire mesh pad or small stiff brush.

* Refer to Glossary – Page 470

Polipetti in casseruola
Baby octopus with onion & tomatoes

Serves 4

Ingredients

60ml olive oil

1 small brown onion, finely chopped

1 garlic clove, crushed

1kg whole baby octopus, cleaned

150ml dry white wine

300g ripe cherry tomatoes

250ml water

Flaked salt

Freshly ground black pepper

¼ cup fresh flat-leaf (Italian) parsley, chopped

2 tablespoons finely chopped fresh basil leaves

Small whole basil leaves, to serve (optional)

Cooked polenta or potatoes, to serve

Octopus (polpo) and baby octopus (polipetti) are popular throughout Italy, but this particular dish hails from Liguria. The slow braise helps tenderise the seafood; if you use larger octopus you might need to cook it for longer. Some recipes include a couple of small red chillies, which are cooked with the onion and garlic, and black Ligurian olives, which are added with the fresh herbs just before serving.

Method

Heat oil in a large saucepan over medium heat, cook onion and garlic for 5 minutes or until onion is soft.

Add the octopus and cook a further 2 minutes, stirring occasionally. Add wine then increase heat to high and cook until the wine evaporates.

Add the tomatoes and water, stirring to combine ingredients. Cover with a lid and reduce heat to low. Cook octopus for 30-40 minutes or until tender, stirring occasionally. Season with salt and pepper.

Stir through the parsley and basil. Serve with cooked polenta or potatoes.

Tip: The best way to test if the octopus is cooked is to remove a piece to a side plate and taste. If it is still a little firm, just cover and continue cooking.

Aceto (Vinegar)

In Italy, vinegar is so much more than a salad dressing.

One of the newest cult food products from Italy is also the oldest – as aged balsamic vinegar, *aceto balsamico tradizionale*, makes its contribution to the gourmet food scene globally.

Aceto Balsamico Tradizionale di Modena and *Aceto Balsamico Tradizionale di Reggio Emilia* are each protected by a DOP (Denominazione di Origine Protetta) and a PDO (Protected Designation of Origin), and have been produced in Modena in Emilia-Romagna for many centuries. If this sounds extreme, it is because these are perhaps the best (and most expensive) vinegars in the world. So it is important that no cheap imposters are allowed.

Only a few thousand litres of this amazing product, aged for at least 30 years, are produced each year, making it the world's rarest and most desirable vinegar.

The best of the best

Of the three grades of *balsamico* (traditional, commercial and condiment-grade) only the first is made by cooperatives in Modena using *mosto cotto*, literally cooked 'must', which is freshly pressed grape juice that still contains the pips and skins of the fruit.

Aged *Tradizionale* balsamic is at the 'pointy end' of vinegars, a dense dark, potent, syrupy elixir, so rich that just a few drops on a chunk of *Parmigiano-Reggiano* is all that is needed for a quick trip to food-lover's heaven. Just a hint of it on mortadella, steaks or strawberries (yes, really!) has to be tasted to be believed.

The intense sweet-sour flavour of *balsamico* reminds us that these parts of the Mediterranean were quite heavily influenced by invaders from the south and east, as well as by the Moors from Spain, who brought their tastes with them. Originally it was seen as having medicinal properties, and the name, 'balsam', which means a 'balm', reflects this.

It may come as a surprise that treacle-coloured traditional *balsamico* begins with the juice of white grapes. Freshly harvested *Trebbiano* grapes are usually used, and their *mosto* is cooked down until it is concentrated to about a third of the original volume. This syrupy result is called *saba*, which is then matured in a succession of wooden barrels, intensify the flavour over decades.

An after-dinner balsamic, perhaps?

True artisan-made balsamic has only been available to the general public, as such, for the past few decades - for centuries, it was only made and served for the royal houses of Italy.

Even today, tiny casks are given to new brides in the Modena and Reggio-Emilia regions. Aged balsamic has a taste so incredible that some Italians actually prefer to sip it as an after dinner liqueur.

Below & Opposite: Aceto Balsamico cooperative, Spilamberto, Emilia Romagna.

Only consortium-sealed bottles of *Tradizionale* balsamic vinegar can command the very highest price. Balsamic Vinegar of Modena is an unaged commercial version without the complex flavours and viscosity – and the cost – of the traditional *balsamico*. However, less expensive balsamico may be used in other dishes, such as salad dressings.

Sweet as ... vinegar

Vincotto differs slightly. It is not a true vinegar, although it may be used to make a sweet vinegar, *aceto di vincotto*. Its name simply means 'cooked wine' as it is the greatly reduced must from Puglian red *Negroamaro* and black *Malvasia* grapes. Made in Italy since Roman times, vincotto was found to be a safe and stable sweetener and was used extensively in cooking. *Vincotto* made in Puglia, *Calogiuri Originale Vincotto*, reduces must for 15 hours, and then barrel-ages the syrup for four years, similarly to *balsamico*. It is best used drizzled over foods as a sweet condiment.

Other vinegars available in Italy include *aceto di frutta* or *aspretto di frutta* and *aceto di vino*, or wine vinegar. The first two are fruit vinegars made from barrel-fermented berry juices, these too are expensive due to the involved process with which they are made.

Red and white wine vinegars, however, are made in large quantities and various styles, including some infused with herbs, garlic or chilli, are readily available. Use it liberally with the staples of the Italian codeing, especially tomatoes.

Le Marche (The Marches)

There is much that is misunderstood about Le Marche. It is one of Italy's lesser-known regions, facing the Adriatic, and generally overlooked in favour of the more glamorous adjoining regions – Tuscany, Umbria, Lazio, Emilia-Romagna. Think of it as Umbria without a press agent.

Visitors come for the beaches in summer, but for those seeking hidden treasures, the countryside offers many pleasures throughout the year. In spring, the blossom from apricot trees in Sassoferrato and Macerata cloud the valleys in the palest pink. There are also pears to be found near Serrungarina, as well as peaches from the Asco valley, and pink apples in Amandola.

Sometimes called Marche, sometimes Le Marche, the name has nothing to do with 'marshes', despite the region's long coastline. Once a number of autonomous regions called *marca*, it is simply the collective name for them.

Gone fishing

The Marche coast is a treasure trove of all sorts of crustaceans – squid, shrimps and cuttlefish – and 10 per cent of Italy's fish catch comes from this region. Some of the country's best *vongole* (clams) come from here and the local mullet appears in several traditional dishes. One of the most charming local food festivals is the *Sagra dei Garagoj*, held during the last week of April in Marotta di Mondolfo. *Garagoj* is local dialect for a fish cooked by local fishermen on the beach.

Pork is important in this region, which produces the highly regarded *prosciutto di Carpegna*, as well as *ciauscolo*, a spreadable pork, garlic and herb salami from inland, salami from Fabriano and *lonza*, cured pork loin, from Macerata. This area raises the same white bullocks that are so beloved for their meat in Tuscany, and *cavallo del Catria*, an especially fine horsemeat.

There are olive groves on hills near the sea (mainly around Pesaro to the north and Ascoli Piceno to the south), mushrooms and truffles to rival those from Norcia (in Umbria) inland in the mountains, as well as honey, *porcini* mushrooms, snails, and wild rabbit from the Marche hills. Acqualagna, which calls itself the truffle town, is so proud of its truffles that it celebrates them three times a year – in February, August and October.

Le Marche is the 'quiet achiever' of Italian cuisine, boasting a large repertoire of regional specialities, minus the fuss.

Ancona

Opposite: farmland in the coastal Conero National Park, Marche.

The capital, Ancona is right on the coast, jutting into the Adriatic, and it is here people come to enjoy fish broths and seafood at scenic waterside restaurants, while bars serve *turchetto*, a unique mix of strong coffee, rum and lemon juice.

Broccoli is grown in the region, tender artichokes in Monteluponese and Jesi, and cauliflower around Jesi and Fano. In places the land rises quite steeply into the mountains from the coastal strip and it is here sheep are raised and sheep's milk cheeses are made, including *casciotta di Urbino*, which uses a mixture of sheep's and cow's milk, and *formaggio di fossa*, a sheep's milk pit-cheese, matured in caves in Talamello, similar to the one made in Emilia-Romagna.

Lasagne lovers

Macerata, in the centre of the region, is said to be the birthplace of the world's best *lasagne*. Cooks make *vincisgrassi*, in which they bake pieces of chicken livers and sliced truffles with cream between very thin sheets of pasta. Then there's *bue brasato*, a tasty braised beef; *coratella d'agnello* - lamb with onion, garlic and herbs; *maiale ubriaco*, literally drunken pig, rabbit and *tagliatelle* with white truffles; and Italy's favourite starter, *ripiene all'ascolana* – large *Ascolane* olives, grown around Ascoli Piceno, stuffed with meat, crumbed and fried.

On the coast, beachside *trattorie* usually serve one of four different *brodetti* (fish broths) depending on the fishing region where they are located. The best ones will be made with fish only, and one, *brodetto all'anconetana*, combines 13 types of fish.

The perfect pairing

Desserts are often sweetened with *sapa*, a twice-cooked must, or partially fermented grape juice, and may include aniseed (which is also used in biscuits) and dried fruit.

Grapes are grown on the lower hills near the sea, and produce very good white wines, ideal for pairing with seafood, plus some good reds such as *Rosso Cónero* and *Rosso Piceno*. The locals also enjoy *mistrá*, an aniseed *digestivi* (after dinner liqueur).

The best aspect of Le Marche? It's still largely ignored by the swarming hordes of Tuscany-weary tourists. Enjoy its seafood, its beaches and its truffles, but shhhh … keep its charms quiet for just a little longer.

Liguria

The rugged terrain of this narrow province, following the crescent-shaped coast of the Ligurian Sea, is not easily cultivated, but the challenges of its geography have been more than made up by the innovation of the native cooks and farmers.

Liguria is rich in olives, producing fine olive oil, alongside mushrooms, truffles, chestnuts, vegetables and fruit. The region itself is much like its famous olives – soft and luscious, with a delicious tang to be remembered by.

Essentially a microcosm of some of the larger northern regions, Liguria features alpine valleys and meadows, woods and coastal areas. In many places the steep land has been terraced to wrestle back usable space to grow produce or raise livestock. Seafood is understandably bounteous, and Genoa and the surrounding ports have been key players in commerce and international trade since medieval times.

Abutting the French Riviera to the west, the natural beauty of the area has lured visitors for centuries. For this is the Italian Riviera, and the picturesque towns that hang precipitously to its cliff sides – including the famous five towns of the *Cinque Terre* – make this area memorable for its scenery alone.

Ligurian specialties

Here you find small, dark, intensely flavoured Ligurian olives from Taggia to Imperia. Chestnuts come from around Savona and Imperia. Asparagus and purple artichokes are grown in Albenga, eggplant and basil are grown in Prà, and haricot beans from the fertile soils around Imperia are used in many local dishes.

Along the Gulf of Portovenere large and luscious farmed mussels are served marinated, stuffed or with pasta. Octopus has long been a valuable by-catch of local fishermen, along with other seafood, such as cuttlefish and calamari. *Bottargà*, or dried mullet roe, is also a Ligurian speciality. Inland from San Remo, Molini di Triora is known as the 'city of snails'.

Home to the famous Ligurian olive – this region may be small, but it has made its culinary mark.

Genoa

Opposite: Manarola, Liguria, one of the five picturesque cliff hugging villages of the Cinque Terre (literally 'five lands').

The steep, terraced vineyards of the Cinque Terre are an unforgettable sight - a verdant cascade to the very edge of the Mediterranean.

Caprino cheese made with goat's milk comes from the hills, but sheep *ricotta* is also popular, and *pecorino* made from ewe's milk is one of the most widely produced cheeses of this region. The *formaggio di Santo Stefano d'Aveto* was originally made with sheep's milk, and over a century ago was so highly prized that it was often bartered for olive oil and other products. Today, it is mostly made from cow's milk.

Ligurian cuisine is historically known for its simplicity, poverty and originality. *Burrida*, a hearty seafood stew-soup, features air-dried stockfish (cod), which is found in many local recipes. In ancient times, Scandinavian and other northern traders would swap this durable foodstuff for more perishable delicacies, such as olive oil. Perhaps they also shared their preserving techniques, which would explain the origins of the delicious local salt-cured anchovies.

Liguria's cuisine bears witness to its trading connections, with different flavours and techniques appearing unexpectedly on menus. Pork- and beef-based *salami genovese* may be sliced and layered on focaccia. *Farinata*, a chickpea flat bread, appears almost North African in its flavour and style. *Pissadella*, a kind of pizza, resembles the French Provençal *pissaladiere*, and it is not surprising that in Imperia, the westernmost province of Liguria, near the French border, there is a trans-border Provençal slant to local dishes.

Opposite: terraced market garden, Corniglia, Riomaggiore, Liguria.

Above: the terraced vineyards of the Cinque Terre, Liguria.

Pasta pioneers

It is said that pasta was used here before Marco Polo is supposed to have brought it back from the East. Did traders before him smuggle ashore some dough that captured the local imagination? Who knows, but today the locals feast on *trenette*, long and flat pasta often served with a pesto sauce, and long twisted *trofie*. *Ravioli di Liguria*, stuffed with meat and breadcrumbs and served with parmesan and pesto, is another Ligurian specialty.

Genoa, the bustling port capital, lends its name to many dishes: *minestrone alla Genovese, torta Genovese* (resembling a sponge) and *pandolce Genovese*. *Canestrelli* are typical Ligurian ring-shaped *biscotti* popular everywhere.

Only two regions of Italy are smaller than Liguria, so wine production, although of a high quality, is limited, and reliant on small producers. Once hundreds of grape varieties were grown here, as it is said Ligurian sailors could not resist bringing back unusual varieties from around the world. Here, whites are generally more notable and there is one truly excellent dessert wine, *Sciacchetrà*.

Each April the Slow Food movement organises a Genoan festival, SlowFish, which focuses on intelligent seafood consumption, thus ensuring sustainability. Again, it's ingenuity at work, ensuring that innovation and a passion for food wins over geographical and environmental challenges.

Verdura e frutta

With fertile soil and farming
know-how, Italy is abundant with
the freshest seasonal produce.

Vegetables & fruit

Verdura e frutta
(Vegetables & fruit)

No one could ever accuse Italy of being a country of vegetarians, yet they are a people who love to cultivate every square centimetre of their own hard-won plots of land. Italians love to turn any scrap of earth into a place that will produce enough to keep the family healthy. They can coax into existence thriving tomato plants, raise fat cabbages, shiny purple eggplants and the longest green beans, which become the envy of all their neighbours.

Vegetables and pulses (the bean, legume and lentil family) feature heavily in Italian cooking. *Minestrone*, originally from Milan and Lombardy, and now synonymous with the entire country, is one of the world's healthiest soups, full of seasonal vegetables, herbs, garlic, sometimes rice and pasta, and not necessarily any meat, although it may have a scattering of bacon cubes.

Salads and *contorni* (side dishes, often vegetables) are a part of most meals. Vegetables are fresh and local, and dishes are based on whatever is in season in the area. Most people prefer something that has been cut or harvested from the garden, just before it is cooked. That's the way to have all the flavour and goodness.

Dried tomatoes are popular – sun-dried, of course – as are the long, red peppers that feature in many southern Italian recipes. Beans and other legumes have always been dried to help tide families over the cold and lean winters. Rather than freezing vegetables, many cooks prefer to pickle small pieces of mixed garden vegetables (*giardiniera*) in vinegar to serve as antipasti.

Vegetable bases

Perhaps the most popular vegetable group used in Italian cookery is the onion-garlic-leek family, cultivated there for hundreds of years. Few savoury dishes do not contain one of these favourites.

Carciofi (globe artichokes), which grow on a strangely unattractive large bush, feature in many Italian dishes. Italy surpasses France with the use of this vegetable, because Italian cooks do not usually spend much time carefully trimming almost all of the artichoke away. They simply trim the outer leaves, remove the choke and simmer, fry or roast them almost whole.

The entire bean family (*fagiolo*), fresh or dried, is popular in Italy - including fresh peas, long, green runner beans, purple-speckled borlotti, little white cannellini beans, lentils and flat green *fava* (broad beans) - believed by Pythagoras to be dangerous (no wonder, as he suffered from an allergy to *fava* called favism). *Ceci* (chickpeas) are popular in the south, and some traditional dishes use chickpea flour.

Opposite: fruit and vegetables line the streets on either side at a market in Frano, Le Marche.

Chillies feature in many southern dishes and *peperone* (bell peppers or capsicum), cucumber, eggplant and zucchini, grow exceptionally well in the Mediterranean climate.

Cooler areas raise the *brassica* family – cabbages (including the uniquely Italian dark long-leaved cabbage, *cavolo nero*), kohlrabi, cauliflower, broccoli, Brussels sprouts and turnip.

From under the soil come beetroot, potatoes (especially valuable for *gnocchi* or thickening soups) and carrots, while above ground a profusion of salad greens are grown – several types of lettuce, chicory (*radicchio*), delicate lamb's lettuce, peppery rocket and other vegetables such as celery, fennel, asparagus and spinach.

Plentiful fruit

Fruit is equally highly prized, and orchards throughout the country provide a wealth of seasonal fruit. In Italy it is bought daily from the market and many homes will have a few fruit trees and grape vines of their own, too.

In the northern and colder regions, apples, pears, persimmons and quinces are grown alongside a wealth of berries such as gooseberries, blueberries, mulberries, strawberries and red and blackcurrants. If there are woods, then some of these may grow wild, along with nut trees as well. A little further south, stone fruit orchards are filled with apricots, peaches, plums, cherries and nectarines, and many Italian desserts feature these delicious fruits.

The south of Italy, particularly Sicily and Calabria, is the best place to find citrus fruits (*agrumi*) of all descriptions – lemons, oranges, mandarins, tangerines, citron, bergamot, limes and grapefruit – in abundance.

Sicily also is richly endowed with *fichi d'India* (literally 'Indian figs'), which are the red and incredibly spiny fruit that grow bizarrely around the edges of the pads of the prickly pear cactus plants lining almost every roadside on the island. Some say the flavour resembles strawberries; others don't risk their fingers trying to get past the fine and incredibly sharp spines to find out.

More recognisable are fig trees, some growing wild on roadsides in the south, especially Puglia, Calabria and Sicily, and this sensuous and luscious fruit is used in many desserts or is dried.

The size of the country with its seasonal bounty of fruit and vegetables ensures that most regions of Italy have more than enough fruit and vegetables to keep their residents happy – and very healthy!

Peperonata
Stewed peppers with tomato

Serves 4

Ingredients

90ml olive oil

2 medium brown onion, thinly sliced

3 garlic cloves, crushed

450g yellow and red peppers*
(capsicums), deseeded, quartered and
thinly sliced

450g ripe tomatoes, skinned and diced

Flaked salt

Freshly cracked black pepper

Extra virgin olive oil, to drizzle

Fresh basil leaves, to serve

Peppers (peperone) came to Italy from the New World in the late 16th century and are now grown widely throughout the country, particularly in Lombardy, Piedmont, Umbria, Basilicata and Calabria. This dish makes the most of the sweeter red and yellow peppers. It's good as a side dish but can also be used as a sugo for pasta.

Method

Heat the oil in a large saucepan over medium heat and cook onion for 10 minutes or until lightly browned.

Add garlic and peppers, cover and cook over low heat for 10-12 minutes.

Add tomatoes and season to taste. Continue to cook uncovered until peppers are tender and sauce has thickened slightly. Taste and season again, if required.

Transfer to a serving dish, drizzle lightly with extra virgin olive oil and serve hot or cold. Top with fresh basil.

Tip: This is delicious with cold meat or as part of an antipasto.

* Refer to Glossary – Page 470

Pomodori estivi della priora
Summer tomatoes

Serves 4-6

Ingredients

6 firm ripe large tomatoes

100ml olive oil

6 anchovy fillets*

4 garlic cloves, crushed

200g ciabatta bread, torn into small chunks

1/3 cup fresh mixed herbs (basil, mint or flat-leaf (Italian) parsley), finely chopped

30g parmesan cheese, grated

Freshly cracked black pepper

Truss tomatoes, to serve (optional)

Method

Preheat oven to 180°C. Cut tomatoes in half and deseed.

Heat the oil in a large frying pan over medium heat. Cook anchovies and garlic until anchovies begin to disintegrate. Add bread and fry until golden. Remove from heat.

Add herbs and parmesan to the bread and anchovies, season with pepper.

Place the tomato halves with the flesh side up into an ovenproof dish and fill with bread mixture. Spoon any extra filling around the tomatoes. If using trussed tomatoes as well place these into the baking dish now.

Bake uncovered in preheated oven for 20 minutes, or until tomatoes are cooked and topping is golden. Serve.

* Refer to Glossary – Page 470

Finocchi gratinati
Fennel bake

Ingredients

800g small fennel bulbs
Flaked salt
1 quantity béchamel sauce*
100g prosciutto*, thinly sliced
160g taleggio cheese*, sliced
60g parmesan cheese, grated

Method

Preheat oven to 200°C.

Wash and trim fennel, cut each bulb into about 6 slices (about 1cm thick). Bring a large saucepan of salted water to the boil, add the fennel and cook for 5 minutes. Remove, drain and then cool fennel for about 5 minutes.

Spoon only half the béchamel sauce into the bottom of a lightly greased 1.3-litre capacity ovenproof dish. Begin to place the fennel into the dish, standing it up in rows. Then in between every 2-3 fennel slices add a slice of prosciutto and taleggio cheese. Sprinkle with only half the parmesan.

Pour remaining béchamel sauce evenly over the fennel.

Sprinkle with remaining parmesan and bake in preheated oven for 25 minutes or until golden. Serve.

Tip: Fontina cheese could be substituted for the taleggio*

Fagioli al pomodoro
Beans with tomato

Serves 4-6

Ingredients

60g butter

2 medium brown onions, finely chopped

2 garlic cloves, crushed

80g anchovy fillets*, finely chopped

500g ripe tomatoes, chopped

60g tomato paste

2 teaspoons dried basil leaves

1 teaspoon white (granulated) sugar

2 x 600g canned borlotti* or cannellini beans, drained

500ml water

Flaked salt

Freshly cracked black pepper

Shredded fresh basil leaves, to serve (optional)

Crusty bread, to serve

Method

Melt the butter in a large saucepan over medium heat. Add the onion and cook for 5 minutes or until soft. Add garlic, anchovies, tomatoes and paste and cook a further 10 minutes.

Add dried basil, sugar, beans and water to the tomato mixture. Bring to a gentle boil then reduce heat to low-medium and cook uncovered for 10 minutes.

Season to taste and sprinkle with fresh basil. Serve with crusty bread.

Tip: Try serving this with cold meats such as salami and pancetta*, or pan-fried chicken breast or fish fillets.

* Refer to Glossary – Page 470

Involtini di cavolo con manzo
Meat stuffed cabbage rolls

Serves 4

Ingredients

1 whole head plain cabbage

100g fresh breadcrumbs

2-3 tablespoons milk

200g lean minced beef

150g minced pork

60g parmesan cheese, finely grated

1 small brown onion, finely chopped

1 egg, lightly beaten

2 tablespoons finely chopped fresh flat-leaf
(Italian) parsley

1 tablespoon chopped fresh oregano
leaves

1 garlic clove, crushed

1½ teaspoons flaked salt

Freshly cracked black pepper

60ml olive oil

1 medium brown onion, finely chopped
(extra)

125ml dry white wine

125ml chicken stock

Flat-leaf (Italian) parsley, to serve

Method

Cut the base from the cabbage then gently remove the leaves, keeping the leaves intact. Choose 8-10 of the best leaves to blanch* in boiling water for 2-4 minutes or until tender. Remove to a colander and run cold water over the leaves to refresh.

Place the breadcrumbs into a large bowl with the milk, soaking for about 5 minutes. Squeeze out any excess milk by hand then transfer the breadcrumbs to a separate bowl. Add to the breadcrumbs the beef, pork, parmesan, onion, egg, parsley, oregano, garlic and salt. Season generously with pepper then mix all ingredients well (preferably with a clean hand to really mix well).

Cut the thicker white steam away from the base area of the cabbage leaves, this will make them easier to roll. Place the leaves onto a clean work surface. Roughly divide the mixture into 8-10 portions. Take one portion and roll into a large egg shape, pressing firmly to shape the mixture.

Place the filling onto the thinner end of the leaf, then as you begin to roll the leaf and mixture away from you turn the sides of the leaf on the left and right inwards to help form a parcel.

Heat the oil in a large deep frying pan or casserole dish (big enough to fit the cabbage rolls in a single layer) over medium heat. Add the extra onion and cabbage rolls. Cook the rolls with the seam side down first, allow to cook for 3-4 minutes or until lightly browned. Carefully turn rolls over and cook the other side for 3-4 minutes. Pour in the wine and stock, bring to a gentle simmer then cover and reduce heat to low. Cook for 15-20 minutes. Remove lid and continue to cook until the remaining liquid has almost gone.

Remove to a serving plate, top with extra parsley. Serve.

* Refer to Glossary – Page 470

Zucchini gratinati
Parmesan crumbed zucchini

Ingredients

8 medium zucchinis (courgettes*)

2 tablespoons olive oil

35g fresh breadcrumbs*

2 tablespoons finely grated parmesan cheese

Flaked salt

Freshly cracked black pepper

Extra virgin olive oil, to drizzle

Method

Preheat oven to 200°C.

Cut zucchini in half lengthways and place cut side down into a lightly oiled roasting pan.

Bake in preheated oven for 10-15 minutes or until the cut sides are lightly golden. Increase oven temperature to 220°C. Turn zucchini over – with cut side facing up.

Combine the breadcrumbs and cheese in a small bowl, season with salt and pepper.

Sprinkle crumb mixture evenly over the zucchini. Drizzle lightly with extra olive oil

Place on the top shelf of oven and cook for a further 10 minutes or until topping is crisp and lightly golden. Or place under a preheated grill until lightly golden.

* Refer to Glossary – Page 470

Gnocchi al formaggio di capra
Potato gnocchi with goats' cheese

Serves 4-6

Ingredients

600g sebago potatoes or potatoes for gnocchi, peeled

1 egg, lightly beaten

Flaked salt

Ground white pepper

125g plain flour (all-purpose), sifted

80g butter

2 tablespoons freshly picked lemon thyme leaves

100g soft goat's cheese*, crumbled

Method

Cut potatoes into quarters then place into a large saucepan of lightly salted boiling water. Cook until tender when tested with a skewer and drain well.

Press the cooked potato through a 'potato ricer*' into a large bowl. Add egg, season with salt and pepper and stir to combine before turning potato out onto a lightly floured work surface.

Mix and knead the flour into the potato to form a soft dough. Add a little more flour, if necessary.

Divide the dough into two pieces. Roll each piece out into a long, thin sausage shape about 2cm in width. Then cut into 3cm-long pieces. Set aside on a lightly floured tray and cover with a clean tea towel until ready to cook.

Bring a large saucepan of salted water to the boil. Melt the butter in a medium frying pan over medium heat until it begins to turn a light brown colour. Add the thyme leaves and remove from heat.

When the water has boiled, cook the gnocchi in batches. The gnocchi is cooked when it rises to the surface. Remove with a slotted spoon and drain well before placing into the melted butter.

Once all the gnocchi has been added return the pan to a medium heat and toss to coat in butter. Season to taste.

Serve immediately topped with crumbled goat's cheese.

Variation – Use fresh sage leaves instead of thyme or a small amount of both.

* Refer to Glossary – Page 470

Parmigiana allai melanzane
Aubergine bake

Ingredients

2 large (about 800g) aubergines* (eggplant)
1 tablespoon table salt
60ml olive oil
Freshly cracked black pepper
500ml tomato purree (passata*) sauce
125g mozzarella cheese*, grated
60g parmesan cheese, grated

This is one of the great dishes from Naples that has spread across the world. Tomatoes, mozzarella and parmesan (which gives the dish its name) are cooked with thick slices of eggplant into a hearty vegetarian dish that's a meal in itself. Salting the flesh of the eggplant before cooking reduces the bitterness and draws out extra water so that less oil is absorbed in cooking, although with some modern eggplant varieties it isn't always necessary to do this. Sicilian recipes for parmigiana alla melanzane sometimes incorporate currants and pine nuts.

Method

Cut aubergine into 1cm thick slices and place into a colander. Sprinkle with salt and allow to stand for 30 minutes with a bowl used to weigh the aubergine down. Rinse under cold running water and pat dry well with kitchen paper towel.

Preheated oven to 180°C.

Lightly brush aubergine slices with olive oil and char-grill or pan fry in batches until lightly golden on both sides.

In a large ovenproof dish make a layer with only half the aubergine, season with pepper then add only half the tomato sauce, and only half the mozzarella and only half the parmesan. Repeat with a second layer, finishing with cheese.

Bake in preheated oven for 30 minutes or until golden. Serve.

Variation – Add some fresh herbs, such as thyme and sweet basil, to the tomato sauce. Or add a layer of cooked onion and 500g lean beef mince in the middle.

* Refer to Glossary – Page 470

Salsa verde
Salsa verde

Ingredients

70g fresh breadcrumbs*

2 tablespoons white wine vinegar

1 tablespoon water

2 cups picked fresh flat-leaf (Italian) parsley leaves

1 garlic clove, finely chopped

2 small gherkins, chopped

2 anchovy fillets*, chopped

1 hard-boiled egg, peeled and chopped

100-150ml extra virgin olive oil

Flaked salt

Freshly cracked black pepper

Salsa verde is traditionally served as an accompaniment to bollito misto (a medley of boiled meats, much more delicious than it sounds), which is common in Emilia-Romagna, Lombardy and Piedmont. However, it's also wonderful with grilled fish; if you're using it in this way, consider substituting the vinegar with lemon juice. Some recipes call for capers instead of gherkins and mustard is also often included.

Method

Combine breadcrumbs, vinegar and water in a medium bowl and allow to stand for about 10 minutes or until the bread soaks up the liquid.

Place the parsley, garlic, gherkins, anchovies and egg into a large mortar and mix with the pestle to form a paste. Add the breadcrumbs and pound to combine. Add enough oil to make a sauce.

Season to taste.

Tip: Serve with vegetables, cold and cooked meats and seafood.

Note – The quantity of oil may vary, depending on the dryness of the bread used. Add enough oil to achieve a thick consistency, similar to pesto.

Minestra della Nonna
Grandmother's soup

Ingredients

2 tablespoons olive oil

1 medium brown onion, finely chopped

1 large carrot, thinly sliced

2 celery stalks, thinly sliced

2 all-purpose potatoes, peeled and chopped

400g can chopped tomatoes

800ml water

1 teaspoon flaked salt

125g mini pasta shapes (such as ditalini rigati)

400g can cannellini beans, drained

2 tablespoons chopped fresh flat-leaf (Italian) parsley

2 tablespoons chopped fresh basil leaves

Flaked salt

Freshly cracked black pepper

Parmesan cheese, grated, to serve

Chopped fresh flat-leaf (Italian) parsley, to serve

Method

Heat the oil in a large saucepan over medium heat and cook onion, carrot and celery for 10 minutes. Add potato, tomato, water and salt. Bring to a gentle boil then cover with lid and cook over a low heat for 40 minutes.

Add pasta and beans and simmer a further 5-8 minutes or until the pasta is cooked and al dente*. Add parsley and basil. Season to taste.

Serve with extra parmesan and parsley.

Variation – Add extra chopped or sliced vegetables, such as fresh beans, zucchini, artichoke stalks, leek, cauliflower or broccoli florets, and spinach.

* Refer to Glossary – Page 470

Piselli alla pancetta
Peas with pancetta

Serves 4

Ingredients

2 tablespoons olive oil
100g pancetta*, thinly sliced
1 large brown onion, finely chopped
400g fresh or frozen peas
250ml salt-reduced chicken stock
Flaked salt
Freshly cracked black pepper

Method

Heat the oil in a large saucepan over medium-high heat and cook pancetta for 5 minutes or until lightly golden. Remove to a side plate. Reduce heat to medium and add the onion, cook a further 5 minutes.

Add peas and cook for 5 minutes. Add stock and cook uncovered on medium heat for 10 minutes or until liquid has evaporated and peas are tender.

Break pancetta into pieces and stir only half of it into the peas. Season to taste. Serve immediately topped with remaining pancetta.

Variation – Add some freshly shredded mint or sweet basil leaves.

* Refer to Glossary – Page 470

Strangolapreti agli spinaci
Spinach dumplings with sage butter

Serves 4

Ingredients

300g stale Italian bread (such as *Ciabatta*)

150ml full cream milk

500g silverbeet, before trimming

60-80ml olive oil

½ leek, white part only finely chopped

2 eggs, lightly beaten

4 tablespoons plain (all-purpose) flour

Flaked salt

Freshly cracked black pepper

35g plain (all-purpose) flour, extra, for dusting

30g butter

2 tablespoons extra virgin olive oil, extra

12 fresh sage leaves

Juice ½ lemon

50g pecorino* romano cheese, finely grated (optional)

Lemon wedges, to serve

Method

Cut the bread into thick slices, remove the crusts and discard. Cut remaining bread into cubes and place into a large bowl. Pour over the milk, turning the bread to ensure it is well moistened. Cover and allow to stand for 2 hours in the refrigerator.

Meanwhile, trim the thick white stalks from the silverbeet and discard. Wash the leaves and blanch* in boiling salted water until just tender. Refresh under cold water and drain well through a strainer, pushing firmly on the leaves to press out as much water as possible. Finely chop the sliverbeet and place into a large bowl.

Heat only 1 tablespoon of olive oil in a large frying pan and cook the leek over medium heat for 2-3 minutes or until tender.

Add the leek and silverbeet to the soaked bread in the bowl. Then add the eggs and flour, stirring well to combine. If the mix seems a little dry add a little more milk, and if too moist a little more flour. The aim is to have a mixture that is slightly tacky and comes together to form dumplings. Season well with salt and pepper. Shape the mixture into walnut-sized dumplings with slightly damp hands and place onto a lightly oiled tray. Dust dumplings lightly with flour, shaking off the excess.

Add the remaining oil to the already used frying pan. Cook dumplings over a medium heat until lightly browned on all sides, about 5 minutes. Remove to serving plate. Drain the oil from pan and wipe clean with kitchen paper towel.

Lastly add the butter and extra oil to the same frying pan cook over medium heat until butter melts. Add the sage then remove from heat. Add the lemon juice. Pour butter over dumplings and serve.

Serve topped with pecorino, if desired. Serve with lemon wedges.

Patate arrostite con olive
Roast potatoes with olives

Serves 4

Ingredients

2 medium red onion, cut into quarters
600g baby new potatoes (chats), halved
2 tablespoons olive oil
2 sprigs fresh rosemary leaves
1-2 teaspoons flaked salt
80g green Sicilian olives

Method

Preheat oven to 200°C.

Place onion and potatoes into a large baking dish, drizzle with oil and add the rosemary leaves. Sprinkle with salt.

Roast in preheated oven on the top oven shelf, or as close to top oven element as possible, for about 30 minutes or until golden and tender. Toss occasionally during cooking.

Add olives and cook for a further 10 minutes. Serve.

* Refer to Glossary – Page 470

Cavolfiore dorato
Golden fried cauliflower

Ingredients

1 small-medium cauliflower
1 slice lemon
75g plain (all-purpose) flour
50g butter
1 tablespoon olive oil
2 eggs, lightly beaten
Flaked salt

Method

Cut the cauliflower into florets. Place into a large saucepan of boiling water with the lemon, cover and cook until just tender. Drain and allow to cool slightly before patting dry with kitchen paper towel.

Place flour into a bowl and coat the cauliflower florets, shaking off any excess flour.

Heat the butter and oil in a large frying pan over medium-high heat.

Dip each floret into the egg. Place into the frying pan and cook for 4-5 minutes or until golden, turning during cooking. Drain on kitchen paper towel.

Season with salt and serve immediately.

* Refer to Glossary – Page 470

Macco di fave
Broad bean soup

Ingredients

250g dried broad beans

1 large brown onion, finely chopped

2 litres water

1 teaspoon flaked salt

250g ripe tomatoes

100g short wide pasta ribbons (such as papardelle)

100ml extra virgin olive oil

Flaked salt

Freshly cracked black pepper

¼ cup roughly chopped fresh flat-leaf (Italian) parsley

40g pecorino cheese*, grated

Both Sicily and Calabria claim this dish as their own, but the ancient Romans were known to have eaten similar dried bean purees. The Calabrian version sometimes includes chilli and is served as a soup over toasted bread; this recipe is closer to the Sicilian version, which incorporates fennel and is used as a sauce over ribbons of flat pasta. The name macco derives from the Latin maccus, meaning crushed.

Method

Place beans into a large bowl and cover with cold water. Allow to soak overnight or for a quicker process cover the beans with boiling water and allow to stand for 2 hours.

Peel the skin from the beans and discard. Place the beans into a large saucepan with the onion, water and salt. Skin and deseed the tomatoes, then dice finely and add to the broad beans.

Cover saucepan and bring to a gently boil over medium-high heat. Reduce heat to low and cook for 1-1¼ hours, stirring occasionally with a wooden spoon. After this time, the broad beans should have completely disintegrated (if they haven't, mash them with a fork), and the soup should be thick and creamy.

Add the pasta and only 80ml of the olive oil and cook until the pasta is al dente*. Season to taste.

Serve the soup drizzle with remaining oil. Add parsley and pecorino.

Tip: If the soup appears a little too thick, add some boiling water.

* Refer to Glossary – Page 470

Tortina di zucca, formaggio e porri
Pumpkin, cheese & leek pie

Serves 4-6

Ingredients

400g plain (all-purpose) flour

1 teaspoon flaked salt

125ml olive oil

60-80ml water (to knead into a soft dough)

500g pumpkin, peeled, seeded and cubed

100g white section leek, roughly hopped

1 tablespoon olive oil, extra

1 tablespoon fresh rosemary

4 free-range eggs*, lightly beaten

100g Gorgonzola cheese*, crumbled

100g ricotta cheese

70g fresh breadcrumbs*

Flaked salt

Freshly cracked black pepper

Method

Preheat oven to 200°C.

Sift flour and salt into a large bowl, add the oil and just enough water to knead into a soft pastry dough. Wrap in plastic wrap and chill for 1 hour.

Meanwhile place pumpkin and leek onto a baking tray, drizzle with the extra oil and add the rosemary. Cook in preheated oven for 20 minutes or until lightly golden, turning once during cooking. Allow to cool.

Cut the pastry into two pieces. Roll out one half as the base, making a circle to fit into a 22cm (base measurement) glass or ceramic ovenproof pie dish. Place pastry into the dish and prick the base with a fork. Secondly, roll out the second piece of pastry slightly larger in circumference to fit as the top. Set aside.

Preheat oven again to 200°C.

Reserve a little egg for glazing pastry top. Place the remaining egg and cheeses into a bowl and mix well to combine. Add the roast pumpkin, leek and breadcrumbs. Season with salt and pepper.

Pour into pie dish and cover with pastry top. Pinch around the edges to seal and cut a small hole in the middle of the pastry top to allow the team to escape. Brush pastry with reserved egg.

Bake in preheated oven for 30-40 minutes until golden and the crust looks cooked. Serve hot or warm.

* Refer to Glossary – Page 470

Funghi all'aglio e prezzemolo
Mushrooms with garlic, parsley & thyme

Serves 4

Ingredients

100ml olive oil

2 garlic cloves, finely chopped

500g button mushrooms, thinly sliced

2 tablespoons roughly chopped fresh flat-leaf (Italian) parsley

1 tablespoon freshly picked lemon thyme leaves

Flaked salt

Freshly cracked black pepper

Extra virgin olive oil, to drizzle

Method

Heat only half the oil in a large frying pan over low-medium heat. Add garlic and cook for 2 minutes.

Increase heat to medium-high and add the mushrooms and remaining oil. Cook, stirring occasionally, for 15-20 minutes or until just tender.

Stir through parsley and thyme leaves. Cook a further 2-3 minutes.

Season to taste and drizzle lightly with extra virgin olive oil. Serve.

★ Refer to Glossary – Page 470

Caponata alla Siciliana
Sicilian caponata

If there's a savoury dish that is the essence of Sicily then this wonderful mix of eggplant, tomatoes and capers is it. Often served as a side dish with fish, caponata is also wonderful as an antipasto or first course; any leftovers can be tossed over pasta. Some recipes incorporate pine nuts and currants, others use olives.

Ingredients

1 large (about 400g) aubergine* (eggplant)

1 tablespoon table salt

120ml olive oil

1 medium brown onion, finely chopped

600g red peppers* (capsicums), cut into about 2cm cube

1 celery stalk, thinly sliced

400g can chopped tomatoes

1½ tablespoon white wine vinegar

1 tablespoon white (granulated) sugar

1 garlic clove, crushed

150g black pitted olives

50g small caper berries*

Flaked salt

Freshly cracked black pepper

Method

Cut aubergine into thick 1cm slices, then into cubes and place into a colander. Sprinkle with salt and allow to stand for 30 minutes with a bowl used to weigh the aubergine down. Rinse under cold running water and pat dry with kitchen paper towel.

Heat only half the oil in a large saucepan over medium heat, add the aubergine and cook for 5 minutes or until lightly golden, then remove to a side plate. Add the remaining oil to the pan and cook the onion over medium heat for 5 minutes. Add peppers and celery and cook a further 5 minutes.

Add the tomatoes, vinegar, sugar and garlic and cook for 2 minutes. Stir in aubergine, olives and caper berries. Reduce heat to low and cook covered for 15 minutes or until thickened.

Season to taste and serve.

* Refer to Glossary – Page 470

Spinaci gratinati
Spinach bake

Ingredients

500g frozen spinach, thawed

1 tablespoon olive oil

2 garlic cloves, crushed

30g butter

20g plain (all-purpose) flour

250ml milk

1 teaspoon flaked salt

80g parmesan cheese, grated

Fresh cracked black pepper

50g mozzarella* or fontina* cheese, thinly sliced

50g extra parmesan cheese, grated, to serve

Method

Preheat oven to 180°C.

Place spinach into a colander and press firmly to remove any excess moisture.

Heat the oil in a large saucepan over medium heat and cook garlic for 2-3 minutes, add spinach and stir well. Remove from heat and set aside.

Heat the butter in a second saucepan over medium heat. Add the flour and cook for 2 minutes. Remove from heat and add the milk, whisking as you add. Add salt.

Return saucepan to medium heat and bring to the boil, allow to gently boil for 2-3 minutes. Stir constantly as the white sauce thickens. Add the spinach mixture, parmesan and season with pepper.

Spoon only half the mixture into one large or two smaller lightly greased ovenproof serving dishes or ramekins. Top with mozzarella cheese then add the remaining spinach mixture.

Sprinkle with a little extra parmesan. Bake in preheated oven for 20 minutes or until golden. Serve.

* Refer to Glossary – Page 470

Broccoli e porri gratinati
Broccoli & leek crumble

Serves 4-6

Ingredients

2 leeks

30g butter

1 tablespoon plain (all-purpose) flour

160ml milk

120ml water

400g broccoli, cut into small florets and pieces

30g parmesan cheese, grated

Flaked salt

Freshly cracked black pepper

Topping

125g plain (all-purpose) flour

1 tablespoon finely chopped fresh basil leaves

Pinch flaked salt

90g chilled butter, cubed

60g fresh breadcrumbs*

Method

Preheat oven to 190°C.

Prepare leeks by cutting the main green top and the root bottom away and discarding these. Cut the leeks in half lengthways and rinse well under cold water then pat dry with kitchen paper towel and thinly slice.

Heat the butter in a large saucepan over medium heat and cook leeks for 3-4 minutes or until tender. Stir in flour and cook for 2 minutes. Remove from heat and gradually add milk and water. Return saucepan to medium heat and bring to the boil, allow to gently boil for 2-3 minutes. Stir constantly as the white sauce thickens.

Add broccoli and cook partly covered for 5 minutes. Stir in cheese and season to taste.

Transfer to a medium-sized ovenproof dish or individual ramekins.

To make the Topping, combine flour, basil and salt. Rub in butter to form a crumb consistency. Lastly, stir in breadcrumbs. Sprinkle crumb over broccoli and bake in preheated oven for 20-25 minutes or until golden.

Variation – Substitute cauliflower for broccoli.

* Refer to Glossary – Page 470

Verdure ripiene
Savoury meat stuffed vegetables

Serves 4-6

Ingredients

4 large zucchini (courgettes*), halved
lengthways

60ml olive oil

1 small brown onion, finely chopped

250g minced beef

250g pork mince

100g prosciutto*, very finely chopped

2 tablespoons chopped fresh flat-leaf
(Italian) parsley

1 egg, lightly beaten

2 tablespoons milk

100g fresh breadcrumbs*

Pinch chilli flakes

Flaked salt

Freshly cracked black pepper

4 firm large tomatoes, halved and
deseeded

2 small-medium peppers* (capsicums),
halved lengthways and deseeded

Topping

30g butter, melted

75g emmenthal cheese*, grated

75g fresh breadcrumbs*

Method

Preheat oven to 180°C.

Cook zucchini in a large saucepan of lightly salted boiling water for 3 minutes, drain and cool. With a spoon, remove flesh from the zucchini reserve this flesh and set aside.

Heat the oil in a large frying pan over medium heat and cook onion for 5 minutes or until lightly browned. Increase heat to high and add minces, cooking until the meat is lightly browned, stirring occasionally and breaking up any large pieces of meat with the back of the spoon.

Remove frying pan from heat and add the prosciutto and parsley. Stir well. Then add reserved zucchini flesh, egg, milk and breadcrumbs to form a soft mixture. Add chilli and season with salt and pepper.

Place zucchini, tomato and pepper halves side by side into two ovenproof dishes. Spoon the prepared meat filling between the vegetable cavities.

To make the Topping, combine topping ingredients and sprinkle over the filled vegetables. Cover with foil and bake in preheated oven 20 minutes; remove foil, bake a further 15 minutes or until golden. Rotate dishes during cooking for even browning. Serve hot.

* Refer to Glossary – Page 470

Carciofi farciti gratinati
Stuffed grilled artichokes

Ingredients

6 whole globe artichokes

1 lemon, juiced and rind finely grated

1 tablespoon olive oil

1 medium brown onion, finely chopped

1 small stick celery, finely chopped

1 garlic clove, crushed

300g lean, pork mince

90g thinly sliced bacon, diced

35g fresh breadcrumbs*

50g parmesan cheese, grated

2 teaspoons freshly picked lemon thyme leaves

Flaked salt

Freshly cracked black pepper

2 tablespoons extra-virgin olive oil

Lemon wedges, to serve

One vegetable that Italian cooks handle better than anyone else in the world is the artichoke. Rome has two notable artichoke dishes, the deep-fried carciofi alla giudia, found on restaurant menus in the former Jewish Ghetto, and carciofi alla Romana, made with young artichokes that are stuffed with garlic and mentuccia (pennyroyal) and poached slowly in water and olive oil. In this recipe, minced pork stuffing transforms what might have been a simple side dish into a hearty meal in itself.

Method

Boil a large saucepan of salted water.

Prepare the artichokes by cutting the stems off, leaving intact about 2cm of stem, directly below the artichoke head. Peel the stem a little as you would peel a carrot. Remove the outer tougher leaves until the leaves begin to appear a lighter green colour, discard outer leaves. Cut about 1cm off the top of each artichoke and discard.

Place the artichokes into boiling salted water with the lemon juice to prevent discoloration. Carefully cover with a plate sitting it directly on top of the artichokes to weigh them down and keep them submerged in the water. Cover saucepan with a lid and cook over medium heat for 20-25 minutes or until the flesh is tender when a skewer is inserted into the thickest part.

Remove artichokes and stand upside down on a plate to allow the water to drain away. When cool enough to handle, scoop out the "furry choke" from the centre of the artichokes and discard. This should leave a hole for the filling.

Meanwhile, heat the oil in a large frying pan over medium heat and cook the onion and celery for 5 minutes, add garlic and cook for 2 minutes. Increase heat to high and add mince and bacon, cook for 8-10 minutes or until lightly browned, stirring occasionally.

Remove from heat and add breadcrumbs, cheese, thyme and lemon rind. Season to taste. Stand the artichokes upright in a round cake pan or ovenproof dish for support. Spoon the filling into the prepared artichokes drizzle the top with extra olive oil and place under a preheated grill. Cook for 5-10 minutes or until lightly golden.

Serve with lemon.

* Refer to Glossary – Page 470

Aglio e pomodori arrostiti
Roast garlic & tomatoes

Serves 4

Ingredients

12 Roma tomatoes, cut in half or left
whole if small

12 garlic cloves, whole unpeeled

60ml olive oil

5 fresh thyme sprigs

1 teaspoon fennel seeds, lightly crushed
with mortar and pestle

Flaked salt

Freshly cracked black pepper

Method

Preheat oven to 200°C.

Place tomatoes and garlic into a baking dish, drizzle with oil and add the thyme sprigs.

Season with fennel, salt and pepper.

Bake uncovered in preheated oven for 40-50 minutes until the tomatoes are soft and slightly crisp around the edges and the garlic is soft and oozes from their skins. Serve.

Tip: Roma tomatoes are also available still on the vine and trussed, they look very attractive and rustic when cooked this way.

* Refer to Glossary – Page 470

Pomodori (Tomatoes)

A relative newcomer to Italy, the tomato quickly became an essential part of the cuisine.

It's hard to imagine Italian food without tomatoes, but until Christopher Columbus returned from the New World in the 16th-century, Europeans were ignorant of this luscious fruit that would change the Italian cuisine forever.

Just 30 years after Columbus's epic journey of discovery, the first tomato is said to have arrived in Naples, possibly as seeds from Spain. These were grown as ornamental plants and those first, small, golden fruit created amazement. They were so different from anything known that most people were afraid of them, some saying they were poisonous.

The Italians instantly and poetically dubbed them *pomo d'oro*, "apples of gold", changing later to today's spelling of *pomodoro*.

Originally all tomatoes were small and yellow, and it wasn't until some time later that Jesuit priests returning from Mexico introduced the red varieties. Now they looked *really* dangerous, and people were even less inclined to eat them.

We now know that tomatoes – the English word comes from the original Mexican, *tomatl* – are part of the deadly nightshade family (although with none of the deadly effects) and also that they are more fruit than vegetable, botanically, a type of berry.

A versatile ingredient

More than two centuries passed before the first tomato dishes were created. Around 1750, there are records of crushed and boiled tomatoes being used to make an early form of tomato sauce that was sealed and bottled, and from then it was not long before the whole population was eating and relishing them.

This was the beginning of Italy's massive love affair with tomatoes, and perhaps explains a lot of the world's love affair with Italian food.

The Italian climate is ideal for growing tomatoes, and they flourish in the hot Mediterranean sun. They are easily sun-dried, or cooked and pureed to make concentrated pastes, *passata* (tomato puree) and *sugo* (tomato sauce), the basis for a multitude of pizza or pasta sauces, *ragùs* and braises. Safely preserved for year-round use, they became the backbone of the cuisine.

Each Italian is said to consume about 50 kilograms of tomatoes a year - a healthy statistic, as tomatoes contain good quantities of vitamin C and are an excellent source of antioxidants.

Fresh, dried, bottled or canned

Many types of tomatoes are grown in Italy. Best for use in sauces are the egg-shaped Roma tomatoes and these are canned for domestic use out of season. Italian cooks have no problem with using canned or bottled tomatoes, possibly because it has long been part of their culture to make their own. Every Italian family with a tomato patch will spend several days each summer making litres of pureed or crushed tomatoes and sauces that will be preserved for later in the year.

Other popular tomato varieties include the large, meaty, ox heart tomatoes, favoured in salads, and the *San Marzano*, *Napoli* and *Marena* strains. Tomatoes grow well in all the southern regions of Italy, and they particularly like volcanic soil, so it follows that they thrive in Sicily, which is known for excellent *pomodorini*, tiny cherry tomatoes.

In the heat of summer, when cooler foods are needed, many families will enjoy a simple salad, *fresella*, in which moistened bread is mixed with olive oil, salt, chopped tomatoes and basil. The clean and bright *insalata caprese (see page 18)*, which alternates thin rounds of buffalo mozzarella with slices of ripe tomatoes and torn basil leaves drizzled with olive oil, is another standout summer dish.

To ripen or not to ripen

Southerners prefer their tomatoes rich and rosy red, while northerners prefer them slightly less ripe. Red or green (or golden again, with the recent introduction of some varieties) one thing is certain: Italian food would not be the same without this amazing, relatively recent import.

Funghi e tartufi
(Mushrooms & truffles)

For those in the know, a walk in the Italian countryside can result in some delicious - and valuable - findings.

Visitors to Italy are often amazed at the numbers of cars parked on the roadside in country areas, and imagine that this must be a nation of dedicated picnickers and ramblers. Maybe so, but they are more than likely foraging for mushrooms and other fungi.

Collected and enjoyed since Roman times (hence *amanita Caesarea* - Caesar's mushroom), Italians still love to pick their own when the conditions encourage these delicacies to spring up in the fields and forest glades.

Picker beware!

Warnings abound, however. There are endless rules connected with mushroom picking throughout the country. Pickers must have a license (*tesserino*) proving they are registered, and may be required to attend a course to teach them what to look for. Rules vary according to the region. Some insist on a strict quota per day; the size of the mushroom is often stipulated – too small is against the law; other places even decree which *day* is legal to go picking!

Below: Dealers at the truffle market in Alba, Piedmont.

Inspectors may ask to see what you have collected, too – and they certainly inspect mushrooms that are for sale. There's a good reason for this. It is estimated that about 40,000 people become ill with mushroom poisoning in Italy each year, because popping up amongst the many perfectly harmless and absolutely delicious orange, brown, spotted and speckled fungi, are about 300 quite similar *in*edible varieties, a few of which may hardly leave you time to call an ambulance if you become ill after eating them. Even handling some can prove dangerous.

So it is absolutely essential for anyone foraging in the countryside for *funghi* to either have a license or go with someone who has – or to simply buy *funghi* from a reputable market.

Italy's mushrooms are some of the tastiest and most diverse in Europe, growing wild mainly in the high valleys of all the northern regions, and in many places in the south as well. Up to 60 varieties may be found in markets of regions known for mushrooms, such as Piedmont, Lombardy and Trentino-Alto Aldige.

The elusive truffle

The king of the *funghi* is the truffle, eloquently described by Plutarch as "mud cooked by lightning". Both white and black truffles are found in many parts of the country and used in a range of dishes. Their famous aroma is so strong that it can permeate whole eggs, which when scrambled will retain the truffle flavour.

Highly valuable white truffles are located mainly in the northern regions of Italy, and occasionally in the highest areas of Calabria and Basilicata. They should not be cooked or they will lose their delicate flavour, and are best shaved with a special cutter, a *mandolino*, over egg dishes, pasta or risotto in order for diners to enjoy them fully. Alba in Piedmont is the key centre for white truffle production, producing the finest in the world.

Black truffles are less expensive, but still secure high prices and even the smallest may still be priced way over most people's normal shopping budgets. They remain very much in the "special occasion" bracket, unless, of course, you happen to be a lucky person living in a truffle-producing area, and know where to find your own. In that case you can be liberal with them, even if you have a glut of black truffles (oh, the idea of that!), roasting and eating them whole.

Foraging for *funghi*

For that's the thing. While there are commercial plantations now in Italy, truffles still grow in the wild in many places, due to their unique method of attaching spores to the rootlets of hazelnut and oak trees. Only the locals (with their pigs or dogs, which have been trained specially to sniff them out) know where they can most likely be found and their location is jealously guarded. In local markets throughout the north in truffle season, the lucrative and sometimes furtive business of selling truffles takes place, and many thousands of euros change hands in the process.

sott'olio

With this wealth of food springing up, seemingly each time it rains, Italian cooks sometimes have more funghi than they can use. If this happens they will dry the excess, or store them *sott'olio*, in oil, until later in the year, for use when needed.

Opposite: Fruit and vegetable market, Catania, Sicily.

Of course, for Italians, the opportunity to make a celebration out of it is tempting, and so there are a number of truffle festivals and markets throughout winter. For white truffles, Alba's is perhaps the biggest and best in early November. Others take place around the same time in **San Miniato**, Tuscany, **Acqualagna** in **Le Marche**, **Savigno** and **Sasso Marconi** in Emilia-Romagna, and also a couple of places in Umbria. Even without the money to buy them, visitors can almost feel they have feasted on this black gold just by inhaling the heady scent in the air at such events.

Second only to truffles is a much more common fungus found throughout most of Italy. It is worthwhile hunting down *porcini* or *cep* mushrooms, of which there are several species all belonging to the *boletus* genus. These mushrooms have a round, light-coloured cap and thick rounded stem, hence the name, which means piglet.

The colour of this mushroom, which stays white throughout the cooking process, and the rich, meaty flavour, makes it much prized for the substance it can add to dishes, such as pasta sauces and risottos. *Porcini* may be simply grilled or roasted as a side dish for meat or polenta, or served with salads. Although commonly found growing as companions of pine trees, inexplicably some say *porcini* are best when found around chestnuts, oaks or other trees.

There are more than 50 types of fungus in Italy and some are quite familiar worldwide, such as common field mushrooms, many of which are commercially farmed around the country.

Others include Caesar's mushroom with its large and delicate orange cap. However, it closely resembles some other highly dangerous mushrooms so pickers should *always* check with someone who can positively identify it.

Other common *funghi* include saffron milk caps, slippery jacks, *cantarella* (another name for the French *chanterelles* or *girolles*), oyster mushrooms, and *spugnola*, better known as morels, greatly favoured by chefs for use in exotic dishes.

Some have names that make you think twice, though. Shaggy inkcaps, hedgehog mushrooms, even piglets, but – given the many caveats on mushroom collecting in Italy – the black *trombetta dei morti* (trumpet of death) is enough to make anyone take a backward step. However, it is also known as *craterello*, which translates much more benignly as 'horn of plenty', because even though it looks lethal enough, it is delicious and can be used similarly to *chanterelles*.

Mushrooms and other *funghi* are, after all, the ultimate "free food". In Italy, for the ultra-careful and those in the know, mushroom hunting can literally turn a simple walk in the fields into the makings of a gourmet meal.

Celebrando 'Slow Food'
(Celebrating 'slow food')

In the era of fast food and even faster living, Italy has spawned a global counter-revolution.

Piedmont has many claims to fame in the food world, but perhaps particularly notable is that Bra, a town near Turin and Alba, is the birthplace of Carlo Petrini, who founded Slow Food in 1989.

Petrini's aim in founding the Slow Food movement was "to counteract fast food and fast life, the disappearance of local food traditions and people's dwindling interest in the food they eat, where it comes from, how it tastes and how our food choices affect the rest of the world".

Bringing together pleasure and responsibility (and making them inseparable) is a seemingly simple and eminently sensible solution, and one now embraced by over 100,000 members of the movement in 132 countries worldwide.

In odd-numbered years, the Slow Food movement in Bra hosts an international cheese festival in September alongside other events in the area, such as the world's largest food and wine fair, the *Salone Internazionale del Gusto*, in Turin each October.

Degrees of gastronomy

In addition to this, the main campus of the University of Gastronomic Sciences (UNISG) in Bra, founded by Carlo Petrini in 2004, offers a three-year undergraduate program. Affiliated with the Slow Food movement, it continues to foster the movement's objectives of bringing agricultural science and gastronomy into closer alignment. A second campus in Colorno, near Parma, Emilia-Romagna, offers Italian and English language graduate and masters programs.

The first *Terra Madre* (Mother Earth) conference was held in Turin in 2004, and was attended by 5000 delegates from more than 150 countries. Carlo Petrini and others at Slow Food hoped that this meeting, aimed at bringing together various previously unconnected food communities, would enable them to work together to "create sustainable food systems". Slow Fish, a festival held regularly in Genoa, aims to help people adopt "good practices of conscious and intelligent seafood consumption".

To quote the movement's stated philosophy, "the movement is founded upon this concept of eco-gastronomy – a recognition of the strong connections between plate and planet".

Mercati e strada alimentari
(Markets & street food)

For an authentic taste of the Italian way of life - head to the market …

Every town and city in Italy has a regular market. Some, like the many fish markets, are huge, undercover and open early on most days of the week (except Sunday). Others may be weekly, and many take place outdoors in the city square or some similar open place – often one that has been used for this purpose since medieval times.

With the passing of the centuries the goods have changed - where once horses, donkeys and chickens were traded, today's *mercato* is more likely to be filled with fruit and flowers, bread, *salami* and cheese. They vary enormously from one end of Italy to the other, depending on the size of the community.

To market, to market

Each market tends to be a social gathering that doubles as the daily (or weekly) shopping expedition. Babies are admired, news, views and gossip are exchanged, and somewhere in it all, food is bought. These day-to-day activities even happen in the *Campo dei Fiori* in the heart of Rome, making this big city seem like a small village after all.

Mobile vans often sell goods that need refrigeration or heating, such as *porchetta*, cheeses or *gelati*. A vendor's 'stand' may be as simple as the back of someone's truck or the bonnet and roof of their car. Some markets offer kitchen equipment, gadgets and perhaps some 'hangers-on' selling knock-off designer handbags and sunglasses from mats on the footpath.

After it is all over, a reviver is needed for all concerned, so coffee or a cool drink, pastries or lunch at one of the cafés around the square are in order.

On the street

Street food is almost always available every day in the same place, although perhaps only at certain times. The food varies according to the region, and tends to reflect the food that the locals grew up with. More importantly, it is quick to buy and easy to eat on the go.

There are some rather strict rules, however. Italian stallholders do not like to have their merchandise prodded and pushed – or, worse still, packed into plastic bags before weighing – by their customers. Haggling is not appropriate, although stallholders may pop in an extra apple for a small child, or some other friendly token gesture. Regulars know to bring their own bags too, and to order in kilograms and *etti* (tenths of a kilogram).

Pizza to go

Breads tend to be flat and easily handled, such as pizza or focaccia almost everywhere, or *piadini* in Emilia-Romagna. Pizza *al taglio* (by the slice) is popular as it is so portable and easily eaten. In fact, it was designed as a quick takeaway when it was first devised in Naples – so nothing much has changed. Focaccias with various fillings feature in the north, savoury chickpea pancakes, in many parts (called *panelle* in Sicily, *farinata* in Liguria), *supplì*, small fried rice balls, in Rome, and *arancini*, filled with peas and meat, in the far south and Sicily.

Fried foods may be sold from *friggitorie*, fried-food stalls, and sliced roast meat, potatoes and polenta are sold from shops called *rosticcerie*, where meat is cooked on large grills.

Porchetta, appetising slices of boned, stuffed and spit-roasted pig, served in a bread roll, are served at cafes and from travelling vans.

Seasonally, the offerings may change. Autumn brings the smoky scents of chestnuts roasting on a brazier on a street corner. Summer calls for wedges of glistening watermelon and other fresh fruits or squeezed juices.

Whatever the season or time of day, Italians manage to eat well whether at home or out and about – and fit in a little socialising at the same time.

Above: Roasting chestnuts for sale as a street snack, Rome.

Below: Shoppers at a cheese stall in the market of Siena, Tuscany

Noci (Nuts)

Used in savoury dishes, desserts and liqueurs – Italy's tasty nuts are extremely versatile.

Italian confetti

Confetti - coloured, sugared almonds, are a traditional Italian wedding gift.

In Abruzzo, where the best *confetti* are made, they are fashioned into elaborate bouquets of daisies - the ultimate edible gift (see below).

Once, when Italian families went for a walk in the woods at certain times of the year, they would take a basket for the nuts they might find. Sometimes, instead, they would fill their pockets with this found food, as it was invaluable in adding taste and nutrition to family meals. This foraging tradition has lived on in the way nuts are used throughout Italian cuisine.

Once home, the nuts could be ground into a paste to add to sugar or honey to fill pastries, added to cakes and bread, sprinkled over other dishes, or simply used as a snack. Best of all, they could be stored in a cool dry place and eaten all year.

Many Italian families had nut trees of their own – almonds, walnuts, hazelnuts, pistachios – planted amongst their orchard trees.

Di Mandorla

Mandorla (almond) trees grow well in Mediterranean countries, and have been cultivated for thousands of years. Their uses are many and they are often ground to make almond meal, which may be used for marzipan and in other dishes. Perhaps the pinnacle of this is in the beautiful marzipan fruit, *frutta di martorana*, which is handcrafted in Sicily. Many of these sweetmeats are so realistic it is hard to imagine they are only confectionery. Perfectly pretty piles of them can be seen in *pasticceria* windows throughout the island, or carefully arranged in gift boxes.

Many italian sweets feature almonds. *Torrone* (nougat) often includes whole almonds; *amaretti* biscuits are flavoured with ground almonds, and the well-known *Amaretto* liqueur is flavoured with bitter almonds. The famous *panforte di Siena*, a dense cake of chocolate and dried fruit, traditionally given at Christmas, is studded with almonds.

Nocciola for chocolate

Avellana in Campania bears one Italian name for hazelnuts, and of course it is known for growing these trees. Campania is a major producer, but the mountains of Piedmont and the north also produce exceptionally fine hazelnuts. These trees play a crucial role in truffle growing as the tubers attach spores to the rootlets of these and other trees in order to produce yet more *tartufi*.

Nocciola (hazelnut) features in liqueurs such as *Frangelico* and *Nocciola*, as well as in *torrone*, but perhaps hazelnut paste is this nut's greatest contribution to Italian cuisine. Hazelnut is combined with chocolate in many confectionery items – famously in Nutella, the spread that the entire world now loves – truly a match made in

sugar-tooth heaven. Anyone who is addicted to *Perugina Baci*, in which smooth dark chocolate wraps a toasted hazelnut, understands this perfectly.

Peanuts, *pinoli* and *pistacchio*

An unexpected nut product for Italy is peanuts (*arachide*), which are grown mainly in Puglia and Campania. These nuts (which are technically pulses, related to beans) have not found their way onto the Italian table except as snacks, and the majority of crops are made into peanut oil.

But where would pesto be without *pinoli* (pine nuts)? These kernels come from pine cones of naturally occurring trees found on coastal Italy, and are gathered from trees more than 70 years old. A key ingredient in Liguria's *pesto, pinoli* are also used with other nuts in *panpepato*, a spicy Tuscan nut cake.

In Italy, the pistachio (*pistacchio*) tree, native to many of the hotter Mediterranean countries, is grown only in Sicily. Pistachios are used in many sweets - especially *gelati* and biscuits; in stuffings for various meat dishes and as an ingredient in *salami* and *mortadella*.

Walnuts (*noce*) are grown mainly in Emilia-Romagna and Campania, especially around Sorrento, and are used in many sweet and savoury dishes. Liguria's *pansotti al preboggion*, a sauce for a vegetarian ravioli-type dish, makes liberal use of walnuts as well as pine nuts. The distinct flavour of *Nocino*, made near Modena, comes from the green walnuts infused in the alcohol.

Castagne - the versatile chestnut

Castagne (chestnuts) are found on trees growing in mountain and upland areas. They are widely used in cooking, ground into a flour to make *castagnaccio*, a flat raisin and rosemary cake, or roasted and eaten as a snack or a vegetable. They can be added to soups or sauces, used to flavour desserts, and in the north they may be simmered until tender then served as *ballotta*, a wine bar snack.

In autumn, roasted chestnuts can be bought, still hot, and served in a paper cone, from a roaster's stand on street corners in many cities around the country. One taste of this traditional street food will help you understand why it continues to please the crowds.

With such bounty falling from trees in woods all over the country, it is no surprise that Italian cuisine is so rich with recipes using these tasty and nutritious gifts of nature.

Basilicata

Basilicata's peasant food has evolved over time, but rustic and hearty is still on the menu.

Opposite: Ruins of an old village, near Maratea, Basilicata.

The geographic outline of southern Italy looks so much like a boot that it's impossible not to describe it in those terms. If you think of it finishing at the 'knee' around Rome in the west and Pescara in the east, then Basilicata occupies a wedge of land somewhere around the 'ankle bone'.

Basilicata, formerly Lucania, has coastlines on two seas, the Tyrrhenian to the west and the Ionian to the south. The interior is mountainous and includes the fairytale Lucanian Dolomites, while the southern coastal area is dotted with ancient Greek ruins. Midway is the unique UNESCO World Heritage-listed stone city of Matera with its caves, or *sassi*.

Subsistence living

Historically depicted as the poorest of the southern provinces, Basilicata's cuisine is based on *cucina povera* (peasant food), which refers back to times in recent history when local people were subsistence farmers and life was hard. Forced to eke a living from the soil and eat whatever was at hand, this often meant foraging mushrooms, herbs and nettles from the roadside or catching a wild rabbit for the pot.

However, Italian cooks know how to make the simplest food tasty, so while the region now produces much more, and the variety is greater, dishes still revolve around rustic staples: olive oil, beans and vegetables, chestnuts, mushrooms (including the wild *cardoncelli*), hard homemade cheeses (*Caciocavallo Silano* DOP, *cacioricotta, pecorino di Filiano*), spicy sausages (*lucanica, pezzente*, and *soppressata*) are made with lamb or pork from Basilicatas renowned black pigs, with paprika and chillies to liven things up.

Bread and wine

The tender flavoursome bread of Matera (*pane di Matera*) is widely known and appreciated, so much so that has been awarded the designation IGP (*Indicazione Geografica Protetta*).

The rich red *Aglianico del Vulture* wines produced in the volcanic soils of the north are highly prized, but visitors to the region should also try a shot of delicious *Amaro Lucano*, an aromatic local *digestivi* served at the end of a meal.

Basilicata is still developing its tourist infrastructure, so, should you be lucky enough to visit, look for local trattorias (*trattorie*) and inns where the welcome will be as genuine as the food, or plan to stay at an *agriturismo* (farmstay) property where you can dine as well.

gourmet
pilgrim

Il Pane

Bread

More than a simple dietary staple, Italian breads are prized throughout the world for their amazing taste, aroma, quality and texture.

Il Pane (Bread)

'Man cannot live on bread alone' - but with the delicious array found it Italy, it would be much less of a challenge.

Bread (*pane*) is an essential part of every Italian meal. In Italian restaurants, no matter how humble, a basket of bread and often a packet of *grissini* (breadsticks) will appear on the table the moment diners are seated.

In the home, Italian *mammas* have been kneading large pillows of dough every morning for centuries and baking crusty loaves for their families, often in wood-fired outdoor or communal ovens.

Italian *panetteri* or *panifici* (bakeries) open early, laden with breads of all types – crusty loaves, small breads, sweet breads, long sticks, and much more. Sometimes it's hard to know whether *pane* is a pastry or a small cake, because in smaller places bakeries may double as a *pasticceria*. Cakes that use yeast to make sweet batter rise, such as Neapolitan *babas*, appear in cake shops. Choux pastry *bignole* from Piedmont, or doughnut-like *bombolini* from Emilia-Romagna, are more desserts or sweet snacks too.

And if you are dining in, ask if there are any *fatta a mano* (handmade bread rolls), which will be freshly baked and delicious.

Fare la scarpetta

Italians appreciate their bread, and it is not considered bad manners at all if you use the last of your bread to mop up any remaining sauces from your plate (known as *fare la scarpetta*, meaning to make a 'shoe') at the end of a meal.

In days gone by preservatives were not used and the bread became stale quickly. Today it is still often made or bought daily for this reason, although many bakeries now prepare bread in the modern way. While the result may last longer, many Italians think it will never match the bread they remember their *nonna* (grandmother) making.

Almost certainly *nonna* would have used a strong wheat flour, finely ground (*tipo 00*) – the same one she used for the daily pasta. Sometimes, in the south, semolina was added – especially for pizza dough – and occasionally *integrale* (wholemeal) flour. Many types of Italian breads use little fat, making the loaves (especially the crusts) quite chewy. Tuscan breads don't use salt.

For centuries, bread was a staple food, eaten every day. In some homes it would have comprised a large part of the diet. When the budget is tight, there is little left for extras, and *il pane* at least fed the family. A few traditional peasant pasta dishes use breadcrumbs to eke out the staple a little further.

Breads made with enriched doughs – with eggs, fat and sugar added – were special treats, made for special occasions, and these tended to be lavish, over-the-top and elaborate.

PANE BIOLOGICO

A LIEVITAZIONE NATURALE

CON FARINE MACINATE A PIETRA

IMPASTATO A MANO

COTTO A LEGNA !

Baking for special events

Feast days and religious events are often celebrated with special bread, so there is *casatiello*, the Neapolitan Easter bread, containing lard and cheese, and the egg and butter-rich *Colomba Pasquale* made in the shape of a dove, while Milan has *pan con l'uva*, which, as the name suggests, uses eggs, as well as dried fruit. Rosemary bread is made at Easter in Tuscany; *pane di San Giuseppe*, fashioned like a fish or in other decorative shapes, decorates altars in Trapani, Sicily, to celebrate All Saint's Day.

At Christmas, the Genoese prepare a dense *pan dolce*, made with a sourdough starter and fruit, while Verona and Venice celebrate with light and delicious *pandoro*. *Panettone*, the tall egg-rich bread lightly studded with fruit and baked only for Christmas, is eaten widely throughout the country.

Regional *pane*

With the advent of modern bread-making techniques and distribution, regional differences are blurring, but, in general, people in the north prefer either very white bread and small rolls or, occasionally, loaves made from the local rye or barley flour. *Pane di segale* is a hard, dark rye bread that is popular in Valle d'Aosta.

Focaccia originated in Liguria, but is now a worldwide favourite. A hard bread is generally favoured in Emilia-Romagna; Tuscans prefer their unsalted *pane sciocco*; while *sfilatino*, or *bastone* (like a short baguette), are found in Rome; and the southern regions make very large loaves of bread that keeps longer.

As in many other countries today, square loaves of sandwich bread, *pane a cassetta* (*pan carré*), are now the universal choice for families.

However, regional specialties still survive: *coppia ferrarese*, first made in the 12th century in Ferrara (Emilia-Romagna) is a type of sourdough bread made with flour, lard, olive oil, and malt, and shaped with a twist. *Pane pugliese* is a very large, hard-crusted and chewy loaf, while tender and tasty bread from Matera in Basilicata is said to be the best in Italy.

Smaller breads are popular – ideal to split and stuff with prosciutto, salami or cheese. *Panino*, *ciabatta*, *focaccia* and *pita* are all popular and widely available. Visitors and locals in Rome look for the distinctively marked *rosetta* rolls or, during Lent, for *maritozzo*, sweet brioche-like buns, but made with sourdough. In Sicily, *guastedde*, topped with sesame seeds, is sold in the markets.

The size, shape and texture of loaves varies enormously, from dense lard-enriched *biovetta* in Piedmont to *pan mieno*, a light sweet bread from Lombardy.

The ultimate sandwich

Muffuletta – a whole loaf stuffed with everything you could dream of – is named for the Sicilian loaf with which it was first made in New Orleans last century.

If you are still hungry, don't forget the crisp and long-lasting dried breads of Italy – *grissini* (those ubiquitous breadsticks), *taralli* (fennel-studded rings), and from Campania and Puglia, *fresella*, which are cut in half after baking, then dried again.

Below: Making *montegemoli* bread in a wood-burning oven, Volterra, Tuscany.

Flat breads are quick and easy to make and ideal for wrapping fillings. *Piadini* are unleavened, like pita, and come from Romagna; the variously named Sardinian bread *carta da musica* (*pane fresa, pane carasau*), once made for shepherds' lunches, is a treat on its own or soaked and used in some dishes. It is baked in fearsomely hot ovens that cause the paper-thin dough to puff like a pillow. When cooled, it is carefully split open and baked again to create wafers.

Crostini are small dried breads from Tuscany, and unleavened *farinata* made with chickpea flour (perhaps more of a pancake than bread) comes from Piedmont and Liguria. *Focaccia* has many relatives: *pinza, pissalandrea, pita, sardenara, schiacciata* and *stiacciata*, among others throughout the country.

Large or small, fresh and soft, or crisp and crunchy – *pane* is the essence of Italian eating and its regional variations fresh examples of the living history of the country.

Grissini ai pinoli
Pine nut bread sticks

Makes about 40

Ingredients

300g plain (all-purpose) flour, sifted

7g active dry yeast

1 tablespoon sugar

½ teaspoon salt

½ teaspoon fennel seeds, crushed

¼ teaspoon lemon rind, grated

2 tablespoons olive oil

2 tablespoons sunflower oil

125ml lukewarm water

50g pine nuts, chopped

1 egg, lightly beaten

2 tablespoons flaked salt

Commercially made grissini don't come close to the flavour and texture of the artisanal, or home made, product. Yeasted dough, usually containing olive oil and often flavoured with herbs, is kneaded then pulled and stretched into long thin baton-like shapes. Sesame or poppy seeds are often used to coat the bread sticks; pine nuts add a lovely texture to these grissini.

Method

Combine only 150g of flour with yeast, sugar, salt, fennel, rind, oils and water in a large bowl; beat until smooth.

Add pine nuts and enough of remaining flour to form a stiff dough.

Turn dough out onto a lightly floured work surface and knead until smooth and elastic; place into a lightly greased bowl. Cover with a slightly damp clean tea towel and leave in a warm place to rise until doubled in size – about 40-60 minutes.

Turn dough out again onto a floured board and punch down*. Divide dough in half then divide each half into 20 pieces.

Preheat oven 160°C.

Roll each piece out (using hands) into a 20cm long sausage; place onto 4 baking trays that have been lined with kitchen baking paper, allowing 2cm between each stick. Cover with tea towels and leave to rise for about 20 minutes, or until doubled in size. Brush with egg and sprinkle with salt.

Bake in preheated oven for 15 minutes or until golden. Suitable to freeze.

Tip: Add ½ teaspoon of dried rosemary to the dough at the same time as the pine nuts. Or sprinkle the uncooked grissini with poppy seeds or toasted sesame seeds.

* Refer to Glossary – Page 470

Pane carta da musica
'Music paper' flat bread

Ingredients

Lukewarm water (about 250ml)
7g active dried yeast
½ teaspoon table salt
200g durum wheat semolina
200g plain (all-purpose) flour

Also known as pane carasau, pane carta da musica is a Sardinian specialty, traditionally eaten by nomadic shepherds in the Sardinian mountains. The name carta da musica, which means "sheet music", is used because the bread is so thin. It's made by separating the flatbread into two sheets that are then baked for a second time. Some Sardinian recipes utilise pane carasau as you might use dried lasagna sheets.

Method

Place the water, yeast and salt into a large bowl – sit in a warm place until it begins to foam slightly.

Combine the semolina and flour into a second large bowl. Make a well in the middle and begin to add the yeast and water. Knead the mix with your hand to bring together and form a smooth dough. Add a little more water if it appears too dry and a little more flour if too sticky.

Turn dough out onto a lightly floured work surface and knead lightly. Place into a second clean bowl, which has been lightly oiled. Cover with a clean tea towel and sit in a warm place until dough doubles in size.

Preheat oven to 240° C. Move oven shelves to the lowest position.

Return dough to the floured work surface and knead once more then divide dough into four portions. Roll each portion out into a circle as thin as possible, about 2-3mm thick. It may work well to only cook two bread rounds at a time.

Place dough onto two large round lightly oiled baking tray (a pizza tray would be perfect).

Bake in preheated oven for about 8-10 minutes or until the dough puffs up and has some golden brown colour. Turn and cook a further 2 minutes. Alternate the shelf position of the trays halfway through cooking.

Dust lightly with flour while warm and cool on a wire rack. Cook the remaining portions.

Note – This is delicious served with tomatoes, cheese and cooked egg.

Tip: If upon cooling the bread doesn't seem quite dry enough it can be returned to a warm oven and heated for a further 5-10 minutes to dry it out a little more.

Pagnotto con olive, cipolle e erbe fresch
Olive, onion & fresh herb bread

Serves 6-8

Ingredients

300ml lukewarm water

7g active dry yeast

Pinch sugar

1 tablespoon olive oil

1 large brown onion, finely chopped

450g strong (bakers) flour

½ teaspoon table salt

60g pitted black olives, roughly chopped

20g black olive paste

1 tablespoon finely chopped fresh rosemary leaves

1 tablespoon freshly picked thyme leaves

1 tablespoon finely chopped fresh flat-leaf (Italian) parsley

Method

Place only half the water, yeast and sugar into a bowl – sit in a warm place until it begins to foam slightly.

Heat the oil in a medium frying pan over medium heat and cook the onion for 10 minutes or until soft.

Place the flour and salt into a large bowl. Add the olives and toss in flour to coat. Make a well in the middle, add the yeast mix, olive paste, onions, herbs and remaining water. Stir to combine then begin to knead the mix within the bowl with your hand to bring it together and to form a smooth dough. Add a little more water if it appears too dry and a little more flour if too sticky.

Turn dough out onto a lightly floured work surface and knead lightly. Place into a second clean bowl, which has been lightly oiled. Cover with a clean tea towel and sit in a warm place until dough doubles in size.

Preheat oven to 200°C.

Return dough to the floured work surface and knead once more and shape into a round of about 20cm. Cut a crisscross pattern into the top of the dough then place onto a lightly oiled baking tray. Cover and rest again for about 30 minutes. Dust lightly with flour.

Bake in preheated oven for 20-30 minutes or until the dough sounds hollow when tapped on the top. Serve.

Focaccia con cipolle e olive
Focaccia with onions & olives

Serves 4-6

Ingredients

2 tablespoons olive oil
1kg white onions, peeled and thinly sliced
Flaked salt
Freshly cracked black pepper
½ quantity pizza dough (see page 294)
50g anchovy fillets* in oil, drained
50g black olives, pitted and halved

This yeasted dough spread or mixed with herbs, oil and seasonings is a specialty of Liguria, although it can be found throughout Italy. Early versions were cooked directly on the hearth or on earthenware tiles. This recipe, featuring salty anchovies, olives and sweet caramelised onions, is similar to the Ligurian pissadella or pissalandrea, which is closely related to the Provencal pissaladière from just over the French border.

Method

Preheat oven to 200°C.

Heat the oil in a large frying pan over low-medium heat and cook onions for 10 minutes, stirring occasionally. Season to taste and cook uncovered over low heat for 30 minutes or until the mixture dries out. Stir often to prevent over browning.

Add a little water if necessary to prevent onions sticking and burning (although onions need to be dry at the end of the cooking time). Drain onions and cool slightly.

Lightly grease a 28cm-diameter pizza tray or a large oven tray and roll out dough to size, pushing dough to the edge to make a ridge around the outer edge.

Spread the cooled onions over the dough and add anchovies and olives.

Bake in preheated oven on the bottom shelf of the oven for 30-40 minutes.

Variation – Sprinkle fresh oregano leaves over the onions.

* Refer to Glossary – Page 470

Crostini al formaggio
Grilled open cheese sandwiches

Serves 2-3

Ingredients

2 tablespoons olive oil

300g ripe roma tomatoes, finely chopped

5 fresh basil leaves, shredded

Flaked salt

Freshly cracked black pepper

4-6 slices of rustic Italian bread (e.g. ciabatta)

1 garlic clove, halved

80g provolone cheese*, thinly sliced

Extra virgin olive oil, to drizzle

Method

Heat the oil in a small frying pan over medium heat. Add the tomatoes and cook for 5-7 minutes or until the tomato liquid/juice is almost gone. Stir in the basil and season to taste.

Toast the bread until lightly golden brown. Then rub both sides of the bread with the cut side of the garlic clove.

Spoon some of the tomato mixture over each slice of bread and top with cheese slices.

Place under a hot preheated grill until the cheese melts. Drizzle with extra olive oil and season with pepper.

Serve immediately.

Note – the number of pieces made will depend on the size of your bread slices.

* Refer to Glossary – Page 470

Panettone
Milanese fruit bread

Serves 10-12

Ingredients

100g castor (superfine) sugar

3 x 7g active dry yeast

200ml lukewarm water

4 free-range egg yolks*, at room temperature, lightly beaten

1 teaspoon vanilla extract*

1 tablespoon finely grated lemon rind

½ teaspoon table salt

600g plain (all-purpose) flour, sifted

175g butter, at room temperature

100g sultanas

100g raisins

100g mixed candied fruit

25g butter extra, melted

Christmas in Italy wouldn't be complete without panettone, a large dome-shaped yeasted loaf made with eggs, butter, vanilla and lemon and studded with dried fruit and candied peel. Industrial production of panettone originated in Milan in the 1920s; it is ubiquitous throughout Italy during the festive season, although the quality varies widely from one brand to another. Variations on this yeasted bread include pandoro, another Christmas specialty, which is shaped like a domed star and contains no fruit.

Method

In a small bowl combine only 1 teaspoon of the sugar with the yeast and water. Set aside in a warm place and allow the yeast to dissolve and become slightly foamy.

Place dissolved yeast into a larger bowl with yolks, vanilla, rind, salt and remaining sugar. Add only about a quarter of the flour then the butter, a little at a time. Add remaining flour and mix until a soft dough forms.

Turn dough out onto a lightly floured work surface and knead for about 10 minutes or until smooth and elastic. Place into a lightly greased bowl. Cover with a slightly damp, clean tea towel and leave in a warm place to rise until doubled in size (about 1 hour).

Turn dough out again onto a floured surface and knead the sultanas, raisins and candied fruit into the dough. Continue kneading until fruit is evenly distributed throughout dough.

Place a panettone paper case (see note) into a round 18cm-baking pan. Place the dough into the case then use a sharp knife to score a cross into the surface of the dough. Cover loosely with greased plastic wrap. Allow to stand in a warm place again until dough has risen to fill the paper case.

Preheat oven to 200°C.

Remove plastic wrap and brush top with only about half the melted butter. Place into preheated oven, bake for 20 minutes then reduce heat to 160°C and bake a further 20 minutes. Remove from oven and brush the top with the remaining butter. Allow to cool on a wire rack. Serve warm or cold.

Note – Panettone literally means "big bread". The decorative paper case for baking can be found at kitchen supply shops.

* Refer to Glossary – Page 470

Lombardia (Lombardy)

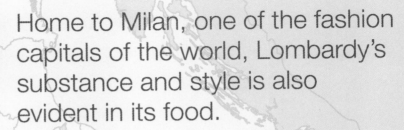

Home to Milan, one of the fashion capitals of the world, Lombardy's substance and style is also evident in its food.

Lombardy, rich and refined, powerful and prestigious, lies at the head of Italy. Home to about sixteen per cent of the Italian population and neighbour to Switzerland, it seems to have it all – stunning mountains, the most scenic lakes in the country and wide, fertile agricultural plains which have been tilled for centuries and are laced with canals and waterways.

Unsurprisingly, this land has been fought over and invaded for much of its long history. It has money and style in abundance and Milan, the style-leading capital of the region, stands secure in its position as the fashion capital of Italy.

Prized produce

From the high valleys come superb cold climate fruits, Valtellina apples and Mantovana pears. Further south there are the prized Viadana yellow-fleshed melons (perfect for pairing with Parma ham from Emilia-Romagna, just across the river), while vegetable stands display pumpkin, cabbage, asparagus and onions in season.

As in neighbouring Piedmont, dairy cattle graze on rich upland pastures and reward their owners with milk and cream used to make the butter and cheeses – *taleggio, gorgonzola, bitto, Grana Padano, stracchino, Parmigiano-Reggiano, provolone* and *mascarpone* – that make this area famous. But goats are also raised here and the local *caprini* is equally highly respected.

Lacking only one thing – a coastline – Lombardy looks to its lakes for fish, which are small but delicious. More popular on many tables are cured meats such as Brianza, Varzi and Milanese *salami*, *bresaola* (cured beef) or *cotechino* (a white sausage) from Valtellina, and *prosciutto crudo*, the cured ham that is preferred here.

Buckwheat grows well in the north, and in warmer areas around the lakes there are olive groves producing olive oil. An annual olive oil market, *Sapor d'Olio*, celebrates and sells the local DOP olive oils of Franciacorta in the province of Brescia from late November to early December – certainly worth a stopover. The Po Valley is a rice-producing area and the strain grown around Lomellina is said to be the best.

Mustard fruits, or *mostarda*, a sort of fruit chutney, is produced in Cremona, although *torrone* (nougat), said to have been created in 1441 for an aristocratic wedding, is the chief product of this city.

Gran Pistà is also prized in Lombardy. This fresh bacon fat is seasoned with parsley and garlic, and is made by farmers from Mantova. Many like to spread it on roasted slices of polenta or add it to soups for richness and flavour.

Risotto, gnocchi and *polenta* still abound on tables in Lombardy, but if there is pasta on the table it is more likely to be *pizzoccheri*, made with buckwheat flour. *Polenta taragna*, a mixture of buckwheat and cornmeal is a local favourite, and for dessert *torta sbrisolona*, a crumbly grape and cornmeal cake, may feature.

Lombardy is not famous for its wines although many are exported to Europe, and good reds are made here with Barbera grapes.

Famous favourites

Perhaps the key dish of the area is the rich and gelatinous *osso buco (see page 136)*, which is usually served sprinkled with *gremolata*, a fresh and aromatic mixture of lemon zest, garlic and parsley. Risotto abounds too, most notably as *risotto alla Milanese*, a creamy dish featuring saffron and bone marrow. Other traditional dishes include *minestrone* and *tortelli de zucca* (pasta filled with *amaretti* and pumpkin).

At Christmastime in Milan there is *panettone*, a lightly fruited egg-rich bread, now popular throughout the world and presented beautifully, of course, as befits the style capital. Panettone is believed to be developed thanks to a long feud between two Milanese bakers early last century, as with all Italian feuds, it has created great things. After all, food and style are everything in Lombardy and Milan – fashion is fleeting.

Lombardians are commited eaters of meat and poultry - and here risotto and polenta still easily surpass pasta in the popularity stakes.

Previous left: The 14th century "Rocca Scalgera" - Scaliger Castle - overlooks Sirmione at the southern end of Lake Garda, Lombardy.

Previous right: Lake d'Iseo, Lombardy.

Below: Mantova's Old Town skyline from 'Lago Inferiore', Lombardy.

Toscana (Tuscany)

Welcome to Tuscany – the Italy of romance, art, and amazing food and wine. This large and ancient region's particularly rich history stretches back to the Etruscans and beyond, via the Renaissance and the powerful Medici family. Geographically, it covers some of Italy's loveliest country, from the Apennines to the Tyrrhenian and Ligurian seas.

But it's not just a pretty face. In recent years the region has introduced environmentally friendly measures for its agriculture, emphasising low-impact and organic methods. The *Toscano* tag is a sign of the provenance of local produce.

This is a region of abundance, evident in the kitchen and on the long, groaning tables, which are often set up outdoors under grape-covered pergolas. No doubt this generosity and homespun goodness of the food are two of the many things that attract so many visitors and encourage them to return yet again.

Good food in abundance

With good soil, sunshine to ripen fruit and an equable climate, it is not surprising that Tuscany is a region of plenty. Olive trees grow in many areas, their silvery groves punctuated by the dark exclamation points of cypress trees. Olive oil is used in most dishes, and many agree that the best in the region comes from Lucca to the west of the capital, Florence (*Firenze*).

Cheese is used liberally too, and the hard local sheep's milk *pecorino Toscano* (especially the one produced near Pienza towards the Umbrian border) is especially prized, and often grated over pasta or other dishes. It is one of only four in the country to have a Protected Designation of Origin (PDO). Other local cheeses of note are the silky *caciotta Toscana*, and *marzolino* from Chianti, which uses sheep milk and has been made here for centuries.

In season, the local markets are vibrant with fresh offerings – chestnuts from the Alto Fiorentino area and the Grossetto mountain slopes in the south, honey from the Magra Valley, saffron from the unbelievably postcard-pretty San Gimignano. There will be cannellini and borlotti beans from Sorana and from Prato to the north, wild mushrooms, bags of *farro* (spelt, an ancient strain of wheat) from near Lucca, flour from Garfagnana, and fat hard-crusted loaves of the unsalted, fat-free Tuscan bread (*pane Toscano*) – again, the best originating from lucky Lucca.

World-famous for its beauty and charm, even visitors who arrive with the highest of hopes won't be disappointed.

Opposite: Countryside around Pienza, Siena province, Tuscany.

Sensational steaks

Florence is steak-central. The white bullocks raised on the central Apennines provide the best meat, and those from Arezzo and Siena have been awarded *classico* status. Sampling *bistecca alla Fiorentina* (see page 140) should be a standard rite of passage for any meat lover.

Like any large city, Florence has gathered together the best of its region's foods and these are showcased in all types of restaurants, many of them enjoying outdoor dining on the city's many piazzas, and affording front row views of the constantly passing parade of people and traffic.

Some piazzas have an interesting addition that is not always palatable to visitors. *Lampredotto* (offal sellers) may set up their stands there to sell tripe sandwiches that, despite the idea and the look of the dark crinkly meat, are surprisingly tasty. Another acquired taste is *Maremmana razza*, horsemeat from Livorno, Pisa and other coastal areas, available in some restaurants.

Diners visiting the region are often eager to try hare or rabbit ragùs and dishes that feature *cinghiale* (local wild boar). The latter's flesh also turns up as sausages or boar prosciutto, and the more traditional pork *prosciutto Toscano* is excellent, too. In addition, Tuscany produces fennel-flavoured salamis from Florence and Siena, *lardo* from the Apuan Alps, and *salsiccia* and *sopressata* across the region.

Florence's trattorias are legendary and ubiquitous. Typical dishes include *ribollita* (literally, reboiled) vegetable soup made with the strong flavoured and distinctive *cavola nero* (black cabbage) and often thickened with bread, also an ingredient in *panzanella*, a bread and tomato salad or soup (see page 38).

On the coast, seafood lovers are equally satisfied with *cacciucco*, a seafood stew from Livorno, made with five types of fish, supposedly to match the five c's in the name of the dish. Pasta is alive and well, too, in Tuscany, with wide flat *pappardelle*, narrower *tagliatelle*, and *pici*, a thick dried spaghetti similar to the Umbrian *umbricelli*.

La dolce vita

Tuscan Dolci (desserts) or sweet snacks include the famous and decadently rich chocolate and nut *panforte (see page 424)* from Siena, *zuccotto fiorentino (see page 350)*, a luscious layering of sponge cake and liqueur cream (perhaps the inspiration for *tiramisù*?) and *ricciarelli*, a *marzipan biscotto* from Siena.

Pizza

Pizza may have started out as simple food sold by street vendors in Naples, but today it's a favourite around the world.

Pizza

Can anyone imagine a weekend without pizza? While it may seem like the epitome of a modern suburban evening meal, pizza does have a long and proud Italian heritage.

The first real *pizzeria* is said to have been Antica Pizzeria Port'Alba, which opened in Naples in 1830, although the company had been producing pizzas to be sold by street vendors for almost a century before this. Remarkably, it is still in business today.

Almost sixty years later, in 1889, Neapolitan baker, Raffaele Esposito, is believed to have created the first *Margherita* pizza. Esposito devised what is probably the most popular (and certainly most basic) pizza of all, as a special treat for the visiting Queen of Italy and Savoia, Margherita and her husband Umberto I. Obviously trying to make an impression on the couple, he named this new dish after the queen, and used the colours of the Italian flag – red, white and green – to underline his patriotism. What's more it tasted good, and so this basic yet universally loved pizza was born.

Even today the tongue-twistingly named *Associazione Verace Pizza Napoletana* (Association of True Neapolitan Pizza) imposes strict guidelines on its worldwide members, dictating the type and amount of ingredients that may be used to create 'true' Neapolitan pizza. An authentic *Margherita*, for instance, may be topped with only tomato, olive oil, grated parmesan, and *fior-di-latte* or mozzarella. The Pizzaiolo may add a leaf or two of basil. According to the association's mandate, true Neapolitan pizzas must be baked in a wood-fired oven (*forno a legna*), and each pizza base must be entirely shaped by hand.

The rules further state that 'variations of pizzas are recognised if they are informed by the Neapolitan tradition of pizzas and are not in contrast with the rules of gastronomy', which brings into question the many variations now dreamed up around the world. Certainly, true Italians baulk at the idea of pineapple on a pizza.

Peasant food gone global

Basically a flat bread baked in an oven with something on top, pizza (the word simply means 'pie') was possibly baked for many centuries before it went commercial. It was originally peasant food; simple to cook, tasty, and similar to breads cooked in many other countries. However, Italy managed to turn the concept into an art form – and an international industry. With widespread Italian migration in the twentieth century, it wasn't long until the whole world knew about – and loved – pizza.

True Neapolitan pizza must be baked in a '*forno a legna*' - wood fired oven - and shaped entirely by hand.

Opposite: The *pizzaiolo* (pizza maker) at work at Pizzeria Trianon, Naples, Campania.

Back to basics

Pizza dough is made with *doppio 00* white flour. The dough is allowed to rise, then often theatrically shaped by the *pizzaiolo* (the pizza maker), as he flings the dough into the air, turning and stretching it each time, until it reaches the size and shape he desires.

Italian pizza bases are much thinner than their overseas cousins, although roughly the same diameter. In Italy, they often have just a crisp cracker base with a smear of topping, and are cooked in just a few minutes in the furnace heat of the wood-fired oven, the heart of every *pizzeria*.

In Italy, pizza may be sold in the familiar round shape or brought steaming from the oven in massive rectangles, and sold by the slice *al taglio*. *Calzone* is a folded pizza with the 'topping' (now the filling) enclosed inside a bread case. Indeed, when eating casually, Italians often fold their slices of flat pizza in half for convenience.

Toppings vary from the unusual but delectable potato and rosemary, to seafood, or mushroom and cheese, and others are topped with *salami* and regional specialties. *Capricciosa* features sausage, prosciutto, or olives – in fact anything according to the 'whim' of the chef, for that is what the word means.

Pizza Pugliese involves tomato, mozzarella and onions, and *pizza Siciliana* mixes tomato, mozzarella, capers, olives and anchovies. Southern pizzas almost certainly will have options that include chilli.

But don't be fooled by traditional *marinara*, which is simply tomato, garlic and oil – and contains no seafood. This topping was the one favoured by fishermen, because they wanted a pizza to eat *with* their fish. It has no cheese, something that Italians are adamant should never be placed on a plate with seafood.

For those who can't decide, there's always the four seasons pizza, *quattro stagioni*, in which each quarter of the pizza is topped differently, or *quattro formaggi*, which uses four types of cheese.

Pizza tradizionzle
Original pizza dough

Makes 4 x 30cm pizzas

Ingredients

1 x 8g sachet dry yeast
270ml lukewarm water
500g strong/pizza flour or plain flour
1 teaspoon salt
1 tablespoon olive oil
Olive oil to grease

Method

Place the yeast and water into a bowl and whisk with a fork to combine. Rest in a warm place for 10 minutes or until it begins to foam a little.

Combine the flour and salt in a bowl and make a well in the centre. Pour in the yeast mixture and gently mix with a spoon to combine.

Once the dough comes away from the sides of the bowl, turn the dough onto a lightly floured work surface. Knead for about 8 minutes or until it becomes elastic to touch.

Place the dough into a clean bowl lightly greased with the olive oil, cover with a slightly damp clean tea towel. Put bowl and dough into a warm place to rest until the dough doubles in size. This may take up to 30 minutes.

To make a 30cm pizza you will need 190g of dough. Once weighed out, flatten out and roll out the dough to a thickness of 5mm. Place onto a lightly oiled pizza pan, or a pizza stone (see note).

Timing wise, try to roll the dough out no longer than 30 minutes before cooking. Keep covered or wrapped prior to rolling to prevent drying out. Should you need to leave the dough for an hour or more, place it into the fridge then remove and bring back to room temperature before using.

Tip: Ideally, less is more when putting your toppings onto the pizzas. And leftover dough can be rolled into balls, wrapped individually and frozen for up to 3 months.

Note – Pizza stones will give the pizza a beautiful, crispy base, but it's important to prepare and use them according to manufacturer's directions.

Pizza Margherita
Margherita pizza

Ingredients

1 freshly prepared, uncooked 30cm pizza base (see page 294)

3 tablespoons tomato puree (passata)* or tomato pizza sauce

150g fresh buffalo mozzarella cheese*, thinly sliced

Fresh sweet basil leaves, to serve

First created in 1889 by a Neapolitan baker, Raffaele Esposito, in honour of the visiting Queen Margherita of Savoy, pizza Margherita is the simplest and most delicious of creations: yeasted dough spread with tomato, olive oil, and mozzarella, sometimes topped with basil leaves, baked (ideally) in a wood-fired oven. With some simple additions, the Margherita can be transformed into an endless variety of other pizzas.

Method

Preheat oven to 250°C.

Place pizza base onto lightly oiled pizza tray or stone and spread the base with passata, leaving the outer rim uncovered. Lay slices of mozzarella onto the pizza base.

Bake in preheated oven on the bottom shelf for 5 minutes or until pizza base and crust is lightly golden and crisp. The top should also be golden brown and the cheese melted.

Remove from oven and scatter the top of the pizza with basil leaves. Serve.

* Refer to Glossary – Page 470

Pizza Napoli
Neopolitan pizza

Ingredients

1 freshly prepared, uncooked 30cm pizza base (see page 294)

60ml tomato puree (passata)* or tomato pizza sauce

125g mozzarella cheese*, grated

½-1 teaspoon dried oregano leaves

50g drained anchovy fillets*

Method

Preheat oven to 250°C.

Place pizza base onto lightly oiled pizza tray or stone and spread the base with passata, leaving the outer rim uncovered. Sprinkle with only half the cheese then add the oregano and anchovies. Top with remaining cheese.

Bake in preheated oven on the bottom shelf for 5 minutes or until pizza base and crust is lightly golden and crisp. The top should also be golden brown and the cheese melted.

* Refer to Glossary – Page 470

Pizza prosciutto e funghi
Ham & mushroom pizza

Ingredients

1 freshly prepared uncooked 30cm pizza
base (see page 294)

60ml tomato puree (passata)* or tomato
pizza sauce

125g mozzarella cheese*, grated

100g prosciutto*, thinly sliced

100g button mushrooms, thinly sliced

50g pitted black olives

Method

Preheat oven to 250°C.

Place pizza base onto lightly oiled pizza tray or stone and spread
the base with passata, leaving the outer rim uncovered. Sprinkle
with only half the cheese then add the ham, mushrooms and
olives. Top with remaining cheese.

Bake in preheated oven on the bottom shelf for 5 minutes or until
pizza base and crust is lightly golden and crisp. The top should
also be golden brown and the cheese melted.

* Refer to Glossary – Page 470

Pizza quattro stagioni
Four seasons pizza

Ingredients

1 x freshly prepared uncooked pizza base
(see page 294)

3 tablespoons tomato puree (passata)* or
tomato pizza sauce

100g mozzarella cheese*, grated

1 small tomato, thinly sliced

20g thinly sliced prosciutto*

2 marinated artichoke hearts, thinly sliced

1 large button mushroom, thinly sliced

Method

Preheat oven to 250°C.

Place pizza base onto lightly oiled pizza tray or stone and spread the base with passata, leaving the outer rim uncovered. Sprinkle the base with mozzarella.

Visually imagine the pizza base is in 4 quarters. Onto 1 quarter place the tomatoes, on the 2nd the prosciutto, the 3rd the artichokes and the 4th the mushrooms.

Bake in the preheated oven on the bottom shelf for 5 minutes or until pizza base and crust is lightly golden and crisp.

The topping ingredients should have melted into the cheese.

* Refer to Glossary – Page 470

Pizza brianzola
Sausage & pepper pizza

Ingredients

1 freshly prepared, uncooked 30cm pizza base (see page 294)

60ml tomato puree (passata)* or tomato pizza sauce

125g mozzarella cheese*, grated

½-1 teaspoon dried oregano leaves

Pinch flaked salt

1 yellow or red pepper (capsicum), char-grilled, peeled and thinly sliced

50g hot Italian salami, sliced to medium thickness

Method

Preheat oven to 250°C.

Place pizza base onto lightly oiled pizza tray or stone and spread the base with passata, leaving the outer rim uncovered. Sprinkle the base with only half the mozzarella.

Sprinkle with oregano and salt. Top with peppers and salami. Sprinkle over the remaining mozzarella.

Bake in preheated oven on the bottom shelf for 5 minutes or until pizza base and crust is lightly golden and crisp. The top should also be golden brown and the cheese melted.

Tip: For extra colour use both yellow and red capsicums

Pizza paradiso
Paradise pizza

Ingredients

1 freshly prepared uncooked 30cm pizza base (see page 294)

60ml tomato puree (passata)* or tomato pizza sauce

125g mozzarella cheese*, grated

½-1 teaspoon dried oregano leaves

Pinch flaked salt

100g whole cooked shrimp* (prawns), peeled and de-veined

50g button mushrooms, thinly sliced

Rucola* (arugula or rocket) leaves, to serve (optional)

Method

Preheat oven to 250°C.

Place pizza base onto lightly oiled pizza tray or stone and spread the base with passata, leaving the outer rim uncovered. Sprinkle the base with only half the mozzarella.

Sprinkle over oregano and salt, then top with shrimp and mushrooms. Sprinkle over the remaining mozzarella.

Bake in preheated oven on the bottom shelf for 5 minutes or until pizza base and crust is lightly golden and crisp. The top should also be golden brown and the cheese melted.

Serve with fresh rucola.

Tip: Small to medium green (raw) peeled shrimp could be used instead of cooked shrimp, however ensure they're dried well with a paper towel so as not to add excess moisture to the pizza.

* Refer to Glossary – Page 470

Pizza quattro formaggi
Four cheeses pizza

Ingredients

1 freshly prepared uncooked 30cm pizza base (see page 294)

60ml tomato puree (passata)* or tomato pizza sauce

125g mozzarella cheese*, grated

½-1 teaspoon dried oregano leaves

Pinch flaked salt

50g edam cheese*, finely chopped

50g Gorgonzola cheese*, crumbled

30g parmesan cheese, grated

Method

Preheat oven to 250°C.

Place pizza base onto lightly oiled pizza tray or stone and spread the base with passata, leaving the outer rim uncovered. Sprinkle the base with only half the mozzarella.

Sprinkle with oregano and salt. Top with edam, Gorgonzola and parmesan cheese. Lastly, sprinkle over the remaining mozzarella.

Bake in preheated oven on the bottom shelf for 5 minutes or until pizza base and crust is lightly golden and crisp. The top should also be golden brown and the cheese melted.

* Refer to Glossary – Page 470

Calzoni
Folded stuffed pizzas

Ingredients

½ quantity pizza dough (see page 294)
Olive oil, for brushing

Filling
150g mozzarella cheese*, grated
100g ham, chopped
100g tomato puree (passata)*
100g parmesan cheese, grated
1 tablespoon chopped fresh sweet basil leaves
Freshly cracked black pepper

Also referred to as pizza ripieno (meaning stuffed or filled), calzone is a pizza folded into a half-circle shape with the "toppings" – perhaps ricotta or mozzarella cheese, tomato, mushrooms, spinach, herbs, ham or salami – sealed inside the crust. Due to its shape, it's actually much more portable than a regular pizza, so great for picnics.

Method

Preheat oven to 250°C.

Lightly oil two baking trays. Divide dough into 2 even portions. Roll each ball out into a 30cm circle, about 5mm thick.

To make Filling, combine all filling ingredients in a large bowl and season with pepper.

Divide the filling between each circle of dough, placing it on just one side and leaving a border around the whole edge of 2cm.

Fold the other half of the dough over to cover the filling. Join the two edges together and press down around the edge. The finished calzoni should look like a half moon shape.

Place the calzoni onto prepared baking trays. Brush the tops lightly with olive oil and bake in preheated oven for 15-20 minutes or until the tops are golden brown and the dough has puffed.

* Refer to Glossary – Page 470

Campania

As if being the birthplace of pizza wasn't enough – Campania mixes historical significance with one of the world's most famous coastal areas.

Opposite above: the ruins of an ancient fast food servery in Pompeii.

Opposite below: The picturesque Amalfi coast, south of Naples.

Earthquakes, seismic activity, volcanoes and emotive people. Welcome to the exuberant south. Every nearby nation has tramped over these valleys leaving their culinary footprint as they came (and went). However, the mix of cuisines is demographic as well as ethnic, ranging from affordable street food for the poorer classes, to that of the *monzù* – the nobility.

The everlasting contribution of Naples, Campania's capital, to dining (and not just in Italy, but to the world's table) is everyone's favourite – pizza. If Naples had done nothing else in its long and chequered existence, this would be enough. As it happens there is much more.

Campania's very rich volcanic soils and the equable Mediterranean climate mean that almost anything grows well and full of flavour and colour here. Coupled with this is the fact that over centuries, the locals have become most ingenious in finding ways to use this fresh produce. This is the land of luscious sauces, headed by the *mamma* of them all – ragù, originating inland, from the farmland – and today's *agriturismo* (farmstay) cooking is just as good.

History frozen in time

Campania's long history is evident at Pompeii, where the remains of ancient bakeries, millstones and kitchens are still visible. You can still see the evidence of street vendors in the ruined streets as well as the bars, as popular and vibrant then, you can be sure, as they are in Naples today.

It would almost be easier to list what is *not* available from Campania, as it seems to grow almost every temperate-climate produce. There are apricots near Vesuvius, white figs elsewhere, *spadona* pears from Salerno, and lemons from Amalfi. Small red apples are called *melannurca*, and extra virgin olive oil is produced in many parts. Chestnuts come from higher forests, such as Serino, and hazelnuts from Giffoni, while walnuts are from the coast, mainly near Sorrento.

But it is vegetables on which much of the cookery in the south is based. King of all is the *San Marzano* tomato, a plum tomato said to be among the best in the world for sauces, and used extensively here. These, and artichokes, the best grown near ancient Paestum, appear in many dishes.

This land raises sheep as does so much of Italy, and cheeses usually reflect this, but here the *Caciocavallo Silano* is made with cow's milk. *Buffalo mozzarella* comes from near the Lazio border, and *burrino*, similar to that made in Abruzzo and Puglia, is a firm cheese, wrapped around butter, and made in several areas. There is smoked *provola* from the Sele Valley and Caserta, north of Naples, and *provolone* from the Sorrentine Peninsula.

Fishing ports along the coast haul in seafood from the Tyrrhenian Sea daily – fish, crayfish, mussels, clams – to feature in many dishes, especially a popular local seafood salad. Lamb, including a range of offal, is widely available, and pork is used for *salame, capocollo campano* and *cervellatine* sausages.

Naples is a city of pizza places, *trattorie*, wine bars, cafes, grills and restaurants specialising in serving seafood. Food is never far away, and while in the city, many visitors are also lured by the pastry shops with their seductive range of *pasticcerie* – sweet pastries and little cakes. On the islands of Capri and Ischia, off the Bay of Naples, the dining naturally becomes more upmarket to suit the tastes of well-heeled visitors and residents.

Pasta is said to have existed here before Marco Polo, which contradicts the theory that he brought it from China. Pasta is popular and menus throughout the region have dishes that include the words *alla napoletana*, meaning simply that the sauce will contain tomatoes and onion. *Ragù alla napoletana* is chunks of meat, red wine and vegetables, and *ragù napoletano* should combine tomato, minced veal, ham, bacon, parsley and wine.

The birthplace of pizza

Pizza Margherita is the *nonno* (grandfather) of all pizzas, and still popular despite its simplicity – just cheese, tomato and basil. At the other end of the cuisine scale for complexity is *sartù*, a rice ring filled with sausages, cheese, mushrooms and much more, intended as a "shareable" centrepiece for important occasions.

Insalata caprese (see page 18), a fresh salad that is simple, tasty and shows the colours of Italian flag, *spaghetti alla vongole* (spaghetti and clams), and *parmigiana de melanzane* (eggplant and cheese - see page 224) are all found in this region. Not to be missed are the sweet delights of *sfogliatella*, ricotta and glacé fruit in flaky pasty and available either baked crisp or fried, and the nougat indulgence, *torrone di Benevento*.

Wines from the Greeks

The wines of Campania can be traced back to times when ancient Greeks colonised the area some 2000 years ago. Many of the grapes grown for wine near Naples come from old-stock vines, hundreds of years old, many labelled as DOC. More recently, the region has become famous for a red wine called *Taurasi* made from *Aglianico* grapes which have been grown here for centuries.

Notable among liqueurs are *Strega*, a yellow herbal liqueur from Benevento, often sipped after a meal or used to flavour desserts, and the famous *Limoncello* produced both from the renowned Amalfi Coast lemons and another variety found on the isle of Capri.

If you wish to sample the food up close, the Naples food market is the best place to get a good overview of the food of Campania – it's a vibrant and noisy display of colour and aromas that could only be found in southern Italy. Emotive, passionate and *delicioso*!

Some say the food of Campania is the food of Italy.

Opposite: a typical streetscene in the neighbourhoods of Naples.

Above: a fisherman off the fabled Isle of Capri, Campania.

Formaggio e vino

Each region, no matter how small or remote, has contributed its own abundance of dairy products and *vino* to the world.

Cheese & wine

Il formaggio (Cheese)

Whatever your preference, there's an Italian cheese to tempt your tastebuds, from hard to soft, *dolce* to *piccante*.

Cheese is an inextricable part of Italian cooking. Where would pasta be without *parmesan?* Pizza without *mozzarella?* Or *tiramisù* without *mascarpone?*

With climates ranging from alpine to Mediterranean, Italy is blessed with a wide range of cheese styles, from silky and creamy through to hard and aged, using milk from four animals – the cow, sheep, goat and buffalo. *Buonissimo!*

Many Italian cheeses have a PDO (Protected Designation of Origin) status under European Union regulations, replacing the former DO (*Denominazione di Origine*).

Many of these cheeses are known and used all over the world, including *asiago, fontina, gorgonzola, Grana Padano*, buffalo *mozzarella* from Campania, *Parmigiano-Reggiano*, several *pecorino* cheeses, *provolone Valpadana, ricotta Romana* and *taleggio*.

While Italian *ristoranti* traditionally do not offer a cheese course on their menus, *il formaggio* plays an important part of most meals. It may be part of the antipasto platter, will be sprinkled on the pasta – and often turns up as mascarpone or ricotta in the *dolci* (dessert).

A variety of sources

Most Italian cow's milk cheeses originate from cattle raised on the high alpine pastures in summer. In autumn they are brought down by their keepers (a process called 'transhumance') to lower altitudes, where they can be sheltered from the winds and colder weather over winter.

Sheep and goats, hardy enough to withstand harsher conditions and climate, provide milk for the bulk of cheeses made in central and southern Italy, including Sardinia and Sicily.

In earlier times, especially in more remote areas, cheese-making was often for the consumption of the family alone, with cooks making use of whatever was at hand. As a result, some cheeses may be made of a mixture of the two milks, and sometimes milk from sheep, cows and goats is combined. Originally most cheeses were made with unpasteurised milk, and cheese-lovers today will argue that this still makes the best cheese. King of these is the parmesan group, notably *Grana Padano* and *Parmigiano-Reggiano*.

South of Rome, and in Puglia, domestic water buffalo have been raised for centuries. It is their rich milk (almost twice as rich as cow's milk) that is used to make mozzarella, that stringy, elastic staple of so many dishes. Few pizzas would be complete without it, nor would the colourful *insalata caprese*, matching the Italian flag with bright green basil leaves, slices of tomato and pure white mozzarella. The highest quality is trademarked *Mozzarella di Bufala Campana*. *Bocconcini* (meaning 'small mouthfuls') are tiny balls of fresh mozzarella, sold packaged in whey. In several regional specialties, such as Puglia's *burrata*, butter or cream is wrapped in mozzarella.

Other Italian cheeses of note are:

Caciocavallo, the most famous of which is *Caciocavallo Silano*. There are many varieties, all from the south of Italy, mainly made from cow's milk, although sheep's milk may be used. Translating as 'cheese on horseback,' the name possibly came about because it is traditionally left to dry mounted on a stick or rod. This pear-shaped cheese is similar to *provolone*.

Fontina Val d'Aosta is an alpine cheese from the far north of the country closely resembling Swiss cheese, with small round holes, and it also melts well, making it ideal for *fonduta*, Italy's version of cheese fondue (see page 324).

Gorgonzola, from Piedmont and Lombardy, is the country's claim to blue cheese fame. It may be served relatively mild (*dolce*) or sharp and bitingly aged (*piccante*), and is widely appreciated either way.

Grana Padano is an unpasteurised hard cheese made from cow's milk in many of the northern regions. Ripening for a minimum of four months, this can be used instead of parmesan cheese, which is universally used and highly respected. More common is *parmigiano*, named for Parma in northern Italy, and of course *Parmigiano-Reggiano* is the traditional, aromatic, unpasteurised skimmed cow's milk cheese once used as currency because of its value.

Mascarpone is a delicious super-creamy 'cheese' with the merest hint of cultured acidity. Some describe it as a curd cheese, but it is manufactured in a similar way to yoghurt.

Pecorino refers to a range of sheep's milk cheeses (*pecora* is the Italian word for sheep) made all over the country south of Tuscany. Several are named to indicate their region of origin, the most important being *pecorino Romano* (or *locatelli*), one of the country's oldest cheeses, from the Rome area. *Pecorino Sardo* is from Sardinia, *pecorino Siciliano*, from Sicily, and *pecorino Toscano*, from Tuscany.

Likewise, *provolone* is made in many of the northern regions using local cow's milk, the most esteemed one being *provolone Valpadana*. A versatile cheese, *provolone* appears in many dishes and is usually sold as *dolce* (mild) or *piccante*, which is the stronger cheese, some having been aged for up to two years.

Creamy *ricotta* is a soft fresh white cheese made primarily from the whey of cow's milk, although sheep's milk may be used. It is used in lasagne and also appears in Sicilian dessert recipes. *Ricotta salata moliterna* is made from the whey of ewe's milk, *ricotta Piemontese* from the whey of cow's milk, and *ricotta Romana* is a by-product of the manufacture of *pecorino Romano*.

Stracchino is a soft cow's milk cheese from Lombardy. Its name derives from the Italian word for 'tired', because it is made with milk from cows that have been moved from higher to lower pastures. Yet far from being poorer in quality, the milk they produce is actually richer in fat, resulting in a deliciously creamy cheese that melts well.

Taleggio is one of Italy's few washed-rind cheeses. *Taleggio* has been matured by the local cheese makers in the remote caves of the high country near Lombardy since ancient times. A soft cow's milk cheese with a pungent flavour, it can be used in many dishes, and also melts easily.

Overwhelmed with choice? There is no better reason to organise a special tasting session at your local delicatessen. Start with the soft and *dolce* cheeses and work up to the *piccante*.

Thank the Romans

The Romans are credited with perfecting the art of cheese-making. They had seperate kitchens solely for making cheese, and shopfronts where people could bring their cheese for smoking. After the collapse of the Roman Empire, cheese-making regions became isolated - and distinct and unique types of cheeses developed.

Above: Taking a core sample of *Gorgonzola* cheese in the aging rooms of Costa Dairy, Novara, Piedmont.

Fonduta
Fontina cheese dip

Serves 2-3

Ingredients

150g fontina cheese* (not too ripe/
mature)

160ml full cream milk

2 teaspoons butter

4 free range egg yolks*, at room
temperature

Flaked salt

Freshly ground white pepper

Warm slices of ciabatta bread, to serve

A specialty of the Piedmont region, fonduta is similar to Swiss fondue, although the ingredients and method are different (fonduta incorporates egg yolks into the melted cheese and doesn't contain any alcohol). Fontina, an unpasteurised cow's milk cheese from the mountains and valleys of the Valle d'Aosta, has a delicate sweet, nutty flavour and melts easily, making it ideal for this dish.

Method

Cut the rind from the cheese and cut into small cubes. Place into a medium bowl and add the milk. Cover and set aside at room temperature for 2 hours.

Place the butter into a glass heatproof bowl that will sit easily over a saucepan of simmering water. Fill the saucepan with water, ensuring the water does not touch the bottom of the bowl, bring the water to a gentle boil over medium heat.

To the butter add the cheese scooped from the bowl and about only 60ml of the milk. Melt the cheese stirring constantly until the cheese begins to form strings when pulled out with a spoon.

Combine the remaining milk and egg yolks and lightly beat. Add this quickly to the melted cheese. Continue to stir constantly over heat until mixture is smooth and consistency of thick cream. Season to taste.

Transfer to a warmed serving dish and serve immediately with bread.

Note – It is important that the water remains just below the boil and at a simmer to prevent the eggs overcooking and curdling. The fonduta will thicken as it cools.

* Refer to Glossary – Page 470

Mozzarelle in carrozza
Fried mozzarella sandwiches

Ingredients

8 slices rustic bread
175g mozzarella cheese*, thinly sliced
60ml olive oil
30g butter

Method

Lay four slices of bread onto a breadboard and divide the cheese between the slices. Top each with a second slice of bread to make a sandwich.

Heat only half the oil and half the butter in a large frying pan over medium heat. Reduce heat to low and place sandwiches into the frying pan and cook for 3-4 minutes or until golden.

Add the remaining oil and butter then turn the sandwiches over and cook the other side for 3-4 minutes, until golden or until the cheese is melted.

Variation – try using some ham slices with the cheese and use provolone* as an alternative to mozzarella.

* Refer to Glossary – Page 470

Budino di ricotta con salsa di fragole
Ricotta pudding with strawberry sauce

Serves 10-12

Ingredients

200g blanched almonds

200g caster (superfine) sugar

3 teaspoons finely grated lemon rind

60ml lemon juice

600g ricotta cheese

8 free-range eggs*, at room temperature

500g fresh or frozen strawberries

100g caster (superfine) sugar, extra

3 teaspoons finely grated lemon rind.

1 tablespoon icing (confectioner's) sugar, to serve

Fresh mint leaves, to garnish

Method

Place the almonds, sugar, lemon rind and lemon juice into the bowl of a food processor whizz until finely chopped and combined. Transfer mixture to a large bowl and add the ricotta, the eggs one at a time and mix together until smooth. Pour the mixture into a greased 10 litre capacity savarin mould.

Place the mould into a large saucepan (so that it actually sits inside the saucepan) and add enough water so that it comes ¾ of the way up the sides of the mould. Cover the whole saucepan securely with foil, sealing the edges to prevent steam escaping. Bring to a gentle boil over medium-high heat, then reduce heat to low and simmer for about 50-60 minutes or until set.

To check if pudding is ready carefully remove the foil then test the centre with the point of a knife, and when cooked it should come out clean.

Remove saucepan from heat and take the mould out of the water, leave to cool. Turn out the cooled pudding onto a serving plate.

Wash and remove the green stems from the strawberries, place only 300g into the bowl of a food processor or a blender with the extra 100g sugar and the lemon rind. Process until smooth. Place the remaining strawberries into the centre hole of the pudding and dust with icing sugar.

Add mint leaves and serve with strawberry sauce.

* Refer to Glossary – Page 470

Vito e vino (Vine & wine)

Perhaps it is no accident that *vite*, the Italian word for 'lives' and the one for 'vine' are the same. Certainly the lives of millions of Italians have been inextricably entangled with the fruit of the vine for centuries, and the huge success of Italy's wine industry is as much a product of their skill as it is of the Italian terroirs.

The Etruscans are believed to have introduced grapes to the Italian peninsula, and successive inhabitants, notably the Greeks in the south, were very keen to extend the wine-growing capacity of this country – in their case, mainly to share with their fellow Athenians.

Italy is now the world's largest wine-producing country, followed closely by France and Spain. It is a massive industry, accounting for a fifth of global production and with major exports to Germany, the UK and the US.

Italians like to drink wine too, and the consumption of wine in Italy is the highest in the world, about 59 litres per capita each year – and that is separate from wine made privately for home consumption, which is a long-standing tradition in Italy. By comparison, Australians consume 22 litres per capita, and the US just seven litres.

Wine in moderation

Traditionally, wine is often drunk at lunch and dinner. It is usually consumed in the home and has long been a part of family life, with even young children tasting it with their meals. Despite this, excessive youth drinking doesn't seem to be as much of a problem in Italy as it is in some other countries, and much of this is attributed to family values and societal expectations. For instance, Italians generally feel that a person behaving in a drunken manner is displaying a *brutta figura*, and this is viewed with distaste.

Most parts of Italy can grow grapes, and the country has about a million vineyards. While making wine in the home is still common, all commercial winemaking takes place in modern wineries.

Wine and good food go hand-in-hand in Italy, where 'eat, drink and be merry' is life's motto.

Wine for slaves

Around 100 AD, Roman law prohibited viticulture outside of the Italian pennisula. Wine was then exported throughout the empire in exchange for slaves.

Opposite: Cellars of the Montelio winery near Codevilla, Oltrepo Pavese, Lombardy.

Compared to wines from other countries, Italian wines are sometimes judged to be more acidic, or dry. However, while they provide light and easy drinking, they still deliver excellent flavour and bouquet. They are regarded as ideal wines to be drunk with a meal, which is exactly the way Italians prefer to enjoy them, often over leisurely *al fresco (outdoor)* lunches that may last all afternoon, or convivial multi-course dinners that linger late.

Varieties and styles

It would be impossible to list all the wines that Italy produces. Even the grape varieties have been estimated as being almost 2000, although only about 400 are regularly used for wine production with most regions growing only a few varieties. Many are regional specialties and grown in small local areas only.

Trebbiano grapes are the most widely planted, and *Sangiovese* is another major wine grape, used in the famous *Brunello di Montalcino* and *Chianti Classico*. *Nebbiolo* and *Barbera* are common reds in the north, while *Moscato*, a white grape, is used to make *Spumante* in Piedmont. Basilicata's and Campania's *Aglianico* is a highly respected red variety, responsible for Basilicata's notable *Aglianico del Vulture*.

'In vino veritas'

It's believed it was the Romans who learnt that aged wines tasted better, discovered which grapes were suited to certain climates, were the first to use wooden barrels, and glass bottles with corks.

They loved wine - many a pithy wine saying, such as 'in vino veritas' ('in wine is truth'), came from this era. Romans drank it at every meal, tried out various spiced wines, and created wine with much higher alcohol content than ours today.

Above: Frescobaldi Estate, transporting wine barrels on a hand cart, Rufina, Tuscany.

Opposite: Vineyards of Bressanone, Alto Adige.

Wine has been part of Italian life since well before the Romans started planting their own vineyards in the 2nd century BC.

Many wines are protected by various classifications. Most prestigious is the DOCG (*Denominazione di Origine Controllata e Garantita*), awarded only to carefully assessed and checked wines. DOC (*Denominazione di Origine Controllata*), means it is from a 'controlled region', that wine is typical of the region, has used a previously agreed winemaking method and grapes from a particular area.

Table wines (*vino da tavola*) have no classification. Some may be excellent, but remain unclassified because they fall outside of the DOC and DOCG guidelines. Recently IGT (*Indicazione Geografica Tipica*) has been commenced in an attempt to recognise wines that are fine examples of wines of their region.

Italian wine styles include *frizzante* (semi-sparkling wines) and *Spumante* (sparkling varieties), while *Prosecco* is available in both sparkling and semi-sparkling. These are mainly made in the north of the country. Other wines are *vini rossi* and *vini bianchi* (red and white respectively), *vini rosati* (rosé) and sweet wines such as *Marsala*, an aged wine from Sicily, and *vin santo*, which is made using *passito*, a 'raisining' technique of semi-drying grapes before winemaking commences.

Wine by the region

Italy's wine growing regions can be simply divided into four sections that share a similar climate, rather than the country's 20 regions.

The three north-eastern regions, centred around the Veneto, are known for producing modern wines, and have over a third of the country's DOC wines, many of them varietals. *Soave, Amarone di Valpolicella* and *Bardolino* from Verona are perhaps the most recognisable. The relatively cool climate is ideal for growing many fine whites, but actually this region produces more red wine, much of this from Trentino-Alto Adige.

North and north-west Italy is made up of five regions, which include the Alps and the Po River and produce about a fifth of Italy's total wine, about 30 per cent of the total DOC. Emilia-Romagna is a major producer and Piedmont has more DOC or DOCG zones than any other region. Here the climate and terrain (Valle d'Aosta and Liguria are particularly steep and rocky) pose challenges to wine-grape growing.

Barbera, Moscato (for Asti Spumante) and *Nebbiolo* are key grape varieties in the higher regions, and Emilia-Romagna, originally known for bubbly *Lambrusco*, is now producing notable wines made with Barbera, Cabernet, Chardonnay and Sauvignon grapes.

Their grapes may have come from many corners of the globe, but Italians have perfected turning them into wine.

Below: *La vendemmia* - the end of summer grape harvest, Cagliari, Sardinia.

Opposite: winery landscape, Chianti, Tuscany.

In the heart of the country, six regions seem perfectly placed, climatically and traditionally, to create great wine. Tuscany, and especially Chianti, are known worldwide and between them account for close to another third of Italy's DOC or DOCG.

While wine production is not extensive, *Sangiovese*, *Trebbiano* and *Malvasia* grapes reign supreme. Chianti's *Brunello di Montalcino*, the *Vino Nobile di Montepulciano*, is one of the world's great red wines, interestingly still without a formal classification. White *Malvasia* grown in Lazio is used for *Frascati*, and Umbrians favour *Sangiovese* for reds, and a variety of *Trebbiano* to create the well-respected white, *Orvieto*.

Tuscany and Umbria, like Emilia-Romagna, are now turning towards Cabernet Sauvignon, Merlot, Pinot, Chardonnay and Sauvignon. In the Marche, red *Montepulciano* is widely planted, as well as *Sangiovese*, with which it is often blended, plus *Trebbiano*.

Lastly, the six regions loosely grouped together and referred to as 'the south' still grow some grape varieties brought by the occupying Greeks so long ago, such as *Aglianico, Malvasia* and *Moscato*, and vines planted by long-gone Spanish invaders, in Sicily and Sardinia. Calabria's *Cirò* wine (made as a red, white or *rosé*) is said by some to be the world's oldest wine.

Puglia and Sicily are two of the largest wine producers in Italy, although much of their crop is blended or sent away to be used in anonymous bulk wines rather used in creating unique regional vintages. This explains why, although the south produces 40 per cent of Italy's wine, very few have DOC status.

Italy's wines, like the regions they come from and the people who make them, all have different histories, different personalities, and different appeal. It's an enjoyable challenge to get to know them.

Denominazione di Origine
(DOC - Designation of Controlled Origin)

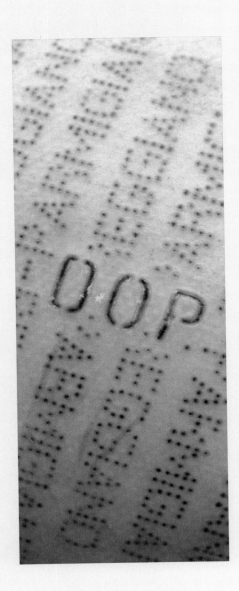

The acronyms of provenance

When it comes to food and wine, Italy seems to be the world capital of acronyms. What do they all mean and are they relevant for good food and wine?

It is important to understand that the appellation of one of these acronyms indicates that a particular food or wine product has a specified origin and has met formally agreed standards of production. Some of Italy's most famous produce – *Parmigiano-Reggiano*, for instance – have strict rules as to how they are made and where they come from. Under Italian law, *Parmigiano-Reggiano*, which is a parmesan cheese, must come from the cheese-producing areas near Parma, Reggio Emilia, Modena, Bologna and Mantua and be made in a certain way to be labelled. Similarly, Parma ham may only be made using pigs from a certain area, and must be prepared in a very specific way.

So when a country puts its imprimatur on a product, it is a code that tells any buyer or consumer that this food complies with an already identified standard and traditional methods, and comes from a clearly defined place of origin. More than 4000 Italian products are registered in some way, according to distinct and strict guidelines.

What's up, DOC?

DOC (*Denominazione di Origine Controllata*) is a quality assurance label for food and serves as an appellation for wines. There are about 350 of these throughout the country, and they monitor the geographic area of production and grape varieties used in each wine, as well as look at appearance, colour, bouquet and flavours of the wines. Consumers unused to Italian labels can find that by buying and drinking DOC-labelled wines that they will be guaranteed a quality product.

The DOC classification system denotes produce of specified origin and production technique.

DOCG (*Denominazione di Origine Controllata e Garantita*), or Controlled and Guaranteed Designation of Origin, signals that this region, or sub-region, produces outstanding products. These products are subjected to regular assessment and even more stringent production and quality standards than products from the surrounding DOC region, and the accreditation is in effect a "guarantee" of a product's provenance and that it is of the highest quality.

To qualify for either, food products must be produced within the specified region using carefully defined methods and prepared to a strict quality standard. Wines are further classified into two categories: *classico*, describing regional wines produced traditionally; and *riserva*, used only for wines that have been aged for at least two years longer than is usual for its particular type.

Joining the union

Two European Union classifications are PDO (*Denominazione di Origine Protetta* or Protected Designation of Origin) and PGI (Protected Geographical Indication). These recognise similar standards and are under the control of external authorities. PDO guarantees "all the phases of the production cycle are performed in the territory of designated origin". PGI certification guarantees "the most significant phases of the production cycle are performed in the designated origin". This is important to ensure that the product's key characteristics are retained.

The European Union also certifies some Italian food products as DOP, *Denominazione d'Origine Protetta* (Denomination of Protected Origin), and IGP, *Indicazione Geografica Protetta* (Indication of Protected Origin). These marks identify which European food and agricultural products are authentic and genuine. The names of all these products include their place of origin, such as *prosciutto di Parma*.

Quality assured

Understandably, regions and producers are extremely proud of these formal acknowledgements of their accomplishments. In turn, the accreditations enable buyers to feel secure in the knowledge that their purchase is of the highest quality.

Valle D'Aosta
(Aosta Valley)

Italy's smallest region, in the north-west corner of the country, has box-seat views from its perch high in the Alps. Famous for its pretty scenery and picturesque Roman ruins, this region is bordered by France and Switzerland. It draws a steady stream of visitors to the Italian slopes of the Matterhorn and Mont Blanc, and other mountains in the area.

This is high, cold country and the food reflects this – a place for hearty appetites, raised by hard work or skiing. It's little wonder that robust dishes such as *fonduta*, a fondue-like dish using the nutty local *fontina* cheese, and crumbed schnitzel-style *costoletta alla valdostana* (veal slices filled with fontina), are popular. The fragrant local *fromadzo* cow's milk cheese also has a DOP.

The area also produces milk, butter and cream, berries, apples, root vegetables and potatoes, as well as various fungi, honeys, mountain herbs and chestnuts. If you think of food of the forest and high meadows, you'll get the idea of what will be most readily available here.

Winter warmers

Goats are raised for their milk to create *capra* cheese and also provide *capretto* (kid), a popular meat in dishes. *Salumi* is made from a variety of meats that well suit the richer northern cuisine, but they also provide a way to enjoy meat throughout those long, icy winters. The local and highly prized ham, *Jambon de Bosses*, from a remote valley, also has a DOP accreditation.

In Valle d'Aosta you can also expect to find goose, veal and pork in abundance. Another specialty is lardo (especially *Lardo di Arnad* DOP), the pork fat used in many sausages, especially *boudin* – and the unusual but very tasty beetroot and potato *boudin* should not be missed! So revered is it that there is a *lardo* festival each August in Arnad. Salami, tripe and polenta also get a turn at a festival each February in La Thuile, and the silky, stretchy *fontina* cheese stars at a similar *sagra* (food fair) in Oyace in mid-August.

Mountain bread

Copa, a hard rye bread, accompanies many meals, along with wines from small local producers of Italy's highest altitude vineyards, or maybe a cup of coffee "corrected" with *grappa*. If there's a group of people, this may be drunk from a "cup of friendship", a carved wooden pot with several spouts.

Perhaps this, as much as anything, underlines the core attraction of this area – its sociability & interaction, whether it's having fun on the ski slopes or sharing a *fonduta* or a warming friendship cup.

A small alpine region, Valle D'Aosta packs a big punch in the gourmet stakes.

Aosta

Opposite: The castle of Sant Pierre, Valle d'Aosta.

Trentino-Alto Adige

The long and fertile Adige Valley flanks the river of the same name as it flows south from Austria, neatly bisecting the region, and providing a thoroughfare into the rest of Europe. It is not surprising that this part of Italy hardly knows whether to brand itself as the Italian Alps or the South Tyrol.

Nothing expresses the mixed nature of this area more than the food. Menus read like Italian classics in some cases, Austrian in others, or more commonly with the names of dishes mixed or used interchangeably. The Alto Adige (the high part of the river valley) is more Teutonic, while progressing south of Salorno, into Trentino, the climate – and the ambience – becomes more Italian.

Cold climate food

Chefs in this region have a lot of food to play with. Cool-climate fruits, such as Renetta Alto Adige apples and berries, grow well in the north, and further south where the climate becomes warmer, there are olives and vines on the hillsides. Potatoes and cabbage, the latter often used to make sauerkraut, grow well here and feature in many dishes, in true Teutonic style.

Cheeses made with the rich milk from cows, which graze on the higher pastures in summer, include *Graukäse*, and the famous *Grana Padano* is a hard cheese from Trentino. As many parts of the region are quite remote, often very small family producers make cheeses that are available only in their own valley. It's worth taking the time to hunt them down.

Trentino's chilly streams flowing from the mountain are ideal for the farming of a freshwater trout-like fish called char. Many types of meat may be smoked to keep them longer, as with *pancetta affumicata*. The prosciutto of this area is usually served cotto (cooked) and *speck dell'Alto Adige* is more common towards the north. *Hauswurst* – as the name suggests – is "homemade" sausage, and is available in many places.

Apart from these staples, there is fine honey from Bolzano province (halfway to Austria), mushrooms and game (such as rabbit, hare and venison), as well as lard and butter, and – again with a nod to the proximity of Austria – excellent caraway and rye breads, often baked to keep for weeks, and chewy pretzels. *Garda Trentino* olive oil has DOP accreditation, and the word from the locals is that *gelati* in the capital, Trento, is definitely worth trying.

> Far from suffering an identity crisis – this area has taken the best from two cultures and united them to make new culinary creations.

Opposite: Vineyards beside Lago Toblino, in the Trentino.

Classic cuisine

A typical Trentino-Alto Adige menu might include *cotto e cren* (cooked ham and horseradish) as a starter, followed by *crauti* (sausages and sauerkraut) or *gulasch*, and finishing up with strudel. The pasta course might include *canederli* (large bread dumplings) or *spà'tzle*, which clearly shows the mixed influence in this region.

North of Salorno diners may find more delicate flavours in their dishes, including tart sauces using berries and fruits. Expect to see plenty of *polenta* in Trenton and robust, rustic dishes, such as *pasta e fagioli* (pasta and beans), *knödeln* (bread dumplings) around Bolzano, as well as *Gulaschsuppe*, literally goulash soup.

Wines here reflect climatic variations with more aromatic whites (Pinot Grigio, Moscato, and Traminer, or Gewürztraminer) in the higher altitudes and fine reds in Trentino on the slopes of the river valley where a 40-kilometre "wine route" follows the river from Salorno to Bolzano. About half the wine produced here is DOC, and much is exported, although mainly just over the border to Austria. Italian Alps, or the South Tyrol? Does it really matter when the two cuisines join together so well?

Calabria

The 'toe' of Italy kicking Sicily out into the Mediterranean – that's how some people picture the outline of Calabria. Isolated for so long because of poverty and oppression, malaria was still a major threat to people's health in the lowland areas of Calabria in the mid 1900s. Often the poor soil did not yield enough to feed the families that relied on it, and this was a land pervaded by poverty, even brigands and kidnappings.

Calabria has more than 700 kilometres of coastline on two seas – the Tyrrhenian and Ionian – and a wildly beautiful mountainous interior. Just inland from Reggio Calabria, the Aspromonte rises like a knuckle on Italy's 'big toe'. Beyond that there are more mountains, state parks, ruins, lakes and remote villages that have hardly changed in centuries. In some, Greek or Albanian is still spoken, the legacy of foreign occupation in ancient times.

Catanzaro

Eating influences

Legends aside, the Calabrian cuisine captivates many with its simple use of ingredients and the influence of a thousand or more years of occupation by foreign peoples – Moors, Normans, Greeks, Arabs and others who came to establish their base here.

Subsisting in harsh conditions, *cucina povera* ('peasant' cookery) prevailed, and the local vegetables – which are excellent, prolific and inexpensive – along with mushrooms, grains and pulses, formed the nucleus of cookery. Meat was scarce and added sparingly, and some foods were preserved in oil, vinegar and salt, or a *scapece* – oil, vinegar, and onion.

A history of poverty and foreign domination has shaped Calabria's cuisine.

Many dishes are closely related to Sicilian food, as they have a shared heritage, which explains the local love for *agrodolce* (sweet and sour) flavours.

Cheeses are essential to the food of the area. *Caciocavallo silano*, formed into a ball which is tied and aged for a year, and may be smoked, is widely available. *Abbespata* is a smoked cheese from Sila and Crotonese, and *butirro* is yet another regional cheese formed around butter. The curds and whey *giuncata* from Sila, *pecorino crotonese, ricotta* and a pear-shaped *provolone* made with cow's milk are highly regarded too.

The coastal ports of Pizzo, Palmi and Scilla are well known for the seafood that is landed here by fishing boats – in particular swordfish, tuna, anchovies, sardines, and mackerel (or blue fish). Tropea is noted for its whitebait. These tiny immature fish are marinated in salt and chilli to produce *rosamarina* (or *sardella*), a prized delicacy that some feel is ecologically unsound.

From sweet to fiery

Rossano Calabro, on the Ionian Sea, is the centuries-old home of traditional Italian licorice (*liquirizia*), and Bagnara (north of *Reggio di Calabria*) is known for nougat. Anyone looking for the best *gelati* heads for Pizzo.

Calabrian dishes can be fiery, using fresh or dried peppers, and flavoured with Calabrian oregano. While the ear-shaped *orecchiette* is found here, the signature pasta, *fileja*, is rolled around thin rods or wires. A box with wires (a 'guitar') is used to create *spaghetti alla chitarra*. For this, freshly rolled sheets of pasta are pressed through the wires to create long strands of spaghetti. Pasta with *ragù alla maiale* or *vitello* (pork or veal) or *ciufftì* spaghetti with olive oil and chilli are popular and *cuccìa* (boiled wheat grains), also found in Sicily, accompany some dishes.

A typical Calabrian menu might include *vrasciole* (pork chops), *frisulìmiti*, resembling brawn in a pork fat skin, *cìcculi* (spicy lamb's innards), with *morseddhu* (stuffed tomatoes or artichokes), anchovies in breadcrumbs, or stewed vegetables served as an accompaniment. *Dolci* (desserts) may include *mosto cotto*, Moorish-influenced cooked grape must, stuffed figs, or sweet ravioli with candied citrus or ricotta.

In cities, locals dine in *trattorie, osterie* and *rosticcerie* (grills) and the capital, Catanzaro, is known for its *putiche* (food stores) and the Saturday morning market in the stadium square.

Land of legends & wine

Calabria is a land of legends. Does the six-headed Scylla still rise from the Messina Straits to capture unsuspecting sailors? Some Calabrians swear they see her in the half light of the Mediterranean evenings.

The ancient Greeks called this part of Italy the 'land of wine', and introduced many grape varieties. Cirò is grown on perhaps the world's oldest vines.

Above: Farm compound, Cirò, Calabria.

Opposite: Castello Ruffo and town of Scilla, Calabria. Overlooking the Straits of Messina, Scilla is the traditional site of the six-headed sea monster Scylla in Greek mythology.

From the fruity *crostata* to the custard-based *zabaglione*, Italian desserts are the sweetest and tastiest of them all.

Dolci
Desserts

Dolci (Desserts)

Nougat (*Torrone*)

Torrone (Italian nougat) is a confection of sugar, toasted nuts and eggwhite, usually shaped into long bars. In the north, local hazelnuts or almonds are used, but *torrone* is made in many other parts of Italy where pistachios or pine nuts may be used. It is very popular as a gift and can be purchased all over Italy in pretty packaged presentation boxes.

The recipe, or something like it, has existed since Roman times, and it was taken to other parts of the empire, where it is still made today.

Opposite: Scaturchio' pastry shop, chefs making the 'baba' (typical yeast cake), Naples, Campania.

Italians love their *dolci*. No matter how big the meal preceding dessert is, there is always room left to partake the sweeter things of life. They are the essence of everything indulgent about Italian food.

The easiest and lightest option, often found on weekday tables, may be simply fresh fruit, *macedonia* (a fruit salad), or compote of stewed apples or pears. Or perhaps fruit preserved in rum or another spirit.

Rich offerings

For grander occasions, the *pasticceria* may be called upon. In Sicily, it could be a richly decorated *cassata* or a selection of *cannoli*, and in Naples it might be a *torta caprese*, a rich walnut and chocolate pie. At Christmas throughout the land it will almost certainly be a gigantic *pandoro* or *panettone*. Usually guests will bring along a boxed gift of a cake, biscuits or pastries they have purchased on the way.

Panna cotta (the name means simply 'cooked cream') is a northern cream dessert that has become a favourite around the world, but it hails originally from Piedmont. In regions in this area, close to the Swiss and Austrian borders and influenced by their neighbours, cooks may also make (or buy) *strudel* and other rich chocolate desserts, cakes and tarts.

Creamy coffee-flavoured *tiramisù* is a recent Italian creation, but simple to make, and universally loved. *Zabaglione* is closely related to the French *sabayon*, and is a light, Marsala-flavoured custard that is ideally served with fresh figs.

A *crostata* may be any sort of fruit tart, sometimes filled with ricotta, especially in Naples or Sicily, but also lavished with jam, making it very rich. *Pastiera*, also from Naples, is an Easter tart filled with ricotta, while at Christmastime, families in this region will indulge in platefuls of *struffoli*, tiny balls of deep-fried dough flavoured with orange zest and drenched with candied fruits and a sweet glaze.

Perhaps all of this explains what Italians refer to as *la dolce vita!* A sweet life, indeed.

Tiramisù del bosco
Fruits of the forest tiramisu

Serves 6-8

Ingredients

200g fresh blackberries
100g fresh blackcurrants
100g fresh raspberries
200g fresh strawberries
1 lemon, juiced
160g caster (superfine) sugar
1 tablespoon brandy
2 eggs, at room temperature, separated
200g mascarpone cheese*
1 tablespoon orange liqueur*
150g sponge finger biscuits*

Method

Combine berries (reserving some for decoration), lemon juice, only 100g of the sugar and brandy in a large saucepan. Cook over a low heat for 10 minutes or until berries are soft and sugar has dissolved. Crush with a fork then set aside to cool.

Combine egg yolks and remaining sugar in a medium bowl and beat with an electric mixer or beaters until light and creamy. Fold in mascarpone and liqueur.

In a second bowl beat eggwhites until stiff peaks form and gently fold into mascarpone mixture in two batches.

Place a layer of sponge finger biscuits over the base of a serving dish or into glasses (as pictured). You can break biscuits into pieces, if necessary.

Drizzle with berry mixture and cover with mascarpone mixture. Repeat layers with remaining ingredients, finishing with mascarpone mixture.

Refrigerate for at least 3 hours before serving. Serve decorated with the reserved fruit.

Tip: When berries are not in season trying using some frozen berries. They are available in most supermarkets

* Refer to Glossary – Page 470

Zuccotto
Sponge bombe

Ingredients

2 x 20cm-round, store-bought sponge cakes (2-3 days old is best)

30ml brandy

30ml hazelnut liqueur*

60g whole blanched almonds, toasted

60g hazelnuts, toasted

300ml thickened cream*

40g icing (confectioner's) sugar

60g dark cooking chocolate, melted and cooled

40g dark cooking chocolate, finely chopped, extra

Cocoa powder or extra Icing (confectioner's) sugar, to serve

Widely regarded as a Florentine creation, zuccotto's rounded shape is said to resemble the cupola of the Duomo, the city's main cathedral. However, different regions have their own stories as to its origin, and the name – which translates as "little pumpkin" – is a reference to the shape of the bowl that's used to make it. Liqueur-soaked savoiardi (lady finger biscuits) or wedges of sponge cake line the bowl, which is then filled with sweetened cream, fruit, nuts and chocolate, and another layer of sponge. It is often lightly frozen to become a chilled semifreddo.

Method

Cut sponge cake into wedges. Slice wedges into 1cm thick triangular slices and brush one side of each slice with combined brandy and liqueur.

Line a 1.25-litre capacity pudding basin with plastic wrap, allowing the plastic to come up the side and out the top of the mould.

Place slices of cake into the mould – placing the dry side against the basin bowl, filling all the gaps with moistened pieces of cake. Trim edges level with top of mould.

Roughly chop almonds and hazelnuts; set aside. Beat cream and icing sugar with an electric mixer or beaters until soft peaks form. Fold in nuts and divide mixture in half and place into two separate bowls.

Fold melted chocolate into one half and chopped extra chocolate into other half. Cover cake slices evenly with whiter cream and nut mixture (leaving a cavity in the centre). Next add the chocolate cream mixture into cavity.

Moisten remaining cake slices with remaining liqueur mixture. Place these slices liqueur side down, onto the top of the cream (this will be the base when the zuccotto is turned out of the pudding basin when set).

Cover zuccotto with plastic wrap and refrigerate overnight. Trim away excess cake from the base sides of the zuccotto.

To serve, turn out onto a serving dish, remove plastic wrap and discard. Dust zuccotto lightly with sifted cocoa powder and/or icing sugar and cocoa powder. Serve chilled.

Tip – The drier (older) the sponge is the easier it is to cut and handle – when it is too fresh it may crumble and break.

* Refer to Glossary – Page 470

Zabaglione
Zabaglione

Ingredients

80g white (granulated) sugar

4 free-range egg yolks*, at room temperature

80ml Marsala or sweet dessert white

200ml thickened cream*

Sponge finger biscuits*, to serve

Recorded in Italian recipes as early as 1570, zabaglione or zabaione is a pale delicate froth of egg yolks beaten with sugar, thickened over hot water and served warm. It's usually flavoured with Marsala although other sweet wines such as vin santo, moscato (or even non-Italian drops such as madeira or sherry) can be used. Make sure you use a large enough bowl as the volume increases as you whisk the zabaglione. The whipped cream in this recipe adds richness to the dessert.

Method

Place the sugar, egg yolks and Marsala into a heatproof bowl that will sit over a pan of simmering water. (Do not allow the bowl to be in contact with the water, as this may result in overheating). Whisk until the mixture becomes lighter in colour and foamy in texture; it is ready when the whisk leaves a 'trail' which remains for a few seconds after the whisk is lifted from the bowl. Remove from heat.

Place cream into a large bowl and beat with electric mixer or beaters until soft peaks form. Fold the cream into the egg mixture and serve immediately with biscuits.

Tip: Alternatively, don't add the cream and serve the zabaglione as a delicious warm dessert sauce with fresh seasonal fruit.

Crostatine all'amaretto
Almond tartlets

Ingredients

1 quantity sweet pastry*
250ml milk
200g white marshmallows
3 teaspoons instant coffee granules
2 tablespoons Amaretto liqueur*
200ml thickened cream*
60g toasted almond flakes, to serve
Icing (confectionary sugar) sugar, to serve

Method

Preheat oven to 180°C. Lightly grease eight 10cm shallow round fluted flan tins with removable bases.

Divide prepared pastry evenly into 8 pieces. Roll out pastry between two pieces of kitchen baking paper and line the prepared flan tins. Trim pastry edges to fit. Refrigerate for 15 minutes, prick base with a fork and bake blind* in preheated oven for 10 minutes, remove baking beans and cook a further 2-3 minutes or until crisp. Remove from oven and set aside to cool completely.

Combine milk and marshmallows in a large saucepan, stirring over medium heat until marshmallows have melted. Remove from heat; add coffee and liqueur and stir until coffee has dissolved. Set aside to cool completely.

Beat cream with an electric mixer or beaters until stiff. Fold into cold marshmallow mixture and spoon into pastry cases. Refrigerate for 1 hour or until set.

Serve topped with almond flakes and lightly dusted with icing sugar.

Tip: Chocolate curls could be used to decorate the tarts.

* Refer to Glossary – Page 470

Tiramisù
Tiramisu

Ingredients

200ml thickened cream*

100g caster (superfine) sugar

4 free range egg yolks*, at room temperature

500g mascarpone cheese*

18 sponge finger biscuits*

60ml strong (espresso) black coffee, cold

60ml hazelnut liqueur*

Cocoa powder, to dust

Both Siena in Tuscany and Treviso in the Veneto claim ownership of tiramisù, a rich, potent dessert containing coffee and alcohol (often rum, brandy or flavoured liqueurs). Some recipes use zabaglione as the custard/cream element while others use mascarpone mixed with whipped cream. It's best made several hours before you want to eat it so that the flavours infuse and the sponge fingers soften.

Method

Beat cream and only 1 tablespoon of the sugar with an electric mixer or beaters until soft peaks form. In a second bowl, beat the egg yolks with remaining sugar until light and fluffy. Fold the mascarpone into the egg mixture a little at a time and lastly fold in the whipped cream.

Place some sponge finger biscuits in a single layer over the base of a 2.25 litre rectangular dish.

Pour over a little of combined coffee and liqueur (do not soak) and cover with only a third of the cream mixture. Repeat with a second layer of biscuits some more coffee mixture and only half the remaining cream mixture.

Finish with a final layer of the biscuits, coffee mixture and cream mixture.

Refrigerate for at least 1 hour before serving. Dust heavily with cocoa.

Note: The number of layers will depend on the depth of the dish used.

Panna cotta caramellata
Caramelised panna cotta

Ingredients

100g caster (superfine) sugar

1 tablespoon water

15g leaf gelatine

500ml thickened cream*

1 vanilla pod*, split lengthways

70g caster (superfine) sugar, extra

4 strips of orange rind

2 tablespoons Marsala*

30g pistachio nuts, to serve (optional)

A dessert from Piedmont, panna cotta essentially contains cream, milk, sugar and vanilla. The ingredients are heated (but not boiled), gelatin is added and when the cream mixture cools, it sets. A good panna cotta should still wobble gloriously on the plate. It's often served with a fruit coulis or poached seasonal fruit. In this recipe the panna cotta is infused with orange flavour and Marsala, and the caramel adds an extra dimension.

Method

Brush six 125ml-capacity heatproof moulds or ramekins with water.

Place the sugar in a small saucepan with the water and heat gently, stirring, until the sugar is melted. Bring to the boil without stirring and simmer until the syrup turns a golden brown.

Pour this caramel into prepared moulds. Set aside to cool.

Place the gelatine in a bowl, add enough cold water to cover and leave to soften for 15 minutes. Place the cream in a medium saucepan with the vanilla pod, the extra sugar and orange rind; stir over a low heat until the sugar dissolves. Remove from heat and stand for 10 minutes before straining through a fine sieve into a large jug.

Add the drained gelatin and Marsala to the warm cream mixture and stir to dissolve.

Divide the cream mixture between the moulds and refrigerate for at least 3-4 hours or overnight, until set.

Dip the moulds into warm-hot water for 1-2 minutes before turning out onto individual serving plates. Garnish with pistachios and serve.

* Refer to Glossary – Page 470

Torta di mela alla panna
Apple cream tart

Serves 6-8

Ingredients

200g plain (all-purpose) flour
½ teaspoon salt
½ teaspoon ground cinnamon
1 teaspoon baking powder
50g caster (superfine) sugar
2 teaspoons finely grated lemon rind
125g cold butter, chopped
1 egg yolk, at room temperature
1 tablespoon Marsala*

Filling
40g raisins
1 tablespoon Marsala*
1 egg, at room temperature
1 eggwhite, at room temperature
75g caster (superfine) sugar
1 tablespoon plain (all-purpose) flour, sifted
2 teaspoons finely grated lemon rind
185g cream cheese, at room temperature
75ml thickened cream*
1 tablespoon candied mixed peel
Pinch salt
2 small green apples, peeled and thinly
sliced into rounds
2 teaspoons white (granulated) sugar

Method

Preheat oven to 180°C. Lightly grease a 33 x 11cm rectangular tart tin with removable base.

To make the Base, sift together flour, salt, cinnamon and baking powder into a large bowl. Add sugar and lemon rind and rub the butter into the flour mixture you're your fingertips until it resembles breadcrumbs. Beat egg yolk and Marsala together and add to dry ingredients. Mix to form a soft dough.

Turn dough out onto a lightly floured work surface and knead lightly until smooth. Press dough into the base and sides of the prepared tin. Prick the base with a fork then refrigerate for 15 minutes while the filling is prepared.

To make Filling, combine raisins and Marsala in a small bowl and set aside. Place eggs and sugar into a medium bowl and beat with an electric mixer or beaters until light and thick. Gradually add flour, then rind and cream cheese, beat again until smooth. Stir in the soaked raisins, cream, peel and salt. Pour into prepared pastry base.

Arrange apple slices on top, overlapping slightly and sprinkle with sugar. Place on a large baking tray and bake for 30-35 minutes or until set, lightly browned and has risen. Cool in tin.

Variation – Use sliced of pears instead of the apples.

* Refer to Glossary – Page 470

Zuppa Inglese
Trifle

Ingredients

6 free-range egg yolks*, separated

180g caster (superfine) sugar

50g plain (all-purpose) flour

700ml milk

30g cocoa powder

100ml rum

100ml dessert wine or Alchermes*

10-12 sponge finger biscuits* or trifle sponge cakes

Assorted fresh berries and thickened cream*, to serve

Zuppa Inglese translates literally as "English soup". It is popularly thought to have been inspired by English trifle, although more recent Italian food historians claim that it was invented in 16th century Siena, and taken to Florence where visiting Brits took to it. The word "zuppa", however, comes from the Italian verb inzuppare which means "to dunk", referring to the sponge finger biscuits soaked in liqueur. The Roman version of zuppa inglese includes diced candied fruits and is sometimes covered in meringe and lightly baked; in Emilia-Romagna half the custard is often flavoured with chocolate, as in this recipe.

Method

Whisk egg yolks, sugar and flour into a medium-sized bowl until thick and pale. Set aside. Bring milk to the boil in a medium saucepan over low-medium heat, remove and cool slightly. Slowly pour milk into egg yolk mixture, whisking constantly. Pour mixture back into saucepan and return saucepan to heat. Stir constantly with a wooden spoon over medium heat until custard boils, thickens and coats the back of the spoon.

Divide custard evenly between two heatproof bowls. Sift cocoa into one of the bowls and stir until smooth. Cover both custard surfaces with plastic wrap and refrigerate until cold.

Combine rum, dessert wine and 150ml of cold water in a bowl. Dip sponge finger biscuits in the rum mixture, break biscuits in half and line the base of serving glasses or one large bowl.

Layer with chocolate custard, more dipped sponge finger biscuits, plain custard and lastly, remaining dipped sponge finger biscuits.

Refrigerate for 2 hours. Serve with berries and whipped cream, if desired

* Refer to Glossary – Page 470

Cassata ricotta
Ricotta cheesecake

Ingredients

185g plain chocolate biscuits, finely crushed

90g butter, melted

Filling

625g fresh firm ricotta cheese

160g icing (confectioner's) sugar

1 teaspoon vanilla extract*

2 tablespoons Crème de Cacao liqueur*

60g dark cooking chocolate, grated

50g glace fruit, finely chopped

Extra dark chocolate, grated, to serve

200ml thickened cream*, whipped (optional)

Method

In a medium bowl combine the biscuits and butter. Press the crumb mix over the base of a lightly greased 24cm-round, shallow flan tin with removable base or springform pan. Refrigerate while preparing filling.

Make the Filling by combining the ricotta, sugar, vanilla and liqueur in a large bowl. Beat with an electric mixer or beaters until smooth and fluffy. Fold in the grated chocolate and glace fruit, mixing to combine.

Spoon filling over base and refrigerate for 6 hours.

Serve chilled, decorated with extra chocolate and cream.

Soufflé al amaretto
Macaroon soufflé

Ingredients

6 almond macaroons, crushed finely
60ml Marsala*
3 eggs, at room temperature, separated
Pinch salt
300ml thickened cream*
150g caster (superfine) sugar
Peach slices, to serve
Chocolate curls, to serve (optional)

Method

Place macaroons into a small bowl with Marsala, allow macaroons to become moist and take in the Marsala. Set aside.

Place eggwhites and salt into a large bowl and beat with an electric mixer or beaters until stiff peaks form.

Beat cream in a separate bowl until stiff then fold into the egg whites in two batches.

Beat egg yolks and sugar until light and frothy. Fold in macaroon mixture then gently fold into egg white mixture in two batches.

Spoon mixture into 6 soufflé dishes or 125ml-capacity ramekins. Place into the freezer overnight or until firm.

Remove from freezer 5-10 minutes before required. Serve decorated with peach slices and chocolate curls.

* Refer to Glossary – Page 470

Crostata di marmellata
Jam tart

Ingredients

375g plain (all-purpose) flour

Pinch of salt

110g caster (superfine) sugar

75g cold butter, chopped

3 eggs, lightly beaten (remove about 1 teaspoon and add to milk for glazing)

475g fruit jam, either raspberry, strawberry or apricot

2 tablespoons milk, to glaze

Cream, to serve

Method

Sift the flour and salt into a large bowl; stir in sugar. Using fingertips, rub the butter into the flour until it resembles breadcrumbs and there are no more buttery lumps.

Add almost all the egg mixture to the flour and work in with a fork until the mixture resembles a dough and holds together. Add remaining egg as needed to form a soft dough.

Wrap the dough in some plastic wrap and chill for 30 minutes.

Preheat oven to 190°C. Lightly grease a 23cm-round, shallow flan tin with removable base.

Reserve a quarter of the dough for the top. Roll out the remaining dough between 2 pieces of kitchen baking paper to a circle large enough to line base and side of prepared tin.

Line the tin with dough and prick the base with a fork. Trim pastry edges and keep trimmings.

Fill pastry case with jam of choice.

Roll out the reserved pastry and trimmings until 3mm thick and cut into strips about 1cm wide. Place over jam in a lattice pattern. Brush the pastry with reserved egg and milk to glaze.

Bake 25-35 minutes or until lightly golden.

Cool completely in tin before removing from tin and cutting into wedges. Serve with cream.

★ Refer to Glossary – Page 470

Schiuma di cioccolata
Chocolate foam

Ingredients

150g dark cooking chocolate, chopped
70g caster (superfine) sugar
½ teaspoon vanilla extract*
50g butter, chopped
3 large or 4 small eggs, at room temperature, separated
9 sponge finger biscuits* (1½ per serve)
60ml rum
Fresh raspberries or mixed berries, to serve

Method

Combine the chocolate, only half the sugar, vanilla and butter in a medium saucepan. Cook over low heat until chocolate melts.

Remove from heat and add egg yolks one at a time, stirring well after each addition. Cool to room temperature.

Beat eggwhites with electric mixer or beaters until soft peaks form. Beat in the remaining sugar a little at a time until stiff and glossy. Gently fold eggwhites into the chocolate mixture in two batches.

Soak the biscuits in the rum and place into the bottom of 6 individual serving glasses (as pictured).

Cover with chocolate foam and refrigerate until time to serve.

Serve topped with fresh raspberries or mixed berries.

* Refer to Glossary – Page 470

Melone al marsala
Marsala honeydew melon

Ingredients

1 small ripe honeydew melon

80ml Marsala*

1 teaspoon caster (superfine) sugar

¼ cup picked small whole fresh mint leaves

1 tablespoon caster (superfine) sugar, to serve

Method

Cut the melon in half horizontally through the middle and scoop out the seeds. Discard seeds then cut melon into chunks or use a melon scoop or baller to make balls from the flesh of the melon.

Place the melon into a large bowl, add the Marsala, sugar and mint and stir gently to combine.

Cover and chill for 1 hour if possible. Sprinkle with extra sugar and serve

* Refer to Glossary – Page 470

Umbria

While not as renowned as its neighbours, Umbria has plenty for the gourmet to discover.

Perugia

Some people describe Umbria as Tuscany with a little more roughness about the edges … and a more affordable price tag.

This landlocked, ancient (pre-Roman, pre-Etruscan) region is just that little bit more 'undiscovered' than its more famous northern neighbour, yet still accessible. Small and dead centre – the very heart of the Italian peninsula – the upper reaches of the Tiber run through it, flowing to Rome.

Some call it a "holy land" because of its hilltop villages crowned with churches dedicated to saints, such as Saint Benedict and Saint Francis, Saint Chiara and Saint Rita. Strategically important in their day, the churches are highly decorative and worth wandering through. There is fantastic dining in the area too, in charming trattorias amongst gentle scenery dotted with cypress, oaks and olives – enough to soothe any soul.

This high country, with its sometimes harsh weather, is not always easy to farm, but the locals, descended from hardy *contadino* (peasant farmer) stock, manage to produce olive oil from the hills, with perhaps the best produced near Spoleto. The Oil Festival (*Festa di Olio*) in Trevi celebrates each year's olive harvest and its olive oil during the first week of November.

Rich pickings

There are also summer figs and plums, lentils from Castelluccio, *farro* (spelt) around Spoleto, red onions from Cannara, black celery from Trevi, and potatoes at Colfiorito. *Porcini* mushrooms and black truffles are found around Norcia, and rare white truffles near Orvieto, itself another picturesque town nestled inside an extinct volcanic crater. And, of course, when speaking of truffles, the town of Norcia celebrates the black truffle at the end of each season, during the third week in February, in restaurants and on street stalls and menus. Definitely a calendar date to remember.

Opposite: The church of *St. Pietro "extra moenia"* (outside the walls) viewed through an arch of the *Ponte delle Torri* (Bridge of Towers), Spoleto, Umbria.

The church of St Pietro was founded in the 5th century AD to house the relics of St Peter and was rebuilt in medieval times in the Umbrian Romanesque style, of which it is one of the finest examples still in current use.

The best Umbrian cheese is generally accepted as *pecorino di Norcia e della Valnerina*, made from sheep's milk, as well as an interesting ricotta rolled in wheat germ, and a sublime *pecorino di tartufo*, meaning, simply, truffled cheese.

Those white bullocks from the Apennines are raised here too for their fine meat, and there is lamb and game: *cinghiale* (wild boar), small birds and deer – although they are in danger of being over-hunted, courtesy of enthusiastic locals.

The pork butchers of Norcia are worth mentioning. Their sign *norcineria* has come to signify high-quality pork and has now been adopted in other parts of Italy. It's to be expected then that the *prosciutto di Norcia* (Norcia ham) is considered to be exceptional, and is said by some to be more fragrant than Parma ham. The tiny, local, thumb-sized boar sausages are worth sampling too, should you be fortunate enough to have the opportunity.

Comfort food, Umbrian-style

Umbrian food is wholesome and rustic (some might say peasant-style), but its simplicity is what the world demands now and it's good – olive-oil based, rich in pork, pasta, legumes, and game, slow-cooked for flavour, often over a wood-fire. *Porchetta*, stuffed and spit-roasted pig, is popular for big gatherings, and the local handmade thick *umbricelli* pasta, roughly hand-cut and made without eggs, is generally served with *ragù*. The other main pasta here is *strangozzi* (or *stringozzi*) a long, squarish pasta, said to resemble a leather thong useful for strangling tax collectors!

Umbria is said to be the home of bruschetta, but at Easter, families celebrate with *pizza di Pasqua*, a pizza topped with sheep's cheese and served with dry-cured pork sausage and hard-boiled eggs (there is a sweet version, too).

Umbria's capital, Perugia, offers regional specialties in its many restaurants, but chocolate-lovers will be on the lookout for its most famous product, *Baci Perugina* chocolate, from a company that was started here more than a century ago.

Umbrian wines include the white *Orvieto Classico* and red *Sagrantino di Montefalco*, while the region produces some of Italy's best *méthode champenoise* (Champagne-style) sparkling wines.

Piemonte (Piedmont)

Home to the revered white truffle, delicious chocolate and world-famous coffee – what more could one ask for?

Far to the north of Italy, at the foot of the Italian Alps, the region of Piedmont has been part of a tug-of-war for centuries with its neighbour France. This is a region that loves to enjoy its food – slowly and with enjoyment. The birthplace of the Slow Food movement and home of the prized white truffle, there is much to take in here. This is the time to stop, slow down and enjoy the view.

It is a large region (Italy's second largest, after Sicily), and while mountains make up almost half of the region, it also comprises the upper reaches of the River Po, plains where two-thirds of Italy's rice is grown, as well as some lakes. These are regarded as Piedmont's "Riviera" and are important for tourism, although snow sports are a major attraction here, too. The 2006 XX Olympic Winter Games were held in Piedmont's capital, Turin.

International influences

Inevitably, Piedmont's cuisine often resembles that of the Savoy region, just across the mountains to the west in France, or parts of Switzerland, which it borders to the north. People who live and visit here require hearty, warming food – lots of stews, broths and dense breads, as well as carbohydrates found in rice, potatoes and corn – to provide the energy they need.

Piedmont's major produce is that which can be gathered or caught in the forests and fields – mushrooms, berries, nuts (notably hazelnuts, chestnuts and almonds), game meats and herbs – or things that can be grown in this cooler high altitude, including vegetables such as pumpkin.

Cattle provide dairy products and meat. Piedmontese beef (*fassone del Piemonte*) is highly respected throughout the region, and the local cheeses are some of the finest in the country. *Gorgonzola*, *Grana Padano*, *taleggio*, and *toma* cheeses are well known outside Italy, but there are many more deemed good enough to have DOP recognition. Some are produced in only one remote valley, the craft of generations of family-producers.

Despite the cold and altitude, this area produces fine wines as well – notable reds (some of the best in the country) such as Barolo or Barbaresco made with Nebbiolo grapes, Barbera from Barbera grapes, and the exceptionally popular sparkling wine, *Moscato d'Asti spumante*. The aperitif Cinzano, essential for a martini, also comes from this region, as well as many DOC and DOCG wines.

The legendary white truffle

But perhaps the most notable claim to culinary fame of Piedmont is the white truffle from the Alba region. While the French revere their "black gold" from the Perigord, and price it accordingly, these beauties sell for twice the price and are so linked to the area that if a dish has *alla Piemontese* added to it, you should expect it to include white truffles.

Snails are also popular in this region and turn up in dishes such as *lumache al Barbera*, snails in Barbera wine sauce, while frog's legs (a by-product of the paddy fields) also make an appearance on menus in season. Hare stew and rabbit dishes make use of the wild game, and *bresaola* and *salami* are prepared from more traditional meats.

Some say that Ferrero chocolates and Nutella from Turin and *torrone* (nougat) from Asti, are two of the area's more important contributions to gastronomy, but few know that peppermint oil, produced near Turin, is an important confectionery product of the area.

Turin is widely accepted as the coffee capital of the north – perhaps even of Italy, as it is the home of Lavazza. It is also the birthplace of modern chocolate bars, and there are many small artisan manufacturers. Do try *gianduia*, an addictively rich mix of hazelnut paste and chocolate, if ever you have the opportunity.

A typical Piedmontese menu will include many dishes known and loved around the world. *Bagna cauda* (literally 'hot bath', a communal dish similar to a beef fondue), *bollito misto* (mixed boiled meats in a rich broth), and *fritto misto* (a lucky dip of battered and fried seafood and vegetables) will almost certainly be there. Risotto is king in this region, and usually makes use of the locally grown *carnaroli* and *arborio* strains of rice, which are ideal for making this versatile and rich, yet simple, dish. To finish, there may be *zabaglione*, the Italian take on the French sweet custard sauce, *sabayon*, and *amaretti* (page 428), crisp little almond macaroons flavoured with almond essence from locally grown almonds.

Festival season

Like almost any part of Italy, the Piedmontese people like to party. Truffles are celebrated with a festival in Alba each October. If you miss that, there are truffle markets on Saturdays during the season from October to December.

Mountainous Piemonte is home to many top-rated cheeses, truffles and more.

Crocera di Barge celebrates Piedmont's other major produce with a rice festival a few kilometres from the source of the River Po in the last week of April each year.

Perhaps the most bizarre event on the Piedmontese food calendar is the Ivrea orange-throwing festival, preceding Lent. Its origin is lost in the Middle Ages, but each year on the appropriate Sunday morning, cooked beans are served at points around the town as a commemoration of a time when food was distributed to the needy. In the afternoon, though, food is actually thrown away as the orange throwing begins in earnest. It continues on to Shrove Monday and Tuesday. Finally, on Wednesday, the first day of Lent is marked by another food handout – this time of polenta and cod that has been cooked in large utensils on the streets.

Bra, a small town near Turin and Alba, has achieved fame in another way. It is the birthplace of Carlo Petrini, the founder of the Slow Food movement, and is also home to the world's first University of Gastronomic Sciences. In odd-numbered years Bra hosts an international cheese festival, and the Slow Food movement has other events in the area. Take a cue from the locals and take Piedmont slowly, and savour all its charms.

Previous right: Ferriolo di Baveno, Lake Maggiore, Piemonte.

Left: Partially aged Gorgonzola cheese, Paltrinieri Dairy, Prato Sesia, Piemonte.

Below: An ancient fortified winery in the famous Barolo wine region, Tenuta la Volta, Piemonte.

Gelato e sorbetto

Gelato & sorbet

Invented in Italy over 500 years ago, a seemingly unending variety of gelati can now be found all over the world.

Gelato

Is there nothing more delightful than finishing a meal on a hot summer day with a refreshing icy delight? *Gelato* actually dates back to the 16th century. Its origins are unclear, but evidence shows that containers were packed in rock salt to lower the temperature of the mix – a simple, yet effective alternative to modern refrigeration. However, it was some time before makers realised they could freeze milk and cream as well as fruit juices and water for an even more sublime result.

From Florence to France

Bernardo Buontalenti, a Florentine chef at the court of Caterina de' Medici, is generally credited with creating the first gelato, and Caterina took the concept with her when she moved to France in 1533 to marry the king's second son, later becoming the Queen of France.

Much earlier, Sicilians had been initiated into sorbet making by the Arabs, who packed snow into caves and then flavoured some with fruit juice. Even today *gelaterie* always feature a range of sorbets, and some serve *granita* too, a slushy flavoured ice dessert.

Just add dairy ...

Some say it was in Naples – others believe it was in Sicily – that the first dairy-based gelato was developed in the 18th century. It hardly matters, of course, as once that trademark creamy flavour was shared with others, there was no turning back. Since then the art has been refined and won fans in every part of the globe.

The major difference between gelato and ice-cream is that ice-cream must contain a minimum of ten per cent fat. Gelato has no such laws, but all milk and cream-based gelati are lower in fat, usually between three and seven per cent. They taste richer and creamier, gelato-makers say, because they use natural ingredients and the dairy products are not homogenised, allowing them to melt more quickly on the tongue. These days gelato is not always made with eggs as it once was, employing other stabilisers instead, such as vegetable gums, kelp, carob and lecithin.

Boasting a kaleidoscope of pastel colours and delicious flavours, an Italian *gelateria* is impossible to resist.

Density matters

The main ingredients of gelato are milk and cream, sugar and other sweeteners, flavourings such as fruits, nuts and essences, as well as air, to provide lightness. Gelato generally has less than 55% air, resulting in a denser product, often with a richer flavour.

Stracciatella
Chocolate chip gelato

Ingredients

450ml full cream milk
300ml pure (single) cream*
150g white (granulated) sugar
1½ teaspoons vanilla extract*
75g dark chocolate, grated coarsely

The name stracciatella comes from the word stracciato, which means "torn apart". Strictly speaking, the term applies to a soup in which cheese, eggs and seasoning are whisked into boiling broth, but it's been commandeered by gelato makers and is probably now better known as vanilla ice-cream that has grated chocolate mixed through it. For best results, use a good dark chocolate with about 70% cocoa solid content.

Method

Place milk, cream, sugar and vanilla into a large bowl or jug and whisk until combined. Allow to stand for about 15 minutes for the sugar to dissolve.

Pour into the chilled bowl of an ice-cream machine and process for 30 minutes or until thick.

Remove from ice-cream bowl, add chocolate and stir to combine.

Serve immediately or transfer to a container and freeze.

* Refer to Glossary – Page 470

Gelato di crema
Creamy vanilla gelato

Serves 4-6

Ingredients

3 free-range eggs*
150g white (granulated) sugar
300ml full cream milk
300ml thickened cream*
1 teaspoon vanilla extract*

Method

Place eggs and sugar into a large bowl and whisk until frothy and pale in colour. Add milk, cream and vanilla, whisk again until combined then allow to stand for about 15 minutes for the sugar to dissolve.

Pour into the chilled bowl of an ice-cream machine and process for 30 minutes or until thick.

Serve immediately or transfer to a container and freeze.

Variations:

• *For a white chocolate ice-cream, add 200g melted white chocolate when adding the milk and cream.*

• *For a coffee ice-cream, add 1 tablespoon espresso coffee when adding the milk and cream.*

Gelato di ciliegie
Cherry gelato

Serves 4-6

Ingredients

225ml single (pouring) cream*
150ml cherry or cranberry juice
180g white (granulated) sugar
450g fresh cherries, pitted and pureed

Method

Place cream, juice and sugar into a large bowl or jug and whisk until combined. Allow to stand for about 15 minutes for the sugar to dissolve.

Add the pureed cherries to liquid and stir to combine.

Pour into the chilled bowl of an ice-cream machine and process for 30 minutes or until thick.

Serve immediately or transfer to a container and freeze.

Tip: Frozen cherries can be used when fresh cherries are not available. Reduce to 420g.

* Refer to Glossary – Page 470

Gelato di bacio
Chocolate kiss gelato

Serves 4-6

Ingredients

120g dark chocolate
450ml full cream milk
1½ teaspoon vanilla extract*
45g ground hazelnuts
1 free-range egg*
1 free-range egg yolk*
150g white (granulated) sugar

Bacio means kiss, and the flavour profile of gelato di bacio – chocolate and hazelnut – is, indeed, a gastronomic match made in heaven. Over the years the term "baci" has become synonymous with the small chocolates of the same name that have been made famous by the Perugina chocolate company. Gelato di bacio is arguably the most popular flavour in any gelateria in Italy. Use the best dark chocolate you can, preferably 70% cocoa solids. If you are grinding your own hazelnuts, gently roast the raw nuts first for a richer, nuttier flavour.

Method

Combine the chocolate, only 100ml of milk and vanilla into a small saucepan. Place over medium heat and stir until chocolate has melted.

Remove from heat and add remaining ingredients and whisk until combined. Allow to stand for about 15 minutes for the sugar to dissolve.

Pour into the chilled bowl of an ice-cream machine and process 30 minutes or until thick.

Serve immediately or transfer to a container and freeze.

* Refer to Glossary – Page 470

Gelato fragole
Strawberry gelato

Ingredients

150ml full cream milk

1 lemon, rind only

1 vanilla bean (pod)*, cut in half
lengthways

180g white (granulated) sugar

1 egg

1 egg yolk

300g strawberries, hulled and pureed

300ml pure (single) cream

Method

Combine milk, rind, vanilla bean and sugar in a small saucepan; bring to a gentle boil, remove from heat and cool.

Place eggs into a large bowl and whisk until pale and frothy, add pureed strawberries and cream. Strain cooled milk mixture and add to strawberries.

Pour into the chilled bowl of an ice-cream machine and process for 30 minutes or until thick.

Serve immediately or transfer to a container and freeze.

* Refer to Glossary – Page 470

Gelato di Nutella
Nutella gelato

Serves 4-6

Ingredients

300ml full cream milk
200ml pure (single) cream
80g white (granulated) sugar
300g Nutella*

Method

Place milk, cream and sugar into a large bowl or jug and whisk until combined. Allow to stand for about 15 minutes for the sugar to dissolve.

Add Nutella and whisk to combine. Pour into the chilled bowl of an ice-cream machine and process for 30 minutes or until thick.

Serve immediately or transfer to a container and freeze.

* Refer to Glossary – Page 470

Sorbetto di champagne
Champagne sorbet

Serves 4-6

Ingredients

500ml water

100g white (granulated) sugar

250ml champagne or dry spumante wine

2 tablespoons lemon juice

Method

Place water, sugar and champagne into a large saucepan bring to a simmer over medium-high heat, remove from the heat and transfer to a jug. Add the lemon juice and refrigerate until cold.

Pour into the chilled bowl of ice-cream machine and process for 30 minutes until almost solid.

Serve immediately or transfer to a container and freeze.

Sorbetto di pesche
Peach sorbet

Ingredients

800g fresh ripe peaches, peeled, stoned
and pureed

300g white (granulated) sugar

2 tablespoons fresh lemon juice

Method

Place peach puree, sugar and lemon juice into a large bowl and allow to stand for about 15 minutes for the sugar to dissolve.

Pour into the chilled bowl of an ice-cream machine and process for 30 minutes or until almost solid.

Serve immediately or transfer into a container and freeze.

Variation – Substitute apricots, nectarines or ripe rockmelon for the peaches.

Sorbetto di pompelmo
Grapefruit sorbet

Serves 4-6

Ingredients

450ml fresh grapefruit juice (about 5
grapefruit)
250g white (granulated) sugar
225ml water
60ml gin

Method

Place grapefruit juice, sugar and water into a large bowl or jug.
Whisk then allow to stand for about 15 minutes for the sugar to
dissolve. Add the gin.

Pour into the chilled bowl of an ice-cream machine and process for
30 minutes or until almost solid.

Serve immediately or transfer to a container and freeze.

Granite Siciliana di limone
Sicilian lemon granita

Serves 4

Ingredients

700ml water
350ml white (granulated) sugar
200ml lemon juice

One of Sicily's great exports to the Italian mainland (and all over the world), granita is in its simplest form a slushy mass of flavoured, sweetened water. Sicilian towns have their own regional variations. In Palermo and the west of the island it's relatively coarse and chunky, while in the east it tends to be smoother and closer to what we regard as sorbet. One of the most popular versions throughout Italy is granita di caffè – icy crystals of strong sweet espresso topped with dollops of whipped cream. This recipe, made with fresh lemon juice, is wonderfully refreshing.

Method

Place water, sugar and lemon juice into a large jug, allow to stand for about 15 minutes for the sugar to dissolve.

Pour into the chilled bowl of an ice-cream machine and process for 20 minutes or until slushy.

Serve immediately or transfer into a container and freeze.

Note – Granita can be made easily without an ice-cream machine. Simply pour the liquid into a deep tray or cake pan that will fit in your freezer. Allow to chill for 30-60 minutes or until ice crystals begin to appear. Then use a fork to flake and break up the ice. Refreeze and repeat this process 3-4 times more until slushy.

Sicilia (Sicily)

Palermo

An island with attitude, Sicily is a place that is separate from Italy, yet part of it. Legend has it that it was once defended by Charybdis, a many-headed watery she-monster in the Straits of Messina, which separate Sicily from mainland Italy. Today people often fear the underworld society of its interior even more.

An island of arid wastes and fertile excesses, this is Sicily, the crossroads of the Mediterranean. Sometimes seemingly more Greek than Greece, other times it is as if North Africa has been transplanted. It is a place of Mafia legends and overshadowed by the threatening peak of Mt Etna, wreathed in cloud. Sicilians themselves often refer to it simply as "the island". So many cultures, so much history; like the mosaics of its churches, they blend together to create a stunning result.

Honey, fruit and nuts

Almost every roadside in Sicily is lined with huge prickly pear cactus, its spiny pads bearing red *Fichi d'India fruit* – as ubiquitous as the endless groves of lemons and oranges (including the glorious, blood oranges) on the island. Figs, table and wine grapes, almonds, pine nuts and hazelnuts are also grown.

A food-centric island with attidude, Sicily is famous for a wealth of delicious reasons.

Below: Piazza San Domenico fruit market, Palermo, Sicily.
Next page: a family meal, Lipari, Sicily.

Pistachios thrive around Mt Etna, carob and figs at Mt Syracuse, with Belice olives and garden vegetables in the river valleys. The Arab-influenced dishes of the region use a lot of honey, so, there are hives wherever there are blossoms, all over the island.

There are olive groves too, producing the high-quality extra virgin olive oil used in almost every Sicilian dish. The best capers come from the isle of Pantelleria to the south, and Pachino tomatoes come from the far south-eastern tip of Sicily itself. Zucchini (courgettes) and artichokes, used in many dishes, are widely grown.

In the sometimes harsh hinterland, sheep and goats thrive, and sheep's cheeses abound. *Pecorino Siciliano* and *ricotta* are made in many places, and *piacentinu* (sheep's cheese coloured with saffron and studded with peppercorns) comes from Nebrodi. It is *ragusano*, though, a hard cow's milk cheese, that is regarded as the "king" of Sicilian cheeses.

Surrounded by water, seafood is a major ingredient in Sicilian cuisine. Lobsters from Trapani in the west, swordfish from the Messina Straits, tuna and other fish and seafood elsewhere contribute rich flavours and excellence to many dishes.

The *Modicana* cattle of Ragusa to the south, and *Madonie* lamb, east of Palermo, are highly rated, and the pork-based *salame di Sant'Angelo di Brolo* rounds out a diet that is already almost perfect.

Salty and sweet

Another traditional Sicilian product is salt, from the salt pans of Trapani on the west coast, some of them still employing eye-catching ancient windmills. Nearby, in the mountaintop village of Erice, nuns make tooth-achingly sweet pastries called *ericini*.

Sicily is temptation island for sweet tooths. In Modica on the south coast, several places produce cold-processed chocolate, and throughout the island *granite* with brioche is a favourite breakfast. These crushed ice drinks may be flavoured with coffee, almond or lemon and are also welcome in the midday heat. If these don't appeal, some of Italy's best *gelati* are made in Sicily.

No visitor to Sicily should miss out on *cassata*, a decadent concoction of sponge cake, ricotta and candied fruit, covered with marzipan, another local specialty with a history stretching back to the Middle Ages. Then there's *cannoli*, crisp fried pastry tubes filled with ricotta and pistachios or fruit. Sicily is noted for its smaller sweetmeats – nut and honey, candied fruit and pastry concoctions, many influenced by the island's Arab history. These magnificent *dolci* are displayed like jewels in *pasticcerie* in every town and city.

On the street

Street food is popular, but nowhere more so than in Palermo, Sicily's teeming capital. Octopus sellers, *polipari*, are found on the Palermo waterfront, and elsewhere *panellari* selling *panelle* (chickpea fritters), and fried food shops called *friggitorie* offer all sorts of fried foods, such as *arancini*, those "little oranges" – fried rice balls often filled with a cube of cheese – for a tasty snack.

In some parts of Palermo, and especially in the north-west of the island, couscous is popular. Shops will display signs when it is being prepared. *Baccalà* with couscous is a popular dish in Sicily, as is *pasta con le sarde*, pasta with sardines, pine nuts and raisins. *Caponata* (see page 244) is a little like Calabria's *peperonata* – mixed vegetables with capers – but here served as a starter.

Flatbreads and filled breads abound: *focaccie* from Messina, *scacciate*, bread pies filled with cheese from Catania, and *scaccie*, filled *focaccie* from Ragusa and Syracuse are popular snacks. For *pane ca'meusa* (bread with innards), locals go to grills or booths in the cities.

Finally, vino! Sicily produces good light reds and whites, but its greatest contributions to the world of liquor are Marsala, developed more than 200 years ago, Moscato from the Aeolian Islands, and Sambuca, an aniseed liqueur. Some areas make *fichi d'India* (prickly pear) or chilli and chocolate liqueurs. The perfect accompaniment to *cannoli*, in fact. Consider them both an extra, essential piece of the mosaic …

Market variety

Palermo's massive Vucciria markets showcase everything in season, from massive swordfish hacked into slices to order, glowing mounds of oranges, tomatoes, red, green or yellow peppers, and shiny purple eggplant, to jars of olives and other condiments, as well as spices and nuts.

Sicily seems to celebrate food every single day with festivals around the island - amongst the biggest are the tuna festival in Trapani in June and the international festival of couscous in San Vito Lo Capo every September.

Torte & piccola pasticcerrie

Cakes & little pastries

Italians love 'the sweet life' – hence their collection of cakes, pastries and biscuits is impressive and delicious.

La pasticceria
(The pastry shop)

La pasticceria is an Italian pastry shop – an innocent-sounding name for a repository of so many irresistible temptations!

Pasticcerie are found in every Italian town, their curved glass-fronted display cabinets filled with the sweeter things of life – *pasticcini* (small cakes), *crostate* or *tartelette* (jam or fruit-filled tartlets), and *biscotti*. A tall cabinet may hold a multi-tiered wedding cake; another will have shelves, sometimes revolving for greater effect, on which are larger *crostate*, *torte* and delectable creations that you may be tempted to buy as a gift – or simply purchase for your own furtive enjoyment.

Pastries, cakes, sweetmeats, they are all here, varying in style as the regions change. In many parts of the country a healthy early morning walk can be so easily hijacked by the sight of these delicacies, especially if they can be found in a *Bar-Pasticceria*, where you can stand at the bar or sit at a table with your coffee and something tiny and crunchily sweet to accompany it. At lunchtime, the *pasticceria* is the place to come for a quick meal of something savoury as well. Most serve *tartine* and little *salatini*, canapé-sized bites of pastries topped with cheese or a tiny taste of something else.

In Sicily, the *pasticcerie* shelves are filled with meticulously executed marzipan fruit, or maybe *cannoli*, those deep-fried pastry tubes filled with ricotta, candied fruit and chocolate, or an over-the-top decorated *cassata* (or its small cousin *cassatina*), more appropriate to take home than to eat on the spot.

The flakiest pastries are Neapolitan – *sfogliatelle* (filled with ricotta and candied peel), often displayed beside *baba* (round cakes oozing rum). In Piedmont, shoppers come for *torrone* (nougat), *bignole* (tiny bite-sized choux pastry balls filled with cream or *zabaglione*), or *baci di dama* (ladies' kisses, which are almond shortbread discs sandwiched together with chocolate icing). Deep-fried pastry strips called *crostoli* will be often found in Trentino-Alto Adige.

Sugar is certainly not sacrilegious here – biscuits, pastries and cakes are displayed for the enjoyment of all.

Opposite: The scrumptious shopfront of Alvino confectioner's, Lecce, Puglia.

A sweet offering

And as far as gifts go, no dinner hostess ever minds if she receives a carefully packed box of assorted pastries and *biscotti*, selected just an hour or so before from the local *pasticceria*. Although the contents will vary enormously, the price is cleverly calculated by weight, per *etto* (100 grams).

Some staples found in almost any *pasticceria* are *amaretti* biscuits, tiny almond-flavoured macaroons, first made in Saronno near Milan. *Biscotti* is the generic name for all the little crispy biscuits that Italian pastry chefs do so well. The regulars love them hard and sweet to dip into their coffees as they stand and chat to each other.

Wafer biscuits are great favourites too, made with flat irons impressed with decorative images and shapes, and cooked on top of the stove, rather like waffles, only their high sugar content and thinness make them ideal for serving with *gelato*.

The recipe for *mostacciolo* goes back to Roman times when it was the sensible (and pleasant) way to use up sweet grape must, the by-product of wine making. These firm finger-shaped biscuits are brushed with a sweet glaze after baking, then left to dry, and are one of the biscuits most favoured for dipping into a glass of *vin santo* (a sweet dessert wine) at the end of a meal.

A few encounters with a *pasticceria* will confirm forever how important a part sugar (and indeed all sweet things) plays in the Italian daily life. As the local saying goes: *Si pigliano più mosche in una gocciola di miele che in un barile d'aceto*, which translates as 'you can catch more flies with honey than a barrel of vinegar'.

Cedro

Candied fruit is popular with Italians as a garnish or sweet snack. *Cedro* is candied citron peel and is used in desserts or yeast-leavened cakes, such as *panettone* at Christmas or *Colomba* cakes at Easter. It is often chopped and added to Neapolitan and Sicilian pastries, such as *cannoli* and *cassata*, and is also added to Sienese *panforte*. *Zucca* (melon) is also often candied and used for similar purposes.

Cassata alla Siciliana
Sicilian ricotta sponge cake

Serves 6-8

Ingredients

350g bought sponge cake (in flat layers is best)

650g ricotta cheese

3 teaspoons finely grated orange rind

1 tablespoon vanilla sugar

100g candied mixed peel, finely chopped

40g pistachio nuts, finely chopped

60ml fresh orange juice

60ml orange liqueur*

30g extra pistachio nuts, finely chopped, to serve

The queen of the Sicilian pasticceria, cassata is a flamboyant cake decorated with pale green icing and luscious glacé fruit. Sweetened ricotta is layered with slices of liqueur-soaked sponge, covered with marzipan and encased in fondant; not surprisingly, it can be cloyingly sweet. Palermo is the true home of cassata, which was traditionally eaten at Easter. This recipe is simpler and more achieveable than any cassata you'd find in the Sicilian capital but still combines the essential ingredients and flavours of sponge cake, ricotta, mixed peel, and nuts.

Method

Lay a piece of kitchen plastic wrap along the length of a 9.5cm x 20cm rectangular cake pan and allow the wrap to over hang the edges. This is to assist in pulling out and removing the cassata once it is set.

Cut the cake into even pieces to fit prepared cake pan. Each slice of sponge should be about 1cm thick and they are placed side by side into the pan when the assembly of the cassata begins.

Combine ricotta, orange rind and vanilla sugar and mix well. Remove only half of the mixture to a separate bowl, cover and refrigerate until later.

To the remaining cheese add the mixed peel and nuts and stir well.

Combine orange juice and liqueur.

Make a single layer across the bottom of the pan with the sponge. Next drizzle with only a third of the combined orange juice and liqueur. Add only half the fruit and ricotta mix, flattening down and pushing mixture into the edges. Add more sponge and repeat with liquid. Next, top with remaining fruit and ricotta mix. Lastly, a sponge layer and add the remaining liquid.

Fold the excess plastic over the final cake layer. Place into the refrigerator and top with a baking tray and something heavy to weigh the cassata down. This is to compact the cassata and bring the layers together.

Chill for 2-3 hours or overnight.

Turn cassata out onto a serving platter by gently pulling on the plastic. Use the reserved ricotta and sugar mixture to spread over the top and sides of the cake. Decorate with extra chopped pistachios.

* Refer to Glossary – Page 470

Torta gianduia
Chocolate hazelnut cake

Serves 6-8

Ingredients

60g quality milk cooking chocolate

80g butter

60g ground hazelnuts

6 free-range eggs*, at room temperature, separated

240g caster (superfine) sugar

60g plain (all-purpose) flour

80g cornflour (cornstarch)

Milk Chocolate Cream

120ml thickened cream*

270g quality milk cooking chocolate, chopped

50ml hazelnut liqueur* (Frangelico)

7 Ferrero Rocher chocolates*, to serve

The word gianduia is often used generically to refer to the flavour combination of hazelnuts and chocolate, which in this recipe transform a simple sponge cake into an impressive dessert. Crema di gianduia (gianduia paste) was first marketed in Turin in the mid 19th century, flavouring chocolates, cakes and many other desserts. It can be seen as the predecessor of the much-loved spread, Nutella, although the latter contains less hazelnut than true gianduia and a lot more sugar.

Method

Preheat oven to 180°C. Lightly grease and line a 24cm-round, deep cake pan or springform pan with kitchen baking paper.

Place chocolate, butter and ground hazelnuts into a small saucepan, cook stirring over low heat until melted, then set aside.

Place eggwhites into a small bowl and beat with electric mixer or beaters until stiff peaks form, set aside. In a second bowl, beat egg yolks and sugar until thick and frothy. Fold in warm chocolate mixture. Fold in sifted flours in two batches and, lastly, gently fold in eggwhites in two batches.

Pour mixture into prepared pan. Bake in preheated oven for 20 minutes. Stand in pan for 5 minutes before turning out onto a wire rack to cool.

To make the Milk Chocolate Cream, place cream in a small saucepan and heat over a low heat (do not boil). Remove from heat, add the chocolate and stir until melted. Stir in Frangelico, cover and refrigerate until cold.

Use a serrated knife to cut cake in half horizontally. Place one layer onto a serving plate and spread with only half the chocolate cream. Top with second layer and spread with remaining milk chocolate cream.

Decorate with Ferrero Rocher chocolates to serve.

* Refer to Glossary – Page 470

Torta di mousse al limone
Lemon mousse cake

Serves 6-8

Ingredients

4 free-range eggs*, at room temperature, separated
200g caster (superfine) sugar
60g plain (all-purpose) flour
60g cornflour (cornstarch)
100g ground almonds
80g butter, melted and cooled
Filling
3 free-range eggs*, at room temperature
150g caster (superfine) sugar
2 teaspoons finely grated lemon rind
200ml lemon juice
30g cornflour (cornstarch)
2 teaspoons gelatine
200ml thickened cream*
Lemon rind threads (blanched), to serve

Method

Preheat oven to 180°C. Lightly grease and line a 20cm-round, deep cake pan.

To make the Base, place eggwhites into a medium bowl and beat with electric mixer or beaters until soft peaks form. Gradually add only half the sugar and beat until thick and glossy.

In a separate bowl beat the egg yolks with the remaining sugar until thick and pale in colour. Combine flour, cornflour and ground almonds and sift into the egg mixture, stir to combine.

Fold in the eggwhites in two batches and lastly the butter (pouring this around the sides of the bowl) and gently fold to combine. Pour into prepared pan. Bake in preheated oven for 25 minutes then stand for 5 minutes before turning out onto a wire rack to cool.

To make the Filling, place eggs and sugar in a medium bowl and use a wire balloon whisk to beat until slightly lighter in colour. Add lemon rind, juice and cornflour. Pour into a medium saucepan and stir constantly with the whisk over medium heat until the mixture gently boils and thickens.

Remove from heat and whisk in the gelatine. Spoon into a bowl, cover surface with plastic wrap and cool to room temperature. Beat cream until stiff and fold in batches into the cooled lemon mixture.

To assemble, slice cake in half horizontally. Place the bottom half of the cake onto a serving plate. Spread with only half the lemon mixture and top with remaining slice of cake and remaining lemon mixture. Smooth the top and refrigerate for 2 hours. Slice and serve with lemon threads.

* Refer to Glossary – Page 470

Dolci di mandorle
Almond cake

Ingredients

250g plain (all-purpose) flour, sifted

2 teaspoons baking powder

250g ground almonds

6 free-range eggs*, at room temperature, separated

240g butter, at room temperature

250g caster (superfine) sugar

1 tablespoon finely grated lemon rind

Filling

340g redcurrant jelly or strawberry jam (Sieve out seeds if using jam)

Topping

400g ground almonds

65g white (granulated) sugar

6 free-range eggs*, at room temperature, separated

75ml rum

60g flaked almonds, toasted

Method

Preheat oven to 180°C. Lightly grease and line base and sides of 2 x 20cm-round, deep cake pans with kitchen baking paper.

Sift flour and baking powder into a medium-sized bowl. Stir in the almond meal and set aside.

Place eggwhites into a clean bowl and beat with electric mixer or beaters until soft peaks form. Set aside.

In a third bowl, place the butter, sugar and lemon rind and beat until creamy, then beat in the egg yolks one at a time. Fold the flour and almonds into the butter mixture in two batches. Gently fold the eggwhites in, also in two batches, until just combined. Do not over-mix or over-beat.

Divide the mixture evenly between the two prepared cake pans.

Bake in preheated oven for 30-35 minutes or until a skewer comes out clean. Stand in the pans for 5 minutes before turning out onto wire racks to cool.

To assemble the Filling, place one of the cooled cakes onto a paper-lined baking tray then spread with only half the jam and top with the second cake – sandwiching them together.

To make the Topping, preheat oven to 220°C. Combine almonds and sugar. Beat together egg yolks and rum, add to almond mixture and mix well. Reserve a third of the almond mixture in a separate bowl. Next add 1 tablespoon of unbeaten egg white to remaining mixture and mix well. Spread this mixture over the top and sides of cake – covering the top of cake thickly.

Add 2 tablespoons unbeaten egg white to reserved almond mixture, mix well and place into a piping bag fitted with a fluted nozzle. Pipe a zigzag or lattice pattern over the top of cake.

Bake in preheated oven for 8-10 minutes or until lightly browned.

Gently heat the remaining redcurrant jelly and drizzle or spoon between zigzag or lattice pattern. Allow to cool for about 10 minutes then spread the sides with remaining melted jelly, and press on flaked almonds.

Cool completely before cutting to serve.

* Refer to Glossary – Page 470

Biscione reggiano
Snake of reggiano

Serves many

Ingredients

1kg ground almonds

800g white (granulated) sugar

3 eggwhites, at room temperature

100ml Sambuca (aniseed liqueur)

Icing (confectioner's) sugar, for dusting

125g apricot jam

100g white (granulated) sugar, extra

100g icing (confectioner's) sugar, extra

3 eggwhites, at room temperature, extra

2 glace' cherries

Glace' fruit

Method

Preheat oven to 180°C. Line a large baking tray with kitchen baking paper.

Process the almonds and sugar in batches in a food processor bowl to combine and transfer to a very large bowl. Add eggwhites and liqueur, stirring well.

Transfer the mixture to a work surface which has been lightly dusted with icing sugar, and roll to form a snake shape – larger at one end to form the head, and smaller at the other end, to form the tail. Place onto the prepared tray, curving it to look like a snake.

Bake in preheated oven for 30 minutes or until golden brown. Heat the jam and strain through a sieve, keep warm. Remove from oven and while still hot brush the snake with the jam. Reduce oven temperature to 100°C.

Combine the extra two sugars in a medium bowl and reserve half for sprinkling. Place the extra eggwhites into a clean bowl and beat with electric mixer or beaters until soft peaks form. Beat in only half the sugar until meringue is smooth and glossy. Spread the meringue over the snake, making it thicker on the head than on the tail. Sprinkle the reserved and remaining sugar over the meringue.

Position the cherries for eyes and use the glaze fruit to decorate, if desired. Return to the preheated oven and bake for 20-30 minutes or until the meringue is cooked.

Remove from oven, cool and serve.

Delizia alla mele
Apple bake

Ingredients

4 apples (Granny Smith or similar)
1 lemon, rind finely grated and juiced
450g plain (all-purpose) flour
1½ teaspoons baking powder
Pinch salt
200g white (granulated) sugar
150g cold butter, chopped
175g plain yoghurt
1 egg, at room temperature
Icing (confectioner's) sugar, to dust

Method

Preheat oven to 180°C. Lightly grease a 27cm x 40cm baking tray.

Peel, quarter, core and slice apples thinly, combine with lemon juice and set aside.

Sift flour and baking powder into a large bowl, stir in lemon rind, salt and only half the sugar. Add butter and rub into the flour until mixture resembles fine breadcrumbs. Make a well in the middle and add the yoghurt and egg, mix well to form a soft dough.

Turn onto a lightly floured work surface. Knead quickly until smooth, halve the dough and roll out into two thin rectangles to fit the prepared baking tray.

Place one rectangle into prepared baking tray, top with apple slices, leaving a slight border of pastry around the edge and sprinkle apple with remaining sugar. Top with the other half of rolled pastry. Gently press the two pastry edges together to seal the apple bake.

Bake in preheated oven for 25-30 minutes or until golden. Cool and serve dusted with icing sugar.

* Refer to Glossary – Page 470

Panforte casereccio
Homemade panforte

Ingredients

200g pure icing (confectioner's) sugar

160g plain (all-purpose) flour

150g walnut halves

150g whole almond kernels

250g chopped candied peel

½ teaspoon coriander seeds, crushed with mortar and pestle

¼ teaspoon ground nutmeg

¼ teaspoon ground cinnamon

150g honey

Traditionally served at Christmas, this dense, chewy, fruit and nut cake is thought to date back to the 13th century. The original name was panpepato (peppered bread), due to the spices used. The historic Tuscan city of Siena is regarded as the panforte capital of Italy; indeed, it is often claimed that an authentic panforte should contain 17 different ingredients, representing the 17 contrade or districts within Siena's city walls. Some richer recipes include chocolate or cocoa.

Method

Preheat oven to 150°C. Grease and line base and side of a 24cm-round springform cake pan.

Place only 1 tablespoon of the icing sugar and only 3 tablespoons of the flour in a small bowl and set aside.

Toast the walnuts and almonds in the preheated oven at 150°C for 10-12 minutes, cool slightly, chop roughly and place into a large bowl with the candied peel, coriander, nutmeg and cinnamon. Add the remaining flour.

Place the remaining icing sugar into a medium saucepan with the honey and 1 tablespoon of water. Heat, stirring continually until well combined. Remove from heat and pour warm liquid over the fruit and nut mixture; mix together well.

Quickly spoon mixture into prepared pan and flatten with a damp hand. Sprinkle the combined reserved icing sugar and flour over the top of the cake.

Bake panforte in preheated oven for 30 minutes. Cool in pan then remove and slice into thin wedges to serve.

Tip: If you have trouble removing the panforte from the pan, run a spatula around the pan between the paper and pan then pull on the paper to lift and remove.

Cannoli Siciliana
Sicilian cannoli

Ingredients

This classic Sicilian pastry, once made as a Carnival specialty, is now enjoyed year round in Italy and beyond. The name comes from the wooden (or metal) tube around which the dough is wrapped, before being deep-fried. Any type of sweet filling, including ricotta, custard and mascarpone, can be used, flavoured with candied fruit (and sometimes wine or chocolate). In Sicily, the most delectable cannoli are filled with sweetened sheep's milk ricotta.

Dough

300g plain (all-purpose) flour, sifted
2 teaspoons cocoa powder
100g caster (superfine) sugar
30g butter, at room temperature
2 teaspoons instant coffee
Pinch salt
125ml dry white wine
Vegetable oil for deep-frying

Filling

300g ricotta cheese
200g icing (confectioner's) sugar
50g candied mixed peel, finely chopped
1 teaspoon orange blossom water*
60g dark cooking chocolate, finely chopped

Topping

75g pistachio nuts, finely chopped, to serve
Icing (confectioner's) sugar, to dust

Method

To make the Dough, sift the flour and cocoa into a large bowl. Add the sugar, butter, coffee, salt and wine and mix to a stiff dough.

Turn dough out onto a lightly floured work surface and knead for 5 minutes or until smooth. Place into a clean bowl, cover and refrigerate for 30 minutes.

To make the Filling, place the ricotta, sugar, peel, orange blossom water and chocolate into a medium bowl. Cover and refrigerate until ready to use.

Divide the dough into 18 pieces and roll each piece out on a lightly floured work surface to form ovals about 3mm thick. Wrap the dough ovals around lightly greased metal cannoli tubes (or similar mould about 10-15cm long and 2-3cm in diameter). Ensure the ovals are long enough so that when you wrap them around the metal tubes the dough edges overlap slightly on one side to seal.

Heat oil in a heavy-based saucepan or for deep-frying and cook the cannoli individually by placing them seam side down into the hot oil. Cook until lightly golden. Remove and drain on crumpled kitchen paper towel, then gently remove the metal tube. Continue until all cannoli are cooked.

Place the ricotta filling into a piping bag with a large, plain nozzle and use this to fill the cannoli. Dip each end of the cannoli into the chopped pistachio nuts to garnish.

Best served immediately or can be refrigerated for 2-3 hours, if necessary.

Dust lightly with icing sugar before serving.

Tip: The pistachio nuts can be added to the filling but the cannoli will need to be served straightaway so the nuts remain crisp.

* Refer to Glossary – Page 470

Amaretti
Almond macaroons

Ingredients

200g ground almonds
200g white (granulated) sugar
2 eggwhites, at room temperature

Topping
400g dark cooking chocolate

Method

Preheat oven to 175°C. Line two baking trays with kitchen baking paper.

Combine almonds and sugar in a large bowl.

Place eggwhites into a clean bowl and beat with electric mixer or beaters until stiff peaks form. Add eggwhites to almond mixture, folding with a spoon to combine.

Drop level tablespoons of mixture onto the prepared baking trays. Bake in preheated oven for 8-10 minutes or until lightly golden. Remove from oven – loosen biscuits while warm and set aside on the trays to cool completely.

To make the Topping, melt chocolate and cool slightly. Dip one half of the biscuit into the chocolate, then place onto a wire rack to allow chocolate to set.

Store in an airtight container.

* Refer to Glossary – Page 470

Baci di dama
Ladies kisses

Ingredients

100g butter, at room temperature
100g caster (superfine) sugar
½ teaspoon vanilla extract*
100g ground hazelnuts
1 tablespoon hazelnut liqueur*
100g plain (all-purpose) flour
80g dark cooking chocolate, melted

Method

Preheat oven to 180°C. Line two baking trays with kitchen baking paper.

Place butter, sugar and vanilla into a large bowl and beat well with an electric mixer or beaters until pale yellow and smooth. Stir in the hazelnuts and liqueur, then fold in the flour.

Roll about 1 teaspoon of mixture into little balls and place in rows on the prepared trays. Flatten slightly.

Bake in preheated oven for 5-7 minutes or until lightly golden. Transfer biscuits to cool on a wire rack. Sandwich biscuits together with melted chocolate. Return to wire racks until chocolate sets.

Store in an airtight container.

Variation – Substitute ground hazelnuts with ground almonds.

Canestrelli
Almond rings

Ingredients

250g ground almonds
175g caster (superfine) sugar
60ml orange blossom water*
2 teaspoons caster (superfine) sugar, extra
1 tablespoon hot water
Extra caster sugar (superfine) for sprinkling

When these biscuits were first created in Liguria in the 12th century, white flour was a luxury only for the rich. Serving fancy treats such as canestrelli reflected wealth, so they were usually offered only at special events, such as weddings. Today these pretty biscuits, often made in the shape of a flower with a hole in the middle, are popular all over Italy. The basic recipe remains the same, with a vibrant tang from citrus zest. In this version, the citrus notes come from fragrant orange blossom water.

Method

Preheat oven to 180°C. Line two baking trays with kitchen baking paper.

Place almonds and sugar into a large bowl; gradually add enough of the orange blossom water to form a stiff, pliable dough.

Roll 2 level teaspoons of mixture into thin cylinders and bring the ends together to form small circles. Place onto prepared trays.

Bake in preheated oven for 15 minutes or until, lightly golden.

Dissolve extra sugar in hot water and brush liquid over hot rings. Sprinkle with sugar. Cool on wire racks.

Tip: It is possible that the mixture will crack a little when it is being shaped into a circle, so just be patient and re-shape or pat out cracks once they are on the trays.

* Refer to Glossary – Page 470

Cantucci (biscotti)
Almond biscotti

Makes about 40

Ingredients

2 teaspoons fennel seeds
200g plain (all-purpose) flour
½ teaspoon baking powder
100g whole almonds kernels
150g caster (superfine) sugar
2 free-range eggs* at room temperature,
lightly beaten

Cantucci were first created in Tuscany as a convenience food for travellers. Twice-cooked, they have a very dry texture which ensured they lasted during long journeys. The traditional Tuscan recipe for cantucci (or the smaller cantuccini) contains almonds, but other nuts, dried fruit or even chocolate can be used. In Tuscany, it's customary to dip cantucci into a glass of vin santo before eating.

Method

Preheat oven to 180°C. Line two baking trays with kitchen baking paper.

Crush only half the fennel seeds finely with a mortar and pestle.

Sift the flour and baking powder into a large bowl, stir in the crushed fennel, fennel seeds, almonds and sugar. Make a well in the middle and pour in the eggs. Mix to form a firm dough.

Divide mixture in half. Roll out each half on a lightly floured work surface into loaves 4cm wide and place onto prepared trays. Bake in preheated oven for 15 minutes or until lightly golden and slightly risen.

Remove from the oven and cool on a wire rack. Reduce oven temperature to 120°C. Carefully cut the loaves with a sharp serrated knife into diagonal slices about 5mm wide. Return slices to the paper lined baking trays, and bake for a further 10-20 minutes or until lightly golden and crisp.

Cool completely on trays before serving.

Store in an airtight container.

Chiacchiere
Chats

Pasticcerie all over Italy produce trays and trays of these crunchy fried treats during Carnevale season, just before Lent. Chiacchiere is the name used in Lombardy; in other regions they're known as cenci, stracci and frappe. Every Italian mamma or nonna has her own take on the recipe, with some adding white wine or Marsala to the dough.

Ingredients

300g plain (all-purpose) flour

1 tablespoon finely grated orange rind

Pinch salt

2 free-range eggs*, at room temperature, lightly beaten

60ml orange juice

50g butter, melted and cooled

Oil for deep-frying

Icing (confectioner's) sugar, to serve

Method

Sift the flour into a large bowl. Stir in the rind and salt. Make a well in the middle and add the eggs, orange juice and butter. Mix to form a stiff dough.

Turn dough onto a lightly floured work surface and roll out until about 5mm thick. Use a fluted pastry wheel to cut into 4cm x 10cm rectangles.

Heat oil in a heavy-based saucepan or deep fryer. Fry chats in batches in the hot oil until lightly golden. Drain on crumpled kitchen paper towel and dust with icing sugar before serving.

Note – These biscuits are made and served at the stalls during carnival time in Italy and are delicious eaten freshly made.

* Refer to Glossary – Page 470

Babà al rum
Rum babà

Ingredients

14g active dry yeast
50ml milk, lukewarm
50g butter, at room temperature
2 free-range eggs*, at room temperature
1 teaspoon white (granulated) sugar
Pinch of salt
1 lemon, rind finely grated
220g plain (all-purpose) flour
Butter, melted, extra
150g white (granulated) sugar, extra
250ml water
125ml rum
160g apricot jam
Thickened cream, to serve (optional)

Method

Place yeast and milk into a small bowl, set aside until it begins to slightly foam.

Next place butter, eggs and sugar into a large bowl, beat with an electric mixer or beaters until smooth. Stir in the salt, lemon rind and, lastly, yeast mixture.

Add the flour in three batches and work into the dough, beating the mixture with your hand (the mixture will appear tacky but will leave the side of the bowl).

Turn onto a lightly floured work surface and knead the mixture to form a soft dough. Transfer to a clean, lightly oiled bowl, cover with a damp, clean tea towel and leave in a warm place for 1 hour to double in size.

Lightly greased 16 timbale, muffin or baba pans (about 25g per pan) with melted butter.

With lightly floured hands punch down* dough and knead lightly within the bowl. Divide mixture evenly between the prepared pans. Brush the tops with a little extra melted butter, cover with the tea towel again and leave in a warm place for about 20 minutes or until doubled in size.

Preheat oven to 160°C.

Bake babas in preheated oven for 15 minutes or until golden.

Place extra sugar and water in a medium saucepan stir over medium heat without boiling, until the sugar is dissolved. Stir in the rum.

Turn out cooked babas onto a shallow tray. Pour the hot syrup over the babas and allow them to soak up the syrup. Turn occasionally.

Heat the jam and strain through a sieve. When cool, top with jam and serve.

Slice and fill with piped whipped cream, if desired.

* Refer to Glossary – Page 470

Tartufi al cioccolato
Chocolate truffles

Ingredients

100g quality dark cooking chocolate
25g unsalted butter, at room temperature
1 egg yolk
1 teaspoon strong coffee
1 teaspoon milk
30g cocoa powder

Method

Line two baking trays with kitchen baking paper.

Place the chocolate into a medium heatproof bowl then sit over a saucepan of simmering water (ensuring that the water does not touch the bottom of the bowl) and stir until chocolate is melted.

Remove from heat and add butter, egg yolk, coffee and milk; mix until smooth. Refrigerate until mixture is just cold then whisk or beat with a wooden spoon until the mixture lightens in colour and is creamy.

Sift the cocoa onto one of the prepared trays then drop teaspoonfuls of the mixture onto the tray. Roll the mixture with your fingertips into small balls coating in the cocoa. Remove truffles to the second tray and refrigerate until ready to serve.

Refrigerate in a sealed container for up to 2 weeks.

Tip: In warmer weather, refrigerate truffles after the first roll in cocoa – then recoat again with cocoa before serving.

Variation – Substitute the coffee and milk for 10ml of coffee liqueur or brandy.

* Refer to Glossary – Page 470

Cioccolato (Chocolate)

Almost everyone has a love affair with this sweet treat – but it was the Italians who introduced hazelnuts to chocolate.

Chocolate entered Europe when Columbus returned from his epic voyage to the Americas, his ships' holds full of strange new seeds & grains, and his memory filled with unusual tastes.

Like the other foods from the New World that Italy eventually embraced with enthusiasm, chocolate took a little while to catch on. In fact, some initially denounced it as a "violent inflamer of the passions" and sought to ban it. It also took a while before it was made into anything more than a drink.

However, Italians have become big fans and today in Italy, chocolate is an integral part of many sweet dishes. The country has a number of famous chocolate manufacturers, such as *Perugina* in Perugia, noted for its hazelnut *Baci* chocolates, *Amedei*, near Pisa, and Piedmont's *Ferrero Rocher*.

Modica, in sweet-toothed Sicily, makes chocolate using the "cold-process" method, merging cocoa fat with sugar until a chocolate mass is formed. Because no heat is used to melt the sugar, the result is interesting – the chocolate is still slightly gritty. A number of liqueurs (one even mixing chilli with chocolate) and other chocolate-based products are for sale in this ancient town.

A perfect match

Chocolate and Italy are synonymous with Nutella - a sublimely smooth, even addictive, mixture of chocolate and hazelnut paste, which was the first product of *Ferrero Rocher* in the late 1940s, and was originally named *Pasta Gianduja*. While originally it was perhaps meant only to be spread on bread, Nutella now also features in recipes for gelati, pastries and desserts.

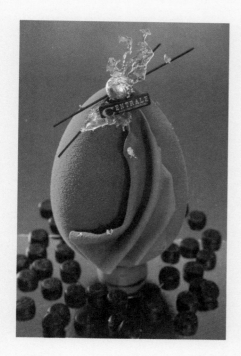

Above: Decorated Easter egg, Bar Centrale, Lecco, Lombardy.

Below: A variety of chocolates on display at Bolzani confectionery, Vicenza, Veneto.

In the cooler north, where Italy borders Switzerland and Austria, (incidentally, the world's top chocolate consumers), the need for *cioccolata calda* (hot chocolate) increases, although it is a popular drink throughout the whole of Italy, especially at breakfast.

A bar is born

The world's first chocolate bars were made in Turin, and it is here too that the famous *Gianduiotto di Torino*, which also mixes hazelnut paste with cocoa and sugar, originated. These flavours were initially combined as a drink in the café that still serves it today, called *Caffè Al Bicerin*, almost 250 years after it first won fans in 1763.

Chocolate eggs are sold all over Italy at Easter, but they are quite unlike the common Easter egg of other Western countries. In Italy every egg is a work of art, mostly handmade and hand-decorated, and some of them are immense creations, wrapped in foil or decorated with icing.

Each year in October the Eurochocolate event in Perugia celebrates this national favourite, with chocolate stands in the streets, as well as tastings, seminars and chocolate-themed celebrations.

Nor is chocolate reserved just for confectionery in Italy. It appears in many cakes and tarts, gelati and soft chocolate Ligurian biscuits called *Baci di Sanremo*, and as a coating for Sicilian biscuits called *sciatore* and crystallised fruit pieces in the south of the country.

Little surprise then that Italians are now eating more chocolate than ever before. With choices such as these, who can blame them?

Easter eggs (Uova di Pasqua)

Easter (*Pasqua*) is an important time in Italy, for both religious and social reasons. There is an Italian saying that translates roughly as, "spend Christmas with your family, and Easter with whoever you choose". Perhaps for this reason, Easter eggs (*uova di pasqua*) are extremely important.

Before Easter, the shelves in every *pasticceria*, bar or supermarket will be stacked to the ceiling with highly decorated chocolate Easter eggs. The biggest may weigh up to eight kilograms, and most have a "surprise" inside. Some adults choose expensive gifts for each other – car keys, rings, watches – and have the chocolatier (*cioccolataio*) put them inside handmade eggs. No wonder they are so popular!

Abruzzo e Molise
(Abruzzo & Molise)

L'Aquila

Tiny Molise and the larger, adjoining region of Abruzzo are often considered as one – and may simply be referred to as Abruzzi. Both have the rugged and heavily wooded Apennines to the west and the Adriatic coast at their doorstep on the east. While Abruzzi is readily accessible from Rome, most visitors to the capital still tend to travel north towards Florence, or south, in the direction of Naples; hence this region has much to offer but remains relatively obscure.

Vines grow on the slopes to the west, although the production is much lesser in volume than some other regions. The magnificent saffron grown on the Navelli plain perhaps makes up for this and for a very brief time each year the fields are awash with the purple of the Crocus sativus blooms awaiting harvest.

Abruzzi produces extra virgin olive oil around Frentano and Vastese as well and near Campobasso, the capital of Molise. Corn, onions, asparagus and chillies grow well here, as does red garlic (at Sulmona), carrots in Fucino, and chickpeas at Navelli, Goriano Sicoli and Isernia. Abruzzi is a land of grains and legumes – *Cicerchie* (chickling), an ancient legume, is raised at **Castelvecchio Calvisio**, cannellini beans at Capestrano, and black lentils at **Santo Stefano di Sessanio**. Spelt, also an ancient cereal, known as *farro* in Italian, is grown at Montereale and Carsoli, while Molise is renowned for its Capracotta lentils.

These healthy foods are accented by *scamorza* – a cow's milk cheese from the Cinquemiglia plain in Abruzzo. *Pecorino* comes from Teramo in the north, and *incanestrato*, a spicy cheese often seen hanging in baskets in delis, is also made here. Cheese in Molise tends more towards the style of neighbouring Puglia with *burrino*, a cheese that is wrapped around butter. The strong *caciocavallo* cheese hails from Agnone, and *fiordilatte* is a delightful fresh milk cheese from Bojano.

The Adriatic provides a bounty of seafood: anchovies, sardines, mackerel, skate, shellfish, and excellent scampi. Inland, mainly lamb and goat are raised, although pigs are kept for making various smallgoods such as *salami* and *mortadellina*. Molise is renowned for its charcuterie, producing *sagicotto* – a matured smoked-pork salami, *salsicce di fegato* – a liver sausage, and *ventricina* – a fennel and paprika-seasoned salami.

Italian food is often celebrated with festivals – and nowhere more than here; home to a 30-course feast and an unusual soup-making ritual.

Above: the dramatic setting of the village of Pietrabbondante, Molise.

Left: skimming saffron from the crocus flower, Navelli, Abruzzo.

Abruzzi often features versions of *spaghetti* or *maccheroni alla chitarra* – pasta cut on a *chitarra* – a board strung with a series of taut wires like a guitar. Sheets of pasta are pressed through the wires to create ribbon-like strands that are usually served with a meat *ragù* – the rough cut edges hold the sauce especially well.

The ultimate degustation menu

Visitors should be warned to bring a good appetite to Abruzzo, because this is the region of *panarda* – a massive meal of 30 or more dishes, where diners are not expected to leave the table before they have a least sampled every dish! The banquet might include broad bean soup, *pizza rustica* topped with ham, hardboiled eggs and cheese, fish broth and *maccheroni alla chitarra* for mains. Dessert is likely to include traditional Abruzzi sweets such as *Cicerchiata*, a dish of fried dough balls in honey, resembling the small legumes of the same name, and *Pizza dolce*, not a sweet pizza this time but rather a rum-soaked sponge cake with chocolate and almonds.

Christmas in Molise means *caucione*, a chickpea flour cake flavoured with Molise liqueur, preceded by *baccalà* griddlecakes or *pollo all'oratinese*, the local fried chicken. A special meal in Abruzzi will almost always finish with *confetti* – coloured sugared almonds, a traditional specialty of the region, the best of which hail from Sulmona in Abruzzo.

Abruzzi is not without its share of local food celebrations. Perhaps the most unique is the soup festival held in the town of Teramo each May, starring *virtù*, the local minestrone. The recipe is full of symbolism – it must contain 49 ingredients, seven from each of seven food categories – and tradition dictates that the soup must be made by seven virgins!

Sardegna (Sardinia)

Because Sardinia is quite isolated from the Italian peninsula, it is not frequented as much as other Italian regions, at least by overseas tourists. It is can appear almost as a separate country, rather than a region. And so much is different – the culture, heritage, ecology, and, of course, the food and wine.

There is a huge disparity between lifestyles on the island, too – ranging from glamorous rich-and-famous visitors frolicking on the beaches, to shepherds eking out a living in the harsh conditions of the inland mountains, as they have done for centuries.

As would be expected, the coastline is rich with all sorts of seafood – tuna, shellfish, lobster, mullet and its roe, *bottarga* (often known as 'poor man's caviar' and delicious over pasta for a simple dish).

Cagliari

A unique island of extreme contrasts, Sardinia is a gourmet paradise for those in the know.

Below: Fishing boats in the port of La Maddalena, Sardinia.

Inland, extra virgin olive oil is produced in several regions, and in the more mountainous areas, honey, bearing the fragrance of herbs, wildflowers and *corbezzolo*, the wild "strawberry tree", as well as myrtle and saffron.

Artichokes grow well at Samassi, Serramanna and many other centres, as do the recently introduced *pomodoro camone di Sardegna*, a hardy and tasty strain of tomatoes.

Sheep are kept in the mountains and their milk is used to make *fiore Sardo* (from the centre of the island), *pecorino Sardo*, *pecorino Romano* (around Sassari and Nuoro) and a creamy and delicate sheep's milk ricotta.

Sardinian lamb is extremely good and is used in many dishes along with goat meat. Young lamb and kid are mostly roasted on a spit, skewered or grilled with herbs – almost Greek style. *Porcheddu*, or suckling pig, is often spit-roasted with herbs too, while inland, a local *prosciutto* is made.

Dining out

Restaurants on the coast, especially in the holiday resorts, are more varied and upmarket, while dining inland is far less sophisticated. Look for *pane carasau* in the north of the island. This is another name for *carta musica*, a paper-thin bread sometimes called "parchment bread". Soaked, it is used to make *pane frattau* and served with tomato sauce and egg. *Pane fresa* is another version, originally devised as a shepherd's luncheon bread, and ideal for daytime snacks. *Pardulus* are typical southern pastries filled with sweetened ricotta cheese flavoured with citrus, and *torrone*, nougat bar, is popular on special holidays.

In trattorias on the coast there will always be a *brodetto* (fish broth) or two, and the *burrida* (fish stew) will often be thickened with nuts. This Moorish influence continues with *impanadas*, little Spanish-style meat pies. *Fregola* - large, toasted couscous, is used in some dishes, and crown-shaped *tillicas* are a sweet almond meal pastry, yet another legacy of Moorish invaders. Restaurants in Sardinia's capital, Cagliari, on the southern coast serve many dishes influenced by Liguria, Piedmont, Spain and North Africa.

Sardinian pasta is made from hard durum wheat. *Gnocchi* or *gnocchetti* are common and *culingiones* (sometimes *culungiones*) are like a rather heavy cross between gnocchi and ravioli, often flavoured with herbs and pecorino. The very fine handmade *su filindeu* pasta is commonly used in soups, and little balls of *su succu* resemble couscous.

Su zurrette is a kind of black pudding made with sheep's blood and grilled or boiled in the stomach of the sheep along with herbs, seasoning and pecorino cheese. Other meat dishes are *trataliu*, skewers of lamb offal larded with caul fat (the fat of the peritoneum), and *cordula*, which is grilled plaited intestines of milk-fed lamb.

Grapes were introduced to Sardinia by the Spanish, and many good DOC red and white table wines match the local dishes well. Most are grown on the west coast and in the south, north of Cagliari. *Moscato* is produced in several places and *Mirto di Sardegna* is a local liqueur made from purple myrtle berries.

Each November the hillside town of Cavoi has a festival for the local bread, potato and wine, while nearby Aritzo celebrates the chestnut harvest in October. The Snail Festival is in August in Senis, and Tonara honours nougat in April.

Right: a Sardinian fisherman displays his catch.

Opposite: a typical street in the old neighbourhood of Bosa, Sardinia.

gourmet
pılgrım

Caffè e liquori

Coffee & liqueurs

Like the country they thrive in, these liquids stimulate appetites, conversation and celebrations.

Il caffè (Coffee)

For all that Italy is seen as being a coffee culture, it is surprising to learn that Italians don't drink very much of it – ranking 18th among the world's top coffee drinking nations. Many Italians might have a cup of milky coffee at breakfast and another later in the day, and often that's it.

However, they are passionate about what they do consume. Italians take their coffee very seriously. It must be served at the right temperature, *tiepido*, please, making it drinkable immediately, and have an excellent golden silky *crema* on top to give the perfect colour, flavour and aroma, which every Italian knows to be the best in the world.

Coffee arrived in Venice from Constantinople in 1560, about six centuries after it is thought to have been discovered in Ethiopia by a young Abyssinian goatherd. Initially the Roman Catholic Church banned it, dubbing it 'the wine of Islam'. This might have slowed its initial progress across Europe, but it instantly became more acceptable after 1600 when Pope Clement VIII is said to have declared: 'This devil's drink is so good … we should cheat him by hallowing it!'

In 1640, the Italian peninsula's first coffee shop opened in Venice, serving thick Turkish coffee – at that time the only known way of preparing it. Soon there were many more canal-side cafes, and from there the trend spread to other major cities. *Caffè Florian*, still operating today on the Piazza San Marco in Venice, began in 1720. *Antico Caffè Greco*, still creating fragrant coffees near Rome's Spanish Steps, opened in 1760 and soon became an elegant meeting spot for many notable artists, musicians and writers.

Coffee shops in Turin and Milan followed the example of grand salons in Vienna and other European cities and soon became popular places for visionaries and radicals, and later, suspected hotbeds of political unrest.

Not far from that first coffee house, the producer of one of Italy's finest coffees, *illycaffè*, has its headquarters in Trieste. Illy was founded by Francesco Illy and his family in 1933, and two years later he invented the first automatic coffee machine. Their coffee is exported to many countries around the world.

Lavazza coffee began in the 1900s in Turin, on the other side of the country, when Luigi Lavazza created the concept of blending coffee beans from different origins. This company too now exports widely. Surprisingly the first roasting company in Italy opened almost at the same time, in 1905, when Alfredo Danesi began his grocery and a coffee-tasting cafe in downtown Rome.

Where would the world be without the papal blessing given to coffee more than 400 years ago?

Italian cafes have their own code of service. Coffee is always served in thick china cups to keep the heat and flavour just right. It may be served pre-sugared by the *barista*, so those who don't want this should say so when ordering. A milky coffee, such as a *cappuccino*, is fine at breakfast, but if you wish to be taken seriously as a coffee drinker in Italy do not order a cappuccino after mid-morning.

The range of options available may seem confusing to newcomers. Everybody recognises *caffè espresso* – short, black, one shot, in a tiny cup & served at any time of day; *caffè decaffeinato* – decaffeinated; *caffè latte* and *cappuccino* - milk coffees to be consumed only at breakfast. *Caffè macchiato* - an espresso just 'stained' with milk, and its counterpart *latte macchiato* - milk stained with espresso, are usually on offer, as is *caffè americano*, *caffè lungo* and *caffè doppio*, all long black coffees, and not usually favoured by the locals.

Macchiatone is not so common. It is a hybrid style with more milk than a *macchiato*, less than a *cappuccino*. *Caffè ristretto* separates the truly serious coffee-drinkers from the rest - a super tiny, very concentrated coffee which captures the first intense burst of liquid from the machine with an amazing flavour.

It is little surprise that the best espresso machines are often stamped 'Made in Italy'. Yet, while these are used almost without exception in cafes in Italy, in the home many people use a stovetop *caffettiera*, a small and effective device that forces boiling water through coffee grounds into a jug on top.

In the hotter southern regions of Italy, iced coffee (*caffè freddo*) and *granita di caffè* – coffee-flavoured shaved ice, is a popular cooler at any time of day, but particularly at breakfast, and of course coffee is used to flavour desserts (think *tiramisu*), cakes and liqueurs throughout the country.

After dinner drinks

After meals, it is customary to offer *caffè corretto*, coffee with a dash of liqueur, or an *affogato* (literally 'drowned'), in which a scoop of ice cream is topped with a shot of *espresso*, turning it into a dessert.

Espresso

Ristretto
Short black

Macchiato
Double

Shakerato
In a shaker

Cappuccino

Affogato

Bicerin

Espresso

The coffee par excellence: served in a tiny 50ml cup (*tazza*). Dark in colour, perfect in taste, with a penetrating fragrance.

Variations:

- *Lungo (long coffee)* – an espresso served in a larger cup for a longer, slightly weaker coffee.

- *Corretto (corrected)* – an espresso 'corrected' with a drop (10ml) of liqueur, such as Grappa, Sambuca or Cognac.

- *Viennese* – an espresso with hot chocolate and cream, topped with whipped cream and cinnamon.

- *Nocciolato (hazelnut)* – an espresso with a teaspoon of hazelnut cream, topped with a layer of cream.

Ristretto

A half-cup of espresso, made with freshly ground coffee tightly packed in the filter of a coffee machine for a very strong drink.

Macchiato

Espresso coffee with a little cold milk or hot milk foam; lightly dusted with cocoa, if desired.

Shakerato

Like an iced coffee, this is an espresso placed into a shaker with crushed ice cubes and sugar to taste then briskly shaken. Sometimes served with cold milk for a smoother taste.

Cappuccino

Espresso served in a long cup, topped with hot, foamy milk and often dusted with cocoa, nutmeg or cinnamon.

Variation:

- *Marocchino (Moroccan)* – a mini cappuccino served in cocoa-dusted espresso cup, topped with extra cocoa.

Affogato

A cup of espresso poured over a few scoops of gelato or ice-cream.

Also served as a dessert with a nip glass of a liqueur, such as Frangelico, which is also poured over the gelato, like the coffee.

Bicerin

A classic coffee from Turin: Hot chocolate, espresso coffee and foamed milk, layered in a glass.

Liquori (Liqueurs)

Aperitivi e digestivi - the opening and closing statements of an Italian meal.

When someone asks, 'What will you have?' in Italy, the liquid choices are many and varied. Beer, wine, liqueurs – there is immense variety to be found, flavours encountered nowhere else and, in some cases, linked to Italy's past.

Liqueurs are flavoured alcoholic drinks, some of which have been made in various regions for centuries. Usually quite sweet, they generally have a lower alcoholic content than spirits, but are still higher in alcohol than wines. Often mixed with water or soda water, or with other drinks to make cocktails, liqueurs may contain fruit extracts or be infused by bark, roots, wood, flowers, fruit peels or aromatic herbs, or distilled from a large number of other sources.

Cocktail hour

Pre-meal *aperitivi* are designed to awaken the appetite and prepare the stomach for food, a tradition in Italy. Bitter liqueurs, such as the easily recognisable crimson *Campari* (which can be drunk straight or with soda or orange juice), are ideal for this. *Negroni* is a cocktail that mixes Campari, gin and vermouth. *Aperol*, another liqueur with half the alcoholic content of Campari, is now becoming popular too. *Crodino* bitters and *Sanbitter* are non-alcoholic carbonated drinks that perform the same function.

Digestivi are taken at the end of the meal to reduce the heaviness and bloating sometimes caused by over-eating. The range of herbal liqueurs with *amaro* (meaning 'bitter') in the name, made throughout southern Italy, fall into this category. Their herbal composition gives them a piquant flavour and helps to settle a rich meal. *Limoncello*, from the Amalfi Coast south of Naples and often made domestically in families, is a fresh lemon-flavoured way to finish a meal, although *Amaretto* is sometimes preferred.

Perhaps the best-known *digestivo* is *grappa*, distilled from the pips and skins of grapes that remain after the juice has been removed to make wine. Its alcohol content is about 40 per cent (although it may be up to 60 per cent), taking it out of the liqueur category. It can be used to preserve fruits or become the base for other liqueurs, such as *limoncello*. Aqua vita is Italian for *eau de vie*, the high-alcohol French fruit-based spirits, and both can be made from many fruits. *Centerba Toro* from *Abruzzo*, said to be distilled from 100 different herbs, is quite potent too. Many Italians make their own *grappa* and families are always proud of their own concoctions - to be offered some of the house *grappa* is a compliment.

Opposite: *Campari*, one of the most famous Italian mixers, distilled from herbs and fruit.

Above: Local *liquori* and wines for sale at the market, Pienza, Tuscany.

Campari

A tall glass of refreshing red *Campari* and soda is a delightful way to prepare for a meal – especially in Italy, where this unique drink was created.

Created as an *aperitivo*, *Campari* is named after Gaspare Campari, who concocted the formula (which still remains a secret) and started selling it in the 1860s.

Campari's distinctive flavour comes from herbal bitters. It has stood the test of time and is now exported to almost 200 countries.

Cynar, made from artichokes and a dozen other herbs and plants, can be used as either an *aperitivo* or *digestivo*. *Genepi* is a specialty of Valle d'Aosta, and as the name suggests, is made from an infusion of gentian and other herbs. The herbal and floral *Fernet Branca*, created in 1845, may be drunk before a meal, used as a *digestivo* or in coffee. Many claims have been made for its usefulness in a number of medical conditions.

In the north-west near the French border, *pastis*, a liqueur favoured in the south of France, is also popular. *Sambuca* was first made in 1800 at Civitavecchia just north of Rome. Using elderberries and flavoured with star anise, this liqueur is sometimes topped with a coffee bean that is set alight when served. *Anisetta* is popular in Sicily and southern regions, and lemon yellow *Strega* and *Galliano* (used in Harvey Wallbanger cocktails) are also herbal liqueurs.

Nocino is made from unripe walnuts. *Nocello* and *Frangelico* owe their delicious flavour to hazelnuts, although *Nocello* uses walnuts as well. The first two come from Emilia-Romagna and the third from northern Italy, where *Frangelico* was developed by monks in the 17th century.

In Italy some Italian liqueurs, such as *Amaretto* and *Sambuca*, are used primarily to flavour desserts and other sweet dishes, and also to 'correct' coffee, as in *caffè corretto*.

One thing is fairly certain, however, exploring the range of Italian liqueurs is a fascinating – and flavourful – experience. *Salute!*

Limoncello
Lemon liqueur

Ingredients

1.8kg unwaxed lemons
750ml 90 proof alcohol or vodka
1kg granulated sugar
1.25 litres water

Method

Remove the rind in strips from the lemons, trying to avoid any white pith. If there is white pith, remove this from the inside of the rind with a small knife.

Place lemon rind and alcohol into a large preserving jar with a tight-fitting lid and leave to mature for 7 days. Dissolve sugar in water and bring to the boil, add to alcohol mixture, replace lid and set aside for a further 7 days.

Strain liqueur through a sieve into sterilised bottles and cap with screw lids.

Serve chilled.

Variation – For an Arancello liqueur substitute oranges for lemons or for a Mandarinello liqueur substitute mandarins for lemons.

gourmet
pilgrim

Reference
Riferimento

Glossario (Glossary)

Al dente
A cooking term used mainly for pasta but also applies to rice and vegetables: meaning cooked until just tender or lightly so as not to be too soft but firm to the bite.

Alchermes
A liqueur made from aromatic herbs, spices and flowers (cinnamon, nutmeg, vanilla, cloves and roses). It's coloured with cochineal, making it red in colour. The convent of Santa Maria Novella in Florence makes it. If unavailable, substitute for any sweet liqueur or red fruit juice.

Amaretto
A rich subtle liqueur with a unique almond flavour.

Anchovy fillets
Are salted and bottled or canned in oil. Available from supermarkets. Drain well on kitchen paper towel before using.

Aubergines
Also known as eggplant. The most common varieties used in Mediterranean cooking are the large aubergines, which range from purple to black skinned, or the finger aubergine. They are available cooked and marinated in oil or barbecued and marinated aubergines can be bought from delicatessens.

Baccalà
Traditionally the fish salted and dried and known as *baccalà* is cod. However, in other countries, such as Australia, Ling is also used.

Bake blind
This is when pastry is pre-baked with weights before placing a filling into the pastry shell. Line the pastry that is in the tart or quiche tin with kitchen baking paper. Two-thirds fill base with uncooked rice, dried beans or baking beads (available from kitchenware shops). Follow timing for individual recipe or a general guide for baking blind, bake at 180ºC for 10-15 minutes or until pastry is firm. Remove rice and paper. Bake for five minutes or until pastry is light golden. This prevents the base of the tart from being too doughy.

Béchamel (cheese) sauce
To make this sauce, combine 700ml milk in a saucepan with a bay leaf. Bring to a gentle boil, remove from heat and set aside for five minutes. In another saucepan melt 115g butter, add 75g (3/4 cup) of plain flour, stir and cook for a minute. Add strained milk and whisk over a high heat until sauce boils and thickens. Season to taste.

Blanching
A cooking method used to slightly soften the texture, heighten the colour and enhance the flavour of food. It involves plunging food, such as vegetables, into boiling water for a few seconds or minutes, then removing it and refreshing it under cold water, if desired.

Bocconcini
Small balls of fresh mozzarella cheese with a mild, slightly sweet flavour. Bocconcini is available in a variety of sizes – 'regular' (walnut size) and 'baby' (cherry size) – and is usually made from cow's milk. It is sold pre-packed in tubs of water or a brine solution and found in the dairy section of delicatessens and supermarkets.

Borlotti beans	A mild-flavoured, reddish-speckled bean. Also known as Roman beans, they can be bought fresh, dried and canned.
Breadcrumbs	'Fresh' crumbs are made from bread (preferably wood-fired bread or sourdough), which is 1-2 days old and therefore a little stale (drier). Process chunks of bread (with or without crusts) in a food processor until fine. Use as needed or store in a sealed bag or container in the freezer. Alternatively, dry packaged breadcrumbs are very fine and available from supermarkets. The two types of breadcrumbs are not interchangeable.
Bresaola	Salt-cured beef, usually served thinly sliced and as an antipasto. Also known as brescola.
Butterflied	To butterfly fish, including mackerel, anchovies and sardines, remove the head, with a sharp knife, just behind the side fin. Discard. Use a small sharp knife to butterfly open the body by cutting through the gut to the tail; open out flat and carefully snap the backbone at the tail end. Starting from the tail end, gently pull away the backbone. Wipe over with damp kitchen paper towel.
Cannelloni tubes	Cannelloni are big, hollow pasta tubes (usually in a dried form) suitable for filling and baking with sauces. A piping bag or small spoon comes in handy when filling them. Larger tubes can be made using fresh lasagne sheets, wrapped around the filling.
Capers and caper berries	Capers are the grey-green buds from a warm climate shrub prevalent in the Mediterranean. They are sold dried and salted or pickled in a vinegar brine. Rinse away the salt or brine before using. They can be found at delicatessens and most supermarkets. Capers come in a baby (small) size, regular (medium) size and as caper berries with the stalks still attached.
Ciabatta	In Italian the word means 'slipper', which is the traditional shape of this popular, crisp-crusted white bread. Available from bakeries, delicatessens and some supermarkets.
Cornflour	Also known as cornstarch, it's a very fine and powdery white flour made from either corn or sometimes wheat and often used to thicken sauces.
Courgettes	See zucchini.
Cream	Pure (single) cream or fresh cream contains 35 per cent saturated fat and can be whipped or used unwhipped. Thickened cream contains 35 per cent saturated fat with a thickening agent, such as gelatine, added to act as a stabiliser. It has a thick pouring consistency and is ideally used for whipping.
Crème de Cacao	This liqueur delivers a powerfully lively, full-bodied chocolate flavour. Available from most liquor stores.
Dry roasted	To dry roast seeds and nuts, including fennel seeds, pine nuts, almonds

and hazelnuts, preheat oven to 180°C. Place seeds or nuts on a baking tray and bake, tossing occasionally, for 10-15 minutes or until lightly golden.

After roasting the hazelnuts, tip them onto a clean tea towel and rub the skins from the hazelnuts.

Durum wheat flour	Also known as semolina flour (see semolina), or substitute with plain flour.
Edam cheese	Red waxed rind Dutch cheese. Substitute with Gouda or Swiss cheese.
Eggs	Generally, eggs used in sweets and baking should be at room temperature. Unless otherwise stated, cold eggs taken from the refrigerator are fine to use in savoury dishes.
	Free-range (open range) eggs, come from hens allowed to roam freely. The eggs have a better flavour than eggs from caged hens. Free-range eggs are preferred in egg-based dishes, such as omelettes and custards, however regular eggs can be substituted.
Emmental cheese	A yellow, medium-hard cheese with holes in it from Switzerland. It is usually used in gratins.
Eschalots	Also known as French shallots or scallions.
Farfalle	A dried, short pasta that's shaped like bow ties or butterflies. You can substitute small shells, penne, spiral or orecchiette for the farfalle, if you prefer.
Ferrero Rocher chocolates	A packaged, crisp hazelnut and milk chocolate-covered specialty with a smooth filling and whole hazelnut. Product of Italy available from most supermarkets, found in the confectionery aisle.
Fontina cheese	A smooth, firm cheese with a few small holes and a delicate sweet, nutty flavour. It has a red or light brown, slightly oiled rind. It can be used instead of mozzarella in a wide variety of dishes.
Free-range eggs	See eggs.
Giardiniera	Pickled mixed vegetables (celery, carrot, cauliflower, baby onions, gherkins, peppers) preserved in vinegar. Often sold in a bottle from speciality food stores.
Gorgonzola	A soft blue-veined cheese made from cow's milk. It is aged for 3-6 months and varies in texture from slightly creamy to extremely creamy.
Grappa	A strong, clear Italian alcoholic drink made from the distilled remains of wine making, including grape skins, seeds and sometimes stems. It is often drunk after meals as a digestive or added to the morning's espresso.
Hazelnut liqueur	The most popular brand is Frangelico, originating in northern Italy. Available at most liquor stores.
Knead	To work dough with palms of your hands, usually on a lightly floured

work surface. A pressing action is used to stretch and fold dough.

Lasagne sheets	See pasta sheets.
Maraschino liqueur	A colourless Italian cherry-flavoured liqueur. Substitute with another liqueur of choice, if unavailable.
Marsala	A sweet, Sicilian, fortified wine that's available at most liquor stores.
Marzipan	A paste made out of ground almonds, sugar and eggwhites. It is available from most supermarkets.
Mascarpone	A cultured cream cheese made in a similar way to yoghurt. It is creamy yellow in colour with a soft, smooth texture and a delicately sweet, slightly acidic flavour. Mascarpone is available in tubs from the dairy section of the supermarket.
Mayonnaise	To make mayonnaise, beat 1 egg yolk (room temperature) and 1 teaspoon lemon juice in a blender or with a stick blender. Add 150ml sunflower oil to the egg in a slow, thin stream, beating continuously until all the oil has been added and is incorporated. Add 60ml olive oil and ½ teaspoon Dijon mustard and season to taste with flaked salt, white pepper and extra lemon juice or vinegar. Mayonnaise can also be made in a food processor, however purists believe the best is handmade. It can keep covered in a fridge for up to seven days. If using bought mayonnaise, choose a good-quality egg mayonnaise, as it will be thicker and have a better flavour than other varieties.
Mortadella	An Italian cooked pork sausage originating in the city of Bologna. The pork is lightly spiced and finely ground with characteristic squares of fat, pistachio nuts and peppercorns visible throughout the sausage. Mortadella is usually served thinly sliced and is available from supermarkets and delicatessens.
Mozzarella cheese	Fresh mozzarella can be found in most delicatessens, packed in whey, and is identified by its smooth, white appearance and ball-like shape. The best is made from buffalo milk. The name 'mozzarella' is also given to a yellow semi-hard cheese used often on pizzas and baked pasta dishes.
Nutella	A chocolate hazelnut spread available from most supermarkets. [Note – The true Nutella that's a product of Italy is different to that available in other countries.]
Orange blossom water	Is also known as orange flower water. It is made from distilled water containing the essential oils of the orange blossom. Orange blossom water is used extensively in Mediterranean and Middle Eastern dishes and is available from kitchen grocery stores. The much stronger orange essence cannot be used as a substitute.

Orange liqueur	A liqueur with an orange flavour, such as Grand Marnier and Cointreau.
Pancetta	Thinly sliced rounds of salt cured pork belly often eaten raw, as in antipasto, or cooked like bacon. Expect it to be rather fatty.
Parboil	A cooking method used to boil food, such as vegetables, for part of the cooking time, and to finish with another cooking method (such as oven, barbecue, grill and fry).
Passata (tomato)	Strained crushed tomato pulp which is added to soups, pasta sauces, pizzas and other savoury recipes. It can be chunky or smooth and is readily available from the supermarket, usually in a bottle or jar. You can make your own using fresh, ripe tomatoes by simply removing the skin and pressing through a sieve to remove the seeds.
Pasta sheets	These are the foundation stone of layered dishes, such as lasagna, and are available fresh and dried. Dried comes in either 'instant' – meaning they can be used directly in the recipe without pre-cooking – or 'regular' – which need to be boiled 3-4 sheets at a time, to soften before use. You may need extra sauce for instant sheets.
Pastry (pre-rolled puff and shortcrust)	These pastries can be bought frozen in block or in ready-rolled sheets from the freezer section of supermarkets.
Pastry cream	To make pastry cream, beat 3 egg yolks and 75g sugar with an electric mixer or beaters until smooth. Next, in a saucepan heat 500ml milk until just boiling then pour milk over yolk mixture, stirring continually. Add 30g plain flour, 1 teaspoon vanilla extract, 30g butter and the finely grated rind of ½ lemon. Return egg and milk mixture to the saucepan and return to heat, stirring constantly over low-medium heat until just boiling (bubbles appear) and the mixture has thickened. If a little too thick, add a small amount of extra milk. Serve with dessert as custard. Variation: for a pastry filling – thicken pastry cream with an extra 10-20g of flour.
Pecorino cheese	Generic Italian name for cheese made from sheep's milk. Hard white to pale yellow cheese, pecorino is usually matured for 8-12 months. If unavailable, use parmesan or romano cheese.
Peppers	Also known as capsicum, available mainly in red, green and yellow.
Polenta	A flour-like cereal made from dried corn (maize), also known as cornmeal. It is also the name of the dish made from it. It is widely available from delicatessens and most supermarkets.
Porcini mushrooms	Available fresh in Europe and the UK and sold dried elsewhere, including Australia and the US. They have an almost meaty texture and earthy taste. Soak dried porcini mushrooms before using (some recipes will recommend using the soaking liquid in the dish). They may also be called cèpes or ceps.
Potato ricer	A potato ricer is a kitchen utensil used to process cooked potato. The potato is forced through the small ricer holes resulting in a very smooth mash.

Prosciutto crudo	Also known as Parma ham, an Italian ham that has been salted then air-dried for up to two years. The paper-thin slices are eaten raw or used to flavour cooked and uncooked dishes. Available from most delicatessens, butchers and supermarkets. Prosciutto crudo from Italy is used in this book, however, locally made prosciutto crudo can be substituted.
Provolone	A pale straw-coloured cheese oval or cylindrical in shape. When fresh it has a mild flavour and is often eaten as is or on sandwiches. Once matured, its flavour is a little stronger. It's used for cooking and is perfect on pizzas and in pasta dishes.
Punch down	A cooking term also known as 'knock back', meaning to re-knead a proven dough after its first rise. It involves punching down the dough (literally one punch) to expel the air and knead again briefly for one minute or until smooth. The dough is now ready for shaping. Handle carefully, avoiding excessive reshaping. Cover dough and allow to stand in a warm place until doubled in size – this is the final rise for the dough before baking.
Pure (single) cream	See cream.
Radicchio	Also known as radicchio rosso, it's a burgundy or red-leafed lettuce from the chicory family – Radicchio di Verona is a round shape and Radicchio di Treviso has an elongated shape. The leaves have a slightly bitter, peppery flavour. Available from most greengrocers and used in salads. If unavailable, substitute with witlof.
Ravioli mould	A kitchen utensil used to make ravioli shapes out of fresh pasta. Available from most specialist kitchenware stores.
Roasted peppers (capsicums)	To roast peppers, quarter peppers and remove seeds and membranes. Place under a preheated grill and cook until skin blackens and blisters. Transfer to a bowl and cover with a tea towel for a few minutes until cool enough to handle. Remove the skin and use as required. Roasted peppers are also readily available from good supermarkets and grocery stores.
Rucola	Also known as arugula, rugula and rocket; a peppery-tasting green leaf that can be eaten raw in salad or used in cooking. Baby rocket leaves are smaller and milder in taste.
Rum essence	A synthetically produced liquid used sparingly to impart a rum flavour to food. Available from most supermarkets.
Saffron	Saffron threads are the dried stigmas handpicked from the saffron crocus flower. It imparts a yellow-orange colour to food once infused. Quality varies greatly and the better quality saffron also adds a unique flavour. It is considered one of the most expensive spices in the world. Also available in ground form.

Semi-dried tomatoes	Unlike sun-dried tomatoes, these are moist and still plump. They are usually sold packed in oil, either loose at delicatessens or in bottles at supermarkets.
Semolina	A kind of wheat flour, semolina is the coarse particles left when wheat is milled, then sifted. Semolina sprinkled in the base of a fruit tart soaks up any excess juice. Generally sold in fine, medium or coarse texture from most supermarkets and speciality food stores.
Shrimp (prawns)	Green shrimp are uncooked and are usually peeled and deveined before use. To devein a shrimp, remove the head then pull out the digestive tract or vein, which can be quite gritty if not removed. Alternatively, make a shallow cut along the back of the shrimp and remove the vein. Uncooked shrimp shells are often reserved to make a strong-tasting stock, which adds more flavour to the shrimp dish.
Soft goat's cheese	Less mature, soft or fresh goat's cheeses are pale in colour, crumbly and spreadable. Often crumbled over pizza, served with pasta and gnocchi or used in savoury pie fillings.
Sponge finger biscuits (Savoiardi)	Also known as savoy biscuits or ladyfingers, these Italian-style crisp biscuits are made from a sponge-cake mixture and often used in tiramisú and trifles.
Spring onions	Also known as green shallots, they are an immature, mild-tasting onion with a straight stem. Often used raw in salads or cooked to impart a mild onion flavour.
Sterilised jar	To sterilise jars or bottles, first wash jars and lids in hot soapy water; rinse well. Place jars and lids into a large saucepan and fill with water. Cover, bring to the boil and simmer over medium heat for 10 minutes. Use tongs to carefully remove jars and lids and drain upside down on a clean tea towel. Transfer to a large baking tray and dry in a 150°C oven for 15 minutes. For bottling hot jams or preserves, use jars while hot. For bottling cold preserves, such as liqueurs, allow the jars or bottles to cool on the tray before using. Avoid touching the inside surface of the jars or lids.
Sun-dried tomatoes	Tomatoes that are salted and air-dried on wire racks in full sun. They can be sold bottled in oil or in a completely dry form.
Sweet pastry (pasta brisé)	To make this pastry, sift 250g plain flour into a large bowl, then, using fingertips, rub in 125g chilled, chopped butter. Add 60g caster (superfine) sugar, 2 egg yolks and 1 teaspoon vanilla extract; mix to form a stiff dough, adding a little cold water, if necessary. Transfer to a floured surface and knead un rolling out.
Swiss brown mushrooms	Also known as Cremini, Honey brown or Italian brown mushrooms, they are more flavoursome than white mushrooms with a brown colour. A larger and more mature variety with a deeper flavour is known as the portabello mushroom.

Tagliatelle	Fresh egg noodles or ribbon pasta, approximately 0.5cm wide. Also available dried.
Taleggio	A mild, creamy salty cheese that is a little sweet when fresh. As it ripens it becomes more pungent. It can be eaten fresh and is perfect for melting.
Thickened cream	See cream.
Truffles	Truffles are highly prized and very expensive. They grow underground, usually near oak trees. They have a round, yet knobbly, shape and a pungent, earthy and delicious flavour and aroma. There are two main types – black and white. Truffles can be eaten raw or cooked.
Vanilla extract	Vanilla extract is made from finely chopped vanilla beans, which have been soaked in alcohol to extract flavour and fragrance. Imitation vanilla should be avoided, as it is inferior.
Vanilla pods	Also known as vanilla beans. The true form of vanilla is in a thin dark bean or pod from a wild orchid that grows in the tropics. The bean is often used in cooking, either whole or slit through the middle to reveal the fragrant seeds nestled inside. The seeds can be scraped out using the tip of a sharp knife.
Zucchini (courgette/s)	Available in dark green, light green or yellow. Zucchini flowers are edible and often stuffed and cooked before serving.

Above: Gondolas at San Marco, San
Giorgio Maggiore, Venice.

Pesi e misure
(Weights & measures)

Volume conversions

1 teaspoon = 5ml

1 Italian tablespoon = 15ml

1 UK, US & NZ tablespoon = 15ml

1 Australian tablespoon = 20ml

1 cup = 250ml (8 fl oz)

Liquid conversions

Metric	Imperial	US cups
30ml	1 fl oz	⅛ cup
60ml	2 fl oz	¼ cup
80ml	2 ¾ fl oz	⅓ cup
125ml	4 fl oz	½ cup
185ml	6 fl oz	¾ cup
250ml	8 fl oz	1 cup
375ml	12 fl oz	1½ cups
500ml	16 fl oz	2 cups
600ml	20 fl oz	2½ cups
750ml	24 fl oz	3 cups
1 litre	32 fl oz	4 cups

Oven temperature conversions

	C°	F°	Gas mark
Very cool	110-120	225-250	¼-½
Cool	140-150	275-300	1-2
Moderate	160-180	325-350	3-4
Moderately hot	190-200	375-400	5-6
Hot	220-230	425-450	7-8
Very hot	240	475	9

Indice (Index)

S

Saffron 66, 289, 444, 475
Sage 120
    Rolled veal with sage & ham 134
    Spinach dumplings with sage butter 232
Salads 208
    Fennel, orange and rocket salad 24
    Fresh fig and proscuitto salad 36
    Mixed salad with gorgonzola and hazelnuts 26
    Russian salad 42
    Tomato and bocconccini salad 18
    Tuscan panzanella salad 38
Salami, see also Sausages 117, 118 - 119, 290, 405
    Antipasto 14
    Sausage and pepper pizza 306
Salami - varieties 119
    Genovese 204
    Milanese 286
    Cappello del prete 119
    Cotechino 119
    Finocchiona 119
    Sagisotto 444
    Soppressata 119
    Ventricina 444
    Salatini 410
Salmon
    Salt-baked fish 174
    Tagliatelle with smoked salmon 90
Salsa d'estate 76
Salsa verde 226
Salsiccia con finocchio 122
Salt 34, 156, 165, 174, 405
Salt-baked fish 174
Salted cod fish cakes 34
Saltimbocca 114, 134
Salumeria 117
Salumi 117, 338
Sambuca 406, 420, 465
Sarde a beccafico 170
Sardine alla pescatore 170
Sardines 165, 166, 186
    Fisherman-style sardines 170
Sardinia 166, 182, 276, 446 - 449
Sardinian-style mackerel 182
Sausage and pepper pizza 306
Sausages, see also Salami 119, 159, 266, 315, 338, 444
    Italian pork and fennel sausage 122
    Pasta bows with sausage & radicchio 94
Sausages - varieties
    Boar 376
    Boudin 338
    Luganiga 119
    Salsicce de fegato 444
Savoiardi 350
Savoury meat stuffed vegetables 250
Scallops 168
Scampi 168
Scampi all'aglio 190
Schiuma di cioccolata 370
Sea bass 166
Seafood, see also Fish and seafood 168 - 169, 202
Seafood risotto 68
Seafood spaghetti 86
Semifreddo 350
Semolina 270, 276, 476
Sepie in nero con polenta 168

Sfogliatella 317, 410
Sgombri alla Sarda 182
Sheep 114, 315, 447
Shellfish 86, 168
Shrimp 168, 476
    Fried mixed seafood 32
    Fish stew 188
    Paradise pizza 308
    Seafood risotto 68
    Seafood spaghetti 86
    Shrimp with lemon, garlic & parsley 190
Shrimp with lemon, garlic & parsley 190
Sicilian cannoli 426
Sicilian caponata 244
Sicilian lemon slush 402
Sicilian rice oranges 62
Sicilian ricotta sponge cake 412
Sicily 7, 10, 146, 166, 170, 209, 224, 238, 244,
    265, 273, 382, 402, 404 - 407, 412, 426, 442
Siena 356, 362, 424
Slow Food 205, 261, 377, 379
Snails 116, 202, 378
Snake of reggiano 420
Sogliano al Rubicone 108
Sorbet, see Gelato and sorbet
Sorbetto di Champagne 396
Sorbetto di pesche 398
Sorbetto di pompelmo 400
Sorrento 265
Sott'olio 260
Soufflé al amaretto 366
Soup 208, 445
    Broad bean soup 238
    Grandmother's soup 228
Spaghetti, see also Pasta - varieties 61
Spaghetti ai frutti di mare 86
Spaghetti alla Bolognese 72
Spaghetti alla carbonara 88, 159
Spaghetti d'estate 80
Spatchcock 148
Spätzle 61, 341
Spelt 289, 374, 444
Spinach 70
    Beef and spinach ravioli 84
    Cannelloni with meat and spinach 82
    Grandmother's soup 228
    Spinach bake 246
    Spinach dumplings with sage butter 232
Spinach bake 246
Spinach dumplings with sage butter 232
Spinaci gratinati 246
Sponge bombe 350
Sponge finger biscuits 476
    Chocolate foam 370
    Fruits of the forest tiramisu 348
    Tiramisu 356
    Trifle 362
    Zabaglione 352
Squid 70, 202
    Fish stew 188
    Fried mixed seafood 32
    Pan-fried squid with squid ink fettuccine 98
    Stuffed grilled squid 192
Squid ink 70
St Stephen's Day 420
Stew, fish 166
Stewed peppers with tomato 210

Gourmet Pilgrim Italy 2nd Edition [English / Metric]

Published by Gourmet Pilgrim Pty Ltd. 181 Station Street, Corio VIC 3214 Australia.
www.gourmetpilgrim.com

Published 2011. Recipe Collection, Text, Photography and Design Copyright © Gourmet Pilgrim 2011.

Commissioning Editor: Jay Stewart

Food Editor: Anna Phillips

Feature Writers: Sally Hammond, Lynne Testoni

Recipe Editing: Nicole Robinson

Sub Editors: Emma Cayley, Nicole Robinson

Food Styling: Anna Phillips

Recipe Testing and Food Preparation: Anna Phillips, Dimitra Stais

Food Photography: Andre Martin

Design: Jamie Lamshed / Juice Visual Communications

Layout and Typesetting: Thomas Groves

Cover Design: Jamie Lamshed / Juice Visual Communications

Cover Photography: Andre Martin, Anna Phillips

Errors and omissions excepted.

Gourmet Pilgrim Italy is not a travel guide, & must not be relied on for any form of travel information. Representations of a local or regional nature, including texts and photography, are conceptual only and by no means complete.

IMPORTANT NOTICE: Any person who may be at risk of any form of adverse reaction to foodstuffs of any kind should exercise due care with regard to recipes and foods included in this publication, including raw foods. Gourmet Pilgrim accepts no responsibility related to the use of this publication or any part thereof, or the consumption of foods included in this publication.

Printed in China

National Library of Australia Cataloguing-in-Publication entry:
Title: Italy : recipes, culture and stories from the kitchen tables of Italy / food editor, Anna Phillips ; photographer, Andre Martin ; texts, Sally Hammond, Lynne Testoni.
Edition: 2nd ed.
ISBN: 9780980768237 (hbk.)
Series: Gourmet pilgrim.
Notes: Includes index.
Subjects: Cooking, Italian
Other Authors/Contributors: Phillips, Anna. Martin, André, Photographer. Hammond, Sally, 1946-
Dewey Number: 641.59251

A catalogue record for this book is available from the British Library.